CompTIA® Healthcare IT Technician (Exam HIT-001)

CompTIA® Healthcare IT Technician (Exam HIT-001)

Part Number: 085710
Course Edition: 1.0

NOTICES

How to Become CompTIA Certified: This training material can help you prepare for and pass a related CompTIA certification exam or exams. In order to achieve CompTIA certification, you must register for and pass a CompTIA certification exam or exams. In order to become CompTIA certified, you must:

1. Select a certification exam provider. For more information, visit **www.comptia.org/certifications/testprep.aspx**.
2. Register for and schedule a time to take the CompTIA certification exam(s) at a convenient location.
3. Read and sign the Candidate Agreement, which will be presented at the time of the exam(s). The text of the Candidate Agreement can be found at **www.comptia.org/certifications/policies/agreement.aspx**.

CompTIA® Healthcare IT Technician (Exam HIT-001)

Lesson 5: Providing Medical IT Support

Lesson 6: Security

Appendix A: Mapping Course Content to the CompTIA® Healthcare IT Technician (Exam HIT-001) Objectives

Appendix B: CompTIA Acronyms

About This Course

Healthcare and information technology are both growing fields. The recent explosion of the use of various IT systems in the healthcare arena presents a tremendous opportunity for IT professionals. Additionally the deployment and utilization of electronic record keeping systems for use in healthcare presents both an opportunity and a challenge to everyone involved. The CompTIA® Healthcare IT Technician certificate (exam HIT-001) was developed as a supplement to both real-world experience and other IT certifications as a way for IT personnel to demonstrate basic understanding of, and competency in, essential healthcare and IT concepts and terminology and the integration of the two realms of practice.

As an IT professional, you are in a unique position to contribute to and benefit from the increasing integration of IT and healthcare systems. This course will provide you with foundational knowledge that is critical to your ability to take advantage of the tremendous opportunity presented by the advancements in healthcare-IT integration. It can also form an important part of your preparation for the CompTIA® Healthcare IT Technician certificate examination (exam HIT-001).

Course Description

Target Student

The typical student for this course is an experienced IT professional in a role such as desktop support technician, network administrator, systems administrator, or database administrator, who is looking for opportunities within the healthcare industry or may already be working within the healthcare industry. Such students want to prove through certification that they have the knowledge and skills required to implement, deploy, and support healthcare IT systems.

Course Prerequisites

While there are no strict prerequisites, CompTIA intends the Healthcare IT Technician certificate to serve as an add-on to the CompTIA® A+® certification.

Students should have experience and comfort with the following concepts and tasks:

- Computer and networking terminology.
- The functional components of a computer and a network (both wired and wireless).
- Installing and troubleshooting Microsoft® Windows®XP and Windows® 7.
- Installing and troubleshooting software, hardware, and networking components.
- Working with computer peripherals.
- Setting up, maintaining, and troubleshooting mobile devices.
- Computer and network security best practices.

An introductory course in a Windows operating system, or equivalent skills and knowledge, is required. Students can take any one of the following Element K courses:

- Introduction to Personal Computers: Using Windows XP
- Introduction to Personal Computers: Using Windows 7
- Windows XP: Introduction
- Microsoft® Windows 7: Level 1

Recommended courses (or the equivalent certifications):

- CompTIA® A+® Certification: A Comprehensive Approach for All 2009 Exam Objectives (Windows 7) is strongly recommended.
- CompTIA® Security+® and CompTIA® Network+® will also be helpful.

Course Objectives

In this course, you will identify essential healthcare and IT concepts and terminology and how to integrate the two realms of practice.

You will:

- Define and describe concepts and terminology that are fundamental to your understanding of the use of IT in a healthcare environment.
- Describe the medical environment including its organization, stakeholders, and the most significant technologies.
- Leverage core medical concepts to describe the use of IT in the medical workplace.
- Describe the essential elements of computing including hardware, software, networking, and change control.
- Provide IT support and solve IT problems in the medical workplace.
- Integrate security best practices into your daily healthcare IT workflow.

How to Use This Book

As a Learning Guide

This book is divided into lessons and topics, covering a subject or a set of related subjects. In most cases, lessons are arranged in order of increasing proficiency.

The results-oriented topics include relevant and supporting information you need to master the content. Each topic has various types of activities designed to enable you to practice the guidelines and procedures as well as to solidify your understanding of the informational material presented in the course.

At the back of the book, you will find a glossary of the definitions of the terms and concepts used throughout the course. You will also find an index to assist in locating information within the instructional components of the book.

In the Classroom

This book is intended to enhance and support the in-class experience. Procedures and guidelines are presented in a concise fashion along with activities and discussions. Information is provided for reference and reflection in such a way as to facilitate understanding and practice.

Each lesson may also include a Lesson Lab or various types of simulated activities. You will find the files for the simulated activities along with the other course files on the enclosed CD-ROM. If your course manual did not come with a CD-ROM, please go to **www.elementk.com/courseware-file-downloads** to download the files. If included, these interactive activities enable you to practice your skills in an immersive business environment, or to use hardware and software resources not available in the classroom. The course files that are available on the CD-ROM or by download may also contain sample files, support files, and additional reference materials for use both during and after the course.

As a Teaching Guide

Effective presentation of the information and skills contained in this book requires adequate preparation. As such, as an instructor, you should familiarize yourself with the content of the entire course, including its organization and approaches. You should review each of the student activities and exercises so you can facilitate them in the classroom.

Throughout the book, you may see Instructor Notes that provide suggestions, answers to problems, and supplemental information for you, the instructor. You may also see references to "Additional Instructor Notes" that contain expanded instructional information; these notes appear in a separate section at the back of the book. Microsoft® PowerPoint® slides may be provided on the included course files, which are available on the enclosed CD-ROM or by download from **www.elementk.com/courseware-file-downloads**. The slides are also referred to in the text. If you plan to use the slides, it is recommended to display them during the corresponding content as indicated in the instructor notes in the margin.

The course files may also include assessments for the course, which can be administered diagnostically before the class, or as a review after the course is completed. These exam-type questions can be used to gauge the students' understanding and assimilation of course content.

As a Review Tool

Any method of instruction is only as effective as the time and effort you, the student, are willing to invest in it. In addition, some of the information that you learn in class may not be important to you immediately, but it may become important later. For this reason, we encourage you to spend some time reviewing the content of the course after your time in the classroom.

As a Reference

The organization and layout of this book make it an easy-to-use resource for future reference. Taking advantage of the glossary, index, and table of contents, you can use this book as a first source of definitions, background information, and summaries.

Course Icons

Icon	Description
	A **Caution Note** makes students aware of potential negative consequences of an action, setting, or decision that are not easily known.
	**Display Slide** provides a prompt to the instructor to display a specific slide. Display Slides are included in the Instructor Guide only.
	An **Instructor Note** is a comment to the instructor regarding delivery, classroom strategy, classroom tools, exceptions, and other special considerations. Instructor Notes are included in the Instructor Guide only.
	**Notes Page** indicates a page that has been left intentionally blank for students to write on.
	A **Student Note** provides additional information, guidance, or hints about a topic or task.
	A **Version Note** indicates information necessary for a specific version of software.

Course Requirements

Hardware

- To perform the research activities and run the various media components of the course, each student and the instructor will need a Windows-based computer with an Internet connection.
- In addition, the instructor will need a projection system to display the course overheads.
- To perform the optional Set Up a Workstation activity, have any hardware and software components that are appropriate for your environment ready and available to install.

Software

- The recommended operating system is Microsoft® Windows® 7.
- A supported web browser: Microsoft® Internet Explorer® 6 or later; Mozilla® Firefox® 3 or later; Opera™ 10, Apple® Safari® 3+, or Google Chrome™.

Class Setup

To prepare for the class, turn on all computers and load a supported web browser.

1 Healthcare IT Fundamentals

Lesson Time: 3 hour(s), 30 minutes

Lesson Objectives:

In this lesson, you will define and describe concepts and terminology that are fundamental to your understanding of the use of IT in a healthcare environment.

You will:

- Identify concepts that are core elements of modern healthcare IT.
- Identify major issues surrounding the use of EHR.
- Describe regulations, standards, and stakeholders that are involved in healthcare IT.
- Describe HIPAA controls and what it means to be HIPAA complaint.

Introduction

In this course, you will identify essential healthcare and IT concepts and terminology and how to integrate the two realms of practice. A strong base in the core concepts of healthcare IT is necessary to begin building healthcare IT-specific skills, so in this lesson, you'll start by examining some of the issues that are key to healthcare IT that are not common to the general information technology profession.

Whenever IT is applied to a specialized area, technicians must make an effort to familiarize themselves with the jargon and concepts that form the foundation of operations in that area, otherwise they will be unaware of key issues and unable to effectively communicate with key stakeholders. This lesson introduces terms and concepts that are central to the use of IT in a healthcare environment, providing you with a foundation upon which you can build your healthcare IT knowledge.

TOPIC A

Core Concepts in Healthcare IT

Your knowledge of healthcare IT begins here with an introduction to the essential elements of the topic. These concepts may seem simple at first glance, but they can be intricate and can vary across organizations.

The surge of opportunity in healthcare IT is based upon the increased use of electronic systems for recording and managing medical information. To ensure success as an healthcare IT professional, you need to establish a framework on which to build your knowledge of the healthcare domain.

Healthcare IT Concerns vs. Traditional IT

Basic IT skills such as user setup and support, hardware and software installation, and troubleshooting are all relevant within the field of healthcare IT. But on top of that, the healthcare field layers some very specific IT requirements, including:

- Specialized hardware.
- Specialized software.
- Specialized working environments.
- Government and other regulations.
- And, above all, a deep concern for the needs of providers, patients, and families for privacy, respect, and confidence in the systems they are relying on in times of physical and emotional stress.

For this reason, many of the specialized concerns in the healthcare IT field relate to medical information and how it is classified, stored, displayed, and handled.

PHI

Definition:

Nearly all information about an individual held by parties that are involved in the healthcare and billing process is considered *Personal Health Information (PHI)*. This information can be in any form including on paper, in a computer, or as part of a verbal conversation. The U.S. Department of Health and Human Services (HHS) further identifies *protected health information* as individually identifiable health information that is transmitted or maintained in any form or medium by a covered entity or business associate. Access to and the dissemination of PHI is strictly controlled by various laws and regulations that lay out guidelines for the use, protection, and release authorization of PHI. These laws require that an individual be able to view and control access to their PHI.

Example:

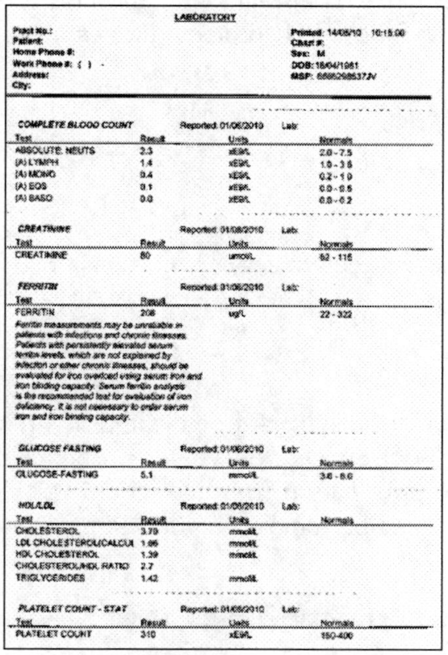

LABORATORY

Pract No.:
Patient:
Home Phone #:
Work Phone #: ( ) -
Address:
City:

Printed: 14/08/10 10:15:00
Chart #:
Sex: M
DOB: 18/04/1981
MSP: 6666298537JV

COMPLETE BLOOD COUNT Reported: 01/06/2010 Lab:

Test	Result	Units	Normals
ABSOLUTE NEUTS	2.3	xE9/L	2.0 - 7.5
(A) LYMPH	1.4	xE9/L	1.0 - 3.5
(A) MONO	0.4	xE9/L	0.2 - 1.0
(A) EOS	0.1	xE9/L	0.0 - 0.5
(A) BASO	0.0	xE9/L	0.0 - 0.2

CREATININE Reported: 01/08/2010 Lab:

Test	Result	Units	Normals
CREATININE	80	umol/L	62 - 115

FERRITIN Reported: 01/06/2010 Lab:

Test	Result	Units	Normals
FERRITIN	208	ug/L	22 - 322

Ferritin measurements may be unreliable in patients with infections and chronic illnesses. Patients with persistently elevated serum ferritin levels, which are not explained by infection or other chronic illnesses, should be evaluated for iron overload using serum iron and iron binding capacity. Serum ferritin analysis is the recommended test for evaluation of iron deficiency. It is not necessary to order serum iron and iron binding capacity.

GLUCOSE FASTING Reported: 01/06/2010 Lab:

Test	Result	Units	Normals
GLUCOSE-FASTING	5.1	mmol/L	3.6 - 6.0

HDL/LDL Reported: 01/06/2010 Lab:

Test	Result	Units	Normals
CHOLESTEROL	3.70	mmol/L	
LDL CHOLESTEROL(CALCUI	1.66	mmol/L	
HDL CHOLESTEROL	1.39	mmol/L	
CHOLESTEROL/HDL RATIO	2.7		
TRIGLYCERIDES	1.42	mmol/L	

PLATELET COUNT - STAT Reported: 01/06/2010 Lab:

Test	Result	Units	Normals
PLATELET COUNT	310	xE9/L	150-400

Figure 1-1: *Results of a lab test contain PHI.*

Information That May Be Part of PHI

Information that can fall under the categorization of PHI includes:

- Demographic information.
- Diagnoses.
- Test, lab, and other work orders.
- Test and lab results.
- Conversations in any form about an individual's health, diagnosis, care, or treatment.
- Nearly all information about the individual contained in a provider's, insurer's, or other concerned party's computer systems.
- Billing information including payment arrangements and insurance information.

Information that is not considered to be PHI includes:

- Employment records.
- Family Educational Rights and Privacy Act (FERPA) records.

Parties Involved in PHI

The parties involved in PHI include any person or organization that is involved in the healthcare process, including:

- The individual whose information is in question.
- Most healthcare providers and other medical professionals.
- Office, IT, billing, and professional staff.
- Health plans including: insurance companies, health maintenance organizations (HMOs), company health plans, government programs that are involved in healthcare, and their staff.

PHI Protection Exceptions

According to the U.S. Department of Health and Human Services (HHS) there are some organizations that are not required to follow PHI protection laws:

- Life insurers.
- Employers.
- Workers' compensation carriers.
- Schools and school districts.
- State agencies such as child protective service agencies.
- Law enforcement agencies.

De-Identification of PHI

In many cases, research or other disclosure will be desired in situations where personal information is not required, could be detrimental, or where consent cannot be obtained. In these cases, it is necessary to remove information from the record that could link that information to an individual. Information that must be removed includes, but is not limited to:

- Names.
- Geographic information more granular than the state.
- Social Security numbers (SSNs).
- Dates.

Types of Health Records

Health records include any documentation that is stored in any format. There are three main types of records.

Type of Record	*Description.*
Public health record 	There are a few reasons that part of a health record may be public: • First, some diseases or conditions are closely monitored by authorities and any occurrences need to be promptly reported. • Second, some public health organizations have the authority to obtain and use PHI in the course of their normal operations. These authorities have a strong history of providing appropriate security for PHI. • Additional reasons that all or part of a record may enter the public domain include: legal requirements, health research; cases of abuse, neglect, or domestic violence; legal proceedings; law enforcement efforts; and workers' compensation proceedings.

Type of Record	Description.
Private health record 	Private records are those that are not for public consumption and require appropriate releases before they can be shared.
Legal health record 	The legal health record is the documentation that a healthcare organization would provide if an official record was requested. It should contain patient-centric, personally identifiable documentation of services provided. In the past, the legal health record was nearly always the paper chart generated during treatment and stored by a provider. The modern healthcare IT environment is far more complex because various systems are involved and an organization must work to define the exact contents and scope of the legal health record within their environment and capabilities. Organizations should consider federal, state, and local regulations as well as community and professional standards when defining what constitutes an legal health record in their environment. The legal health record generally does not include administration or financial information.

> There are additional websites you can visit to read more about legal health records:
>
> **www.ihs.gov/NonMedicalPrograms/BusinessOffice/documents/2010pres/LegalHealthRecord.pdf**

Custodian

A *custodian* is the role, department, or individual that is formally responsible for a record. Responsibilities of the custodian include oversight of systems and services involving the record, collection of data for the record, and protection and archiving of the record. Custodians are usually authorized to certify records, and may be required to testify to the procedures and protections involved in the record-keeping process, and admissibility of the record. Generally, the health information management (HIM) department is the custodian of health records with specific individuals designated for certification and affidavit purposes.

Certification

Formally certifying a record specifies that a copy or the other version of the record is a completely accurate representation of the original record. The custodian is responsible for certifying a record.

EMR and EHR

Definition:

While the terms *Electronic Medical Records (EMRs)* and *Electronic Health Records (EHRs)* are often used interchangeably, there is a subtle distinction that should be noted. EMRs are computerized records of a health encounter. They are the modern equivalent of a paper chart. EMRs are specific to a facility (doctor's office, treatment facility, and more) and its computer system. EHRs are made up of all of the recorded health information about a person stored within a given network and provide an overall view of a patient's health, not just specific medical reports. EHRs generally contain multiple EMRs collected from various systems within a provider network or umbrella organization.

Example:

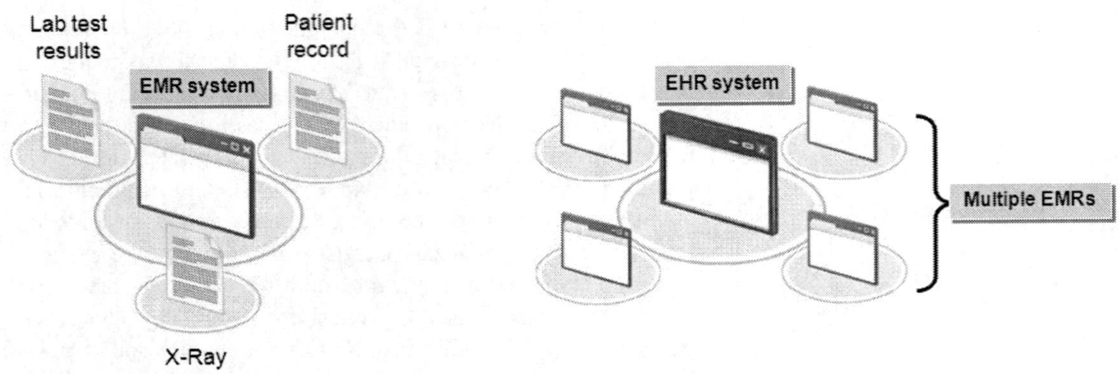

Figure 1-2: *EMRs and EHRs.*

HIPAA

HIPAA is an acronym for the Health Insurance Portability and Accountability Act. Enacted in 1996, HIPAA establishes several rules and regulations regarding healthcare in the United States. The most significant of these rules are the *Privacy Rule* and the *Security Rule*; these rules form the core of HIPAA as most people think of it. They establish a framework for the use, protection, security, and maintenance of PHI that permeates nearly every aspect of healthcare IT from software selection to document printing to archive and backup procedures.

> Visit **www.hhs.gov/** for more information on HIPAA regulations.

ACTIVITY 1-1

Discussing the Implications of IT on Medical Records

Scenario:

In this activity, you will discuss how IT issues impact concerns relevant to medical record-keeping.

---

1. **Which of the following are true of protected health information? (Select all that apply.)**

    a) It is personally identifiable.

    b) It is protected by law.

    c) It is stored by the government.

    d) It is not accessible by the patient.

---

2. **Which one or more of the following are true of legal health records?**

    a) They are personally identifiable.

    b) They are the same everywhere.

    c) They are always on paper.

    d) They contain specific treatment information.

---

3. **True or False? EHRs often contain multiple EMRs.**

    __ True

    __ False

---

4. **What is the significance of the word "accountability" in the HIPAA acronym?**

---

5. **Visit any of the websites mentioned in this topic and spend some time exploring and researching the various core concepts. What were your findings?**

TOPIC B

EMR/EHR Issues

In the first topic of this lesson, you defined some of the most basic information-related elements of healthcare IT. EMR and EHR are probably the most significant components of healthcare IT information needs. In this topic, you will identify major issues surrounding the use of EHR and EMR.

Understanding the uses and benefits of EMR, as well as significant regulations concerning EHR, are central to the growth of healthcare IT. As a healthcare IT professional, you will be interacting with EMR and EHR systems, terminology, and requirements no matter what your role is in the field, so a solid grasp of the issues and constraints concerning EMR and EHR implementations will be an important foundation for you.

Key Features and Uses of EHR

EHR systems are available from several vendors and in many configurations. Generally, these systems will have a robust feature set.

Scope	*Features*
Patient interaction and records	• Checks and balances to ensure complete and accurate encounter notes. • Note taking for encounter and progress notes.
Communication management and practice administration	• Document management for scanned and imported documents. • Ability to share documents, records, and reports with internal and external personnel. • Transcription functionality, or integration with outside transcription software. • Messaging between staff, and notes to self. • Spell checking against common and medical terminology.
Orders and prescription management	• Integration with, or import from, pharmacy, lab, imaging, and billing department systems. • Orders management. • e-Prescription integration. • Formulary checking. • Drug interaction checking. • Referral management.
Data security	• Robust security and access control mechanisms. • Audit trail recording.
Practice workflow management	• Built-in workflow for patient encounters and billing. • Diagnosis and decision making support through forms and integrated logic. • Patient education, care plans, and documentation.

Benefits of EHR

EHR and EMR systems offer many benefits over traditional paper-based systems to both medical providers and to patients.

Stakeholder Group	***Benefits***
Medical providers and organizations	• Easier and faster access to more up-to-date patient information. • Patient information is consolidated into once place. • 24/7/365 access to information. • Decreased information retrieval time. • Consistent history information for one patient across all participating providers. • More complete and accurate patient profiles. • Notes that are nearly always more legible than handwritten ones. • Increased ability to track patients for follow-up care. • Increased quality of care through reduced potential for human error. • Use of intelligent forms and predefined workflows that can reduce the potential for human error and increase care efficiencies. • Easier measurement of outcomes. • Reduced time required for data entry. • Reduced or eliminated work effort to gather data or charts. • Increased efficiency for forms processing and billing. • Increased regulatory compliance. • Increased formulary compliance. • Reduced costs through increased efficiency and reduced rework. • Smaller space requirements to store many more records. • More efficient research across vast volumes of patient data.
Patients	• Increased quality of care through reduced potential for human error. • Easier and faster access to more up-to-date information. • Consistent history information across all participating providers. • Increased treatment compliance through automated follow ups. • Easier and more accurate prescription submissions and refills. • Easier to change address and insurance information. • All care providers get all pertinent information. • Data is more easily shared among providers when working with providers that are part of the same EHR system. • Reduces the time it takes to make a diagnosis or consult for advice or a second opinion. • Patients may have some level of access to their own EMR.

Other EHR Effects on Medical Stakeholders

For medical professionals and organizations, there are many long term benefits of an EHR system. However, shorter term concerns include funding an EHR implementation and qualifying for federal and state programs to help with that funding. There are also concerns about achieving the same level of efficiency as paper charts and the adoption of new workflows and processes.

PHRs

In some systems patients may be granted some level of access to an EHR, most likely through a *Personal Health Record (PHR)* component. The PHR is a place for patients to input their own medical history and status information. This is usually available through a web portal that has been purchased by the provider as an additional feature for the EHR system. While PHRs are not usually part of the Legal Medical Record, they can be shared with medical professionals for use during history taking, diagnosis, and treatment.

Stakeholder Requirements to Consider

Within an organization, consideration must be given to a variety of needs from many job roles. Doctors, nurses, lab technicians, and front office staff will all have different needs and desires from an EMR or EHR system. It is important to have input and buy-in from all concerned roles when selecting a new EMR or EHR system. It is also vital to anticipate challenges when integrating with existing software systems.

ACTIVITY 1-2

Discussing EMR/EHR Issues

Scenario:

In this activity, you will discuss major issues related to EMR and EHR implementations.

---

1. Which of the following are features of an EHR system? (Select all that apply.)

a) Automated diagnosis

b) Note taking

c) Referral management

d) Staff recruiting

e) e-Prescribing

---

2. Which of the following are benefits of an EHR system? (Select all that apply.)

a) More complete patient profiles

b) Reduced potential for audits

c) Increased efficiency

d) Increased regulatory compliance

---

3. Have you had any personal experience with an EHR system?

---

4. What potential road blocks do you foresee with an EHR implementation?

TOPIC C

Stakeholders, Regulations, and Standards

You have reviewed the basic concepts behind and major benefits of EHR systems. To truly understand the context of EHR in today's environment, you also need to see who has a stake in healthcare IT and what standards and regulation influence the entire healthcare IT system.

There are many regulations, standards, and stakeholders involved with any health issue. IT professionals need to be aware of which of these may apply to a given situation and what the effects might be. This awareness will not only increase efficiency, but can also reduce potential liabilities.

EHR Organizational Stakeholders

Various federal organizations have an interest in the implementation of EHR systems. These organizations have set standards that EHR systems providers and medical organizations must meet and then enforce those standards. A properly implemented system allows authorities to verify that standards are maintained and that appropriate access and security controls are in place and functioning. EHR also gives public health authorities a great deal more flexibility and efficiency in researching trends and generating reports. If an emerging outbreak is detected, the quick access to data allowed by EHR systems could save lives.

With regards to funding EHR implementations, some level of reimbursement is available from federal and state stakeholders. This funding is nearly always dependent upon the documented, effective use EHR systems.

Federal Organizational Stakeholders

As a healthcare IT professional, you need to recognize the names and functions of the federal organizations that have a significant effect on the selection, implementation, and maintenance of healthcare IT systems.

Organization	***Description***
HHS	The *U.S. Department of Health and Human Services (HHS)* is charged with protecting the health of the population and providing various human services. HHS is one of the largest federal agencies and works closely with state and local agencies to provide services including the Medicare and Medicaid programs. HHS is involved with healthcare IT through regulations, guidance, and the provision of a great deal of grant monies for the implementation of EHR systems. You can find the HHS website at **www.hhs.gov**.

Organization	Description
ONC	Regulatory requirements related to EHR/EMR systems can be complex, and sometimes conflicting, and come from several different sources. The primary authority is the Office of the *National Coordinator for Health Information Technology (ONC)* within HHS. The ONC is charged with encouraging, administering, and regulating the advancement of IT in healthcare. The ONC has issued the Standards & Certification Criteria Final Rule. The *Final Rule* is an effort to set standards, specifications, and criteria for the implementation, use, and security of healthcare IT systems. The ONC website is **http://healthit.hhs.gov**.
CMS	The *Centers for Medicare and Medicaid Services (CMS)* are responsible not only for overseeing Medicare and Medicaid services but also for administering a children's insurance program, some portions of HIPAA, and other programs. CMS works closely with ONC to encourage, standardize, and incent the efficient adoption and use of compliant EHR systems. You can find the CMS online at **www.cms.gov**.
NIST	The *National Institute of Standards and Technology (NIST)* is an agency of the U.S. Department of Commerce. NIST's mission is to promote U.S. innovation and industrial competitiveness by advancing measurement science, standards, and technology in ways that enhance economic security and improve our quality of life. NIST works to achieve its goal through active participation in research and development projects both independently and with industry organizations and businesses. NIST has provided some guidance on implementing the security components of HIPAA. You can find the main NIST website at **www.nist.gov**. NIST has also published some guidance on implementing the HIPAA Security Rule at **www.nist.gov/healthcare/security/hipaasecurity.cfm**.

ONC Final Rule Information

More information about the Final Rule can be found at **http://healthit.hhs.gov**. Click **Resources & Guidance,** and scroll to the **Final Rule** link under **Meaningful Use.**

Medicare

Medicare is a federal health insurance program for the elderly and some disabled individuals in the United States. It is one of the largest government programs and has significant influence over electronic record integration, coding and billing practices, and coordination of benefits practices. Medicare also has the ability to provide incentives or to discipline providers through financial means.

> Medicare is also used as a program title in Canada and Australia. This discussion is limited to the U.S. Medicare program.

Medicare Information

Extensive information regarding the Medicare programs and related procedures and standards is available at **www.cms.gov**.

Parts of Medicare

Medicare has three main parts.

Medicare Part	***Description***
Part A	Part A coverage (hospital insurance) helps pay for treatment in an inpatient hospital or skilled nursing facility, as well as hospice and some home healthcare. While most individuals do not pay a monthly premium for this insurance, they must meet certain conditions to receive benefits.
Part B	Part B coverage (medical insurance) applies to doctor's services and other outpatient services as well as some services not covered under Part A. Most individuals do pay a monthly premium for Part B coverage.
Prescription drug coverage	Prescription drug coverage is available to all Medicare recipients. Most will pay an additional monthly premium. This insurance is provided by independent, private insurers who offer plans under this program.

Medicaid

Medicaid is the U.S. federal program to provide healthcare for certain low-income individuals and families. Medicaid provides direct payment to providers for their services to these individuals. While each state sets eligibility and service guidelines, having a low income is only one of the milestones that must be met to be eligible for Medicaid coverage. Some states have distinct names for their programs that fall under Medicaid, such as "Soonercare" in Oklahoma. Due to its scope, Medicaid is a very large program, making up a significant portion of federal and state budgets. Due to this size and the complexity of the regulations governing Medicaid, the program works closely with state and local organizations' healthcare IT in general, and EHR systems in particular, to reduce costs and increase efficiency.

Private Health Insurers

Definition:

Private health insurers are private, non-government businesses that contract with individuals or employers to help pay medical expenses. The contract specifies what treatments or activities the insurer will contribute towards, and how much will be contributed. Many of these insurers also have separate contracts with many health organizations that specify negotiated rate structures for that health organization's services. Patients usually pay a portion of the fee in the form of a co-payment or deductible. These varied payment schemes are complex and potentially increase the margin for error in the billing process, making the use of reliable, easy-to-use technology a key factor in billing office efficiency.

Example: U.S. Private Insurers

Major private insurers in the U.S. include the Blue Cross and Blue Shield Association, AARP Health, Cigna, and Aetna.

Laws and Regulations

In addition to government agencies, there are separate laws and regulations that have an impact on healthcare IT.

Regulation	***Description***
ARRA	The provisions of the *American Recovery and Reinvestment Act (ARRA)* included provisions for funding of some healthcare initiatives and the creation of the HITECH Act.
HITECH	The *Health Information Technology for Economic and Clinical Health Act (HITECH),* part of the ARRA, promotes the adoption and meaningful use of healthcare IT through enhanced enforcement and extension of HIPAA policies. HITECH: • Enhances and extends HIPAA Security and Privacy Rules. • Creates four categories of violations and culpability with corresponding increases in penalties. • Adds the notion of willful infringement, and removes allowances for ignorant infringement. • Allows patients to request electronic copies of records.
The Joint Commission	*The Joint Commission* is an independent, non-regulatory, not-for-profit organization that provides accreditation and certification for healthcare organizations in the United States. The Joint Commission's mission statement is to continuously improve healthcare for the public, in collaboration with other stakeholders, by evaluating healthcare organizations and inspiring them to excel in providing safe and effective care of the highest quality and value.

Additional Regulatory Authorities

Additional authorities to be concerned with include:

- HIPAA.
- Medicare and Medicaid.
- HSS.
- The U.S. Food and Drug Administration (FDA).
- State and local regulations and authorities.

Meaningful Use

Definition:

Meaningful use is a regulatory concept that describes the ideal of effectively and efficiently leveraging EHR technology in the medical workplace. There can be many advantages provided by EHRs, but they are only realized after a sound implementation and consistent, well-considered use. The ARRA was the initiator of the push to achieve true, meaningful use for EHR implementations in the United States. This act links billions of dollars in incentives to the achievement of this sometimes nebulous concept.

Example: Meaningful Use in Private Practice

When examining the meaningful use standards, Dr. Bublik, a sole practitioner, has to make some decisions on which items her practice would choose to implement, as she is not required to meet every single objective during the initial deployment. One of the optional items the practice implemented is the inclusion of lab and test results in the EHR—the practice is already associated with a large, regional health information network, so this feature was relatively easy to implement.

The Meaningful Use Process

The process of establishing meaningful use can be complex. There are generally four phases.

Phase	*Description*
Application	In this first phase, the practice or hospital will apply for applicable meaningful use funding or grants and be given the objectives needed to meet requirements.
Implementation	In this phase, the practice, hospital, or organization implements the EMR/EHR system within the environment.
Demonstration	In this phase, the practice or hospital will demonstrate meaningful use by meeting all the objectives established in the application phase.
Reimbursement	In this phase, the practice or hospital receives the reimbursement from the government.

Components of Meaningful Use

There are several components that combine to demonstrate meaningful use:

- Use of a *certified EHR system.*
- Use of the certified system in a meaningful way—such as e-prescribing.
- Use of the certified system to electronically exchange health information to improve the quality of care.
- And, use of the certified system to submit clinical quality and other measures.

Certified EHR Systems

HHS, CMS, and ONC all require the use of a certified EHR system for the implementation to be eligible for incentive payments. Certification falls under the domain of the ONC and assures the purchaser of the EHR system that the system will perform to a minimum standard and will be secure. More information is available at: **http://healthit.hhs.gov/portal/server.pt/community/certification_programs/1196/home/15505**

Stages of Meaningful Use

Meaningful use benchmarks have been broken into three stages that are currently planned to be completed by 2015. Stage 1 is the only stage currently defined. It is to take place in 2011 and 2012. Stage 1 requires professional providers or healthcare organizations to complete a set of meaningful use objectives, the majority of which are mandatory. The requirements for stages 2 and 3 are still in flux.

Meaningful Use Stage 1 Objectives

More information and a detailed lists of the objectives can be found at the CMS website at **www.cms.gov/ehrincentiveprograms/30_Meaningful_Use.asp**.

Eligible Providers

Definition:

An *eligible provider* is a healthcare provider that meets legally defined criteria and thus is eligible for incentive payments for the implementation of EHR systems. There are separate requirements for individual professionals and hospitals, as well as for Medicare and Medicaid. Providers must choose whether they want to participate in the Medicare or Medicaid incentive program; it is not possible to participate in both incentive programs. Providers who meet the requirements are designated as eligible providers.

Example: Typical Eligible Providers

Most private practices and hospitals are eligible to be considered for incentives once they implement an EMR or EHR system.

More Information on Eligibility

Detailed descriptions of eligibility requirements and an easy-to-use flowchart are available from CMS at: **www.cms.gov/ehrincentiveprograms/15_Eligibility.asp**

Covered Entities

Definition:

According to CMS, a *covered entity* is any healthcare provider that conducts certain transactions in electronic form, a healthcare clearinghouse, or a health plan. All covered entities fall under the HHS Administrative Simplification standards adopted as part of HIPAA. All covered entities must adhere to the HIPAA Privacy Rule and Security Rule. In some cases, a business relationship where a third party will be handling PHI also qualifies that provider as a covered entity for compliance and security purposes.

Example: A Covered Entity

A hospital that is utilizing an electronic billing system is a covered entity.

More Information on Covered Entities

Detailed descriptions of entities and an easy-to-use flowchart are available from CMS at: **www.cms.gov/hipaageninfo/06_areyouacoveredentity.asp**

ACTIVITY 1-3

Discussing Regulations, Standards, and Stakeholders

Scenario:

In this activity, you will review your knowledge of healthcare IT regulations, standards, and stakeholders.

---

1. **HHS is responsible for which of the following? (Select all that apply.)**

   a) Medicare

   b) Medicaid

   c) Healthcare IT regulation

   d) Accrediting hospitals

---

2. **True or False? Most healthcare providers and facilities can be considered covered entities.**

   __ True

   __ False

---

3. Visit some of the websites presented in this topic, and perform further research on the various federal organizations.

TOPIC D

HIPAA Controls and Compliance

Of the regulations discussed so far, HIPAA and its rules are probably the largest concern for most medical facilities. Now that you have an understanding of the variety of regulations and government stakeholders, you can focus on the effects of HIPAA.

HIPAA is a large statute with many requirements. Successfully complying with HIPAA requirements can be an arduous task, but the benefits to both patients and providers make the effort pay off. HIPAA has a major influence upon all healthcare IT operations. Being aware of and understanding HIPAA, its requirements, and how they interact with healthcare IT systems will make you a more effective healthcare IT technician by allowing you to communicate with healthcare staff and resolve potential issues.

Medical Record Controls

Definition:

Medical record controls are mechanisms that are put in place to limit access to electronic health information. Processes and procedures are one way of controlling information to ensure records are not released, moved, or edited unless the appropriate steps have been taken and authorizations obtained. These controls can be physical in nature by restricting access to secured areas, computer screens, or building entrances. The controls can also be computer-based through a variety of methods including limited access and permissions. Exactly what controls are put in place and how they are carried out is dependent upon the working environment, and federal, state, and local requirements. The prevailing wishes of the provider's community are sometimes taken into account. It is also important to take into account a patient's wishes—there may be some instances where a patient will want tighter control over certain pieces of information.

Example: Controls in a Physician's Office

When a patient visits their doctor, even if the staff is familiar with the patient, they should verify the patient's identity by asking for the name, date of birth, and probably a third identifying features like part of an address or phone number.

HIPAA Compliance

Complying with the various requirements of HIPAA and subsequent modifications, clarifications, and enhancements can be a daunting task. It is important that IT providers work with healthcare and business personnel to meet and adapt to the relevant requirements. The basic aspects of HIPAA compliance include:

- Implementing mechanisms to track and record the identity of individuals or organizations that access, edit, and release PHI. This audit information should include an identifier for the record accessed, the time and date of access, and an identifier for the accessing individual.
- Establishing policies and procedures to allow individuals to request amendments to their PHI.
- Ensuring that interactions with contractors and other third parties protect any PHI that is transmitted.
- Enacting and enforcing of penalties for the mishandling of PHI.

- Preparing documentation to demonstrate adherence to the HIPAA Privacy and Security Rules.
- And, appointing a privacy officer to oversee the implementation and enforcement of the HIPAA Privacy and Security Rules.

> There are many resources available to assist with identifying and testing which requirements your organization may need to meet and how well you are doing with compliance, including the websites for the HHS, ONC, and CMS.

HIPAA Security and Privacy Rules

There are two rules that HIPAA requirements are based on.

Rule	*Description*
Security	The HIPAA Security Rule requires that covered entities maintain the integrity, confidentiality, and security of PHI. The rule is written to be flexible enough to allow covered entities to implement compliance measures that are appropriate to their organization and risks. The HHS defines several main areas to be addressed under the Security Rule. covered entities must: • Perform and document risk assessments, and work to manage identified risks. • Implement administrative safeguards for security management, information access, workforce training and management, and evaluation. • Implement physical security measures in the form of physical access controls and electronic device security. • Implement technical safeguards, including access, audit, and integrity controls, and transmission security. • Be aware of their responsibilities under the rule. • Maintain written security policies and procedures, and written records of activities undertaken as part of rule enforcement for 6 years after their effective date. Covered entities can be subject to fines when violations against the Privacy Rule occur. The amount of a fine or penalty given is based on the severity of the violation, and whether the individuals involved or the practice has taken necessary measures in correcting the issues.
Privacy	The HIPAA Privacy Rule protects an individual's health information while allowing sufficient access and transfer of information to allow increased effectiveness and efficiency in treatment. The HHS defines several main areas to be addressed under the Privacy Rule: • Ensure quality assessment and improvement activities. • Ensure competency activities are carried out. • Conduct reviews, audits, or legal services when needed. • Insurance functions. • Business management and planning services.

HIPAA Security Rule Information

More information about the HIPAA Security Rule can be found at these resources:

- **www.hhs.gov/ocr/privacy/hipaa/administrative/securityrule/index.html**

- **www.hhs.gov/ocr/privacy/hipaa/understanding/srsummary.html**
- **www.cms.gov/hipaageninfo/04_PrivacyandSecurityStandards.asp**
- **www.nist.gov/healthcare/security/hipaasecurity.cfm**

HIPAA Privacy Rule Information

More information about the HIPAA Privacy Rule can be found at these resources:

- **www.hhs.gov/ocr/privacy/hipaa/administrative/privacyrule/index.html**
- **www.cdc.gov/mmwr/preview/mmwrhtml/m2e411a1.htm**
- **http://privacyruleandresearch.nih.gov/**

PHI Disclosure

It might be helpful to think of PHI disclosure as a "need-to-know" scenario. You only share the minimum amount of information that is necessary for a person to do their job. This can be a very difficult line to find in healthcare because in many situations, providers will have an easier time making a diagnosis when they have complete access to a patient's information, or a lack of information could potentially harm an individual.

Psychotherapy Notes

Due to their sensitive nature, most uses of notes relating to psychotherapy require additional security.

ROI Requirements

HIPAA places many guidelines on the release of PHI, commonly known as *Release of Information (ROI)*. Many institutions have entire departments dedicated to handling the release of information. These ROI departments are often part of a larger health information management (HIM) department. ROI HIPAA responsibilities begin with the Privacy Rule. Any use or disclosure of PHI by a covered entity is subject to the provisions of the Privacy Rule. PHI may only be used or disseminated as the Privacy Rule requires, or when authorized by the individual in writing. There are two cases where disclosure is required:

1. When the individual requests access to, or an accounting of disclosures of, their PHI.
2. When there is a potential breach of security, then HHS will conduct a compliance investigation or review or enforcement action.

Overall, only the minimum necessary disclosures should take place.

ROI and the Privacy Rule

The Privacy Rule lays out additional permitted uses of PHI, including treatment, payment, and healthcare operations. Other aspects of the rule discuss incidental use, opt in or opt out scenarios, public interest, and limited data sets. Some states or counties have stricter rules than the HIPAA Privacy Rule, but there are generally few exceptions of more relaxed rules. Violations of the Privacy Rule can bring about audits that may result in fines or other reprimands.

Permissions Within Healthcare IT

While permissions are a part of any network or computer installation, they become much more important, and complicated, in a healthcare environment. The additional requirements HIPAA places on ensuring privacy and audit trails necessitates increased complexity for the permissions granted to users and systems within the healthcare IT environment and the EMR or EHR system. The analysis and setup phases of an implementation can be lengthened by the need to satisfy these requirements, but usually within an EMR or EHR system, default profiles are available with permissions assigned. After implementation, changes to users' permissions are likely, as the initial analysis can't really simulate working life in the new EHR. When users ask for new or increased permissions, it is likely that they do need the requested access. This access will make both the users' and your working life easier. Be sure to analyze and get authorization for granting the requested access quickly and fairly to ensure a good working relationship with your users.

ACTIVITY 1-4

Discussing HIPAA Controls and Compliance

Scenario:

In this activity, you will review issues related to HIPAA controls and compliance.

---

1. **Which statements are true about ROI?**

   a) It is subject to the HIPAA Privacy Rule

   b) It is usually under the HIM department.

   c) It is more concerned with security than privacy.

---

2. **Research the HIPAA Privacy and Security Rules using the websites listed in this topic. What type of information did you find? Was anything familiar to you?**

Lesson 1 Follow-up

In this lesson, you defined and described the concepts and terminology that are fundamental to your understanding of the use of IT in a healthcare environment. With this basic understanding, you should be able to interact confidently with various stakeholders within a medical environment regardless of your role as a healthcare IT professional.

1. **What regulatory authorities presented in this lesson are familiar to you?**

2. **In your current position, or the position you are seeking, what concepts presented in this lesson do you think will be important on the job?**

2 The Medical Environment

Lesson Time: 3 hour(s)

Lesson Objectives:

In this lesson, you will describe the medical environment including its organization, stakeholders, and the most significant technologies.

You will:

- Describe the structure and key components of healthcare organizations.
- Identify key concepts in medical terminology, equipment, and software.
- Describe the medical coding and billing processes and identify the most significant technological components of these processes.
- Define medical computer interfaces and their role in healthcare IT.

Introduction

Having established the fundamental concepts and definitions about IT in the healthcare industry in the previous lesson, this lesson will focus more in depth on the healthcare industry itself, focusing on material that IT professionals who are not familiar with the healthcare industry will need the most.

Working in a medical environment can be very different from life in other industries. The many unique aspects of this environment will present many new challenges. Having an understanding of how the medical environment is structured and familiarity with essential jargon will allow healthcare IT technicians to meet the challenge of this unfamiliar environment.

TOPIC A

Healthcare Organizations

In this lesson, you will learn more about the medical environment and the myriad of devices, systems, and technologies used within it. In the medical environment, there are a number of different types of organizations that all meet a specific niche of healthcare. In this topic, you will describe these types of healthcare organizations.

Within the medical environment, there are a wide variety of healthcare organizations, each with its own set of requirements, specialties, and capabilities. There are a variety of devices, systems, and technologies used in these organizations. An IT professional will need to know and understand these different organizations and the technologies used in these environments. Identifying these variations and how information flows within them will enable you to more effectively design, implement, and manage healthcare IT systems.

Types of Hospitals

There are numerous types of hospitals, which can be categorized in a number of ways.

Type of Hospital	***Description***
General or community	The majority of hospitals are *general or community hospitals* which treat a wide scope of medical issues, including emergencies and inpatient or outpatient care, and perform general surgeries. A general hospital will have access to a variety of different medical resources, and would follow more formalized procedures for treatment using general medicine standards and practices.
Specialized	*Specialized hospitals* are far more specific in their scope of work, treating a specific disease or condition, such as cancer; or a specific type of patient, such as children. A specialized hospital may have access to particular resources specific to the condition that a general hospital may not have access to, such as research or drug trials. A specialized hospital will follow formalized procedures, but may also utilize techniques or treatments not yet embraced by the more general medical organizations.
For-profit	A *for-profit hospital* is investor-owned, usually by a corporation or a group of individual persons, which may include those on staff. A for-profit hospital aims to gain profits from the services provided to be paid back to those invested. Due to the nature of charging for services and generating funding, for-profit hospital will likely cover a broad scope of issues and treatments, will have access to resources and technologies, and will follow more formalized procedures.
Non-profit	*Non-profit hospitals* are typically owned by not-for-profit organizations, religious organizations, or government organizations, and are usually overseen by a board of trustees. Profits do not go back to the investors, but are reinvested back into the hospital or the community through the owner organization. A non-profit hospital may not cover as broad a scope of medical issues or have the same access to resources as a for-profit hospital, due to the nature of funding. It may also not follow the same standards or formality of procedures, as it may not have the same governance as other types of hospitals.

Type of Hospital	Description
Public	*Public hospitals* are owned and operated by federal, state, or city governments, and are usually located in impoverished inner cities, where they can provide subsidized medical services to patients unable to pay for their medical services. Because these hospitals are found in more poor, urban areas, public hospitals do not always have the same funding available as other types of hospitals. They may not cover as broad a scope of medical issues and treatments and may not have access to the resources that a more well-funded hospital may have access to. A public hospital would still follow formalized procedures.
Teaching	A *teaching hospital* is affiliated with a nearby medical school, allowing medical students and residents to gain hands-on learning and obtain real-world experience by working in the hospital environment. Typically, staff at a teaching hospital will also hold teaching positions at the affiliated medical school. A teaching hospital could be affiliated with a general hospital or a specialized hospital; depending on the affiliation, the scope of work, availability of resources, and formality of procedures that are followed will vary.
Short-stay	*Short-stay facilities*, also known as acute care facilities, provide services aimed to resolve immediate and short-term medical conditions like pregnancy or a heart attack. Short-stay facilities do not provide a wide scope of services for a variety of issues, like a general hospital, but are more "specialized" in nature to treat conditions that can be treated on a short-term basis. Depending on funding sources, specialization and possible affiliations, a short-stay facility may or may not have access to resources, and may or may not follow formalized procedures.
Long-stay	*Long-stay facilities* provide services like rehabilitation to address more long-term medical conditions like mental illness. Long-stay facilities do not provide a wide scope of services for a variety of issues, like a general hospital, but are more "specialized" in nature to treat conditions that require a longer treatment period. Depending on funding sources, specialization and possible affiliations, a long-stay facility may or may not have access to resources, and may or may not follow formalized procedures.

> One individual hospital may be more than one type of hospital; for instance, based on the services it provides and its affiliation with a medical school, one hospital could be categorized as a general hospital, a for-profit hospital, and a teaching hospital.

Other Types of Healthcare Organizations

There are many other types of healthcare organizations besides hospitals.

Healthcare Organization	Description
Private practice	An independent medical practice opened by one or more accredited medical practitioners of any specialty area in an office environment. Depending on the medicine being practiced, a private practice may or may not cover a broad scope of services (a practice of primary care physicians will cover a broad spectrum of services; a practice of dermatologists would only focus on the scope of services related to dermatology). Depending on factors such as funding sources or affiliations, a private practice may or may not have access to available resources such as equipment, the latest technology, personnel, or even specific skillsets and knowledge. By its nature private, a practice may not follow the more formalized procedures found in a general hospital or facility.
Nursing home	A residential facility for patients who need constant medical or nursing care and supervision. Due to the nature of a wide variety of patient types, a facility of this type would need to have a broad scope of services offered. Depending on factors such as affiliations with other facilities, it may or may not have access to resources and may or may not follow formalized procedures.
Assisted living facility	A residential facility or community for patients who may need assistance with some functions of daily living, such as bathing or medication reminders, but can otherwise remain mostly independent. Often it is made up of single resident "apartments" where a resident can live alone or with their spouse in an independent environment, with medical assistance as needed. Due to the nature of a wide variety of patient types, a facility of this type would need to have a broad scope of services offered. Depending on factors such as affiliations with other facilities, it may or may not have access to resources and may or may not follow formalized procedures.
Continuing care facility	A blend of assisted living and nursing home care and may include independent living options. It is a residential facility with "steps" of care based on the residents needs; residents can start out with more independence through assisted living, with the comfort of knowing nursing home care is available at the same facility when they can no longer remain independent. Due to the nature of a wide variety of patient types, a facility of this type would need to have a broad scope of services offered. Depending on factors such as affiliations with other facilities, it may or may not have access to resources and may or may not follow formalized procedures.
Intermediate care facility	A residential facility for individuals with persistent medical conditions who are currently unable to live independently, but do not need constant medical care or supervision. Typically, they provide support or rehabilitative services aimed to enable the resident to regain independence in functions of daily living, with the goal to transition to another care facility or return home. Due to the nature of a wide variety of patient types, a facility of this type would need to have a broad scope of services offered. Depending on factors such as affiliations with other facilities, it may or may not have access to resources and may or may not follow formalized procedures.

Healthcare Organization	Description
Home healthcare	A wide variety of medical services that are provided in a patient's home by an accredited home health aide, often including physical therapy and medication delivery through more complicated methods like injections, intravenous therapy, etc. Due to the nature of a wide variety of patient types, a facility of this type would need to have a broad scope of services offered. Depending on factors such as affiliations with other facilities, it may or may not have access to resources and may or may not follow formalized procedures.
Hospice care	A residential facility for terminally ill patients who have reached the end stages of their condition. Hospice care is designed to provide comfort and care for patients and support for the patient's family during end-of-life. Due to the nature of a wide variety of patient types, a facility of this type would need to have a broad scope of services offered. Depending on factors such as affiliations with other facilities, it may or may not have access to resources and may or may not follow formalized procedures.
Surgical center	Also known as an outpatient surgery center. It is a healthcare facility that performs surgical procedures that does not require hospitalization. Surgeries are usually outpatient, meaning the surgery performed does not require an overnight or extended hospital stay for recovery. Due to the growing number of outpatient surgeries, a facility of this type would need to have a broad scope of services offered. Depending on factors such as affiliations with other facilities, it may or may not have access to resources and may or may not follow formalized procedures.
Urgent care facility	An outpatient facility where treatment can be provided for medical problems or conditions that need immediate medical attention, but are not an emergency, such as ear infections, sprains, etc. Due to the nature of a wide variety of patient types, a facility of this type would need to have a broad scope of services offered. Depending on factors such as affiliations with other facilities, it may or may not have access to resources and may or may not follow formalized procedures.

Inpatient Treatment

Inpatient treatment occurs when a patient's medical condition requires being admitted to the hospital for anywhere from an overnight stay to a long-term stay, due to the fact that the patient's condition must be closely monitored.

Inpatient Treatment Scenarios

Inpatient scenarios may include but are not limited to:

- A patient comes to the Emergency Department (ED) with chest pains, and is admitted to inpatient care to monitor his cardiac stability.
- A patient with a history of drug addiction checks into an inpatient rehabilitation center to address her chemical dependency.
- An elderly patient with dementia and diabetes is checked into an inpatient facility for rehabilitation after he fell and broke his hip, because he needs medical supervision for both the treatment of his diabetes and his rehabilitation, and his dementia prevents him from being able to monitor his own glucose levels carefully.

Outpatient Treatment

Outpatient treatment occurs when medical services can be provided to a patient without the need for the patient to be admitted to any type of healthcare facility. Treatment can be provided in a doctor's office or clinic, even including minor outpatient surgeries, usually supplemented by at-home use of medications to address or control the medical condition. Outpatient care is also referred to as *ambulatory care.*

Outpatient Treatment Scenarios

Outpatient scenarios may include but are not limited to:

- A patient has minimally invasive arthroscopic surgery on her knee to address an ongoing issue. She is released a few hours after surgery is performed and will use outpatient rehabilitation to recover from the surgery.
- A patient visits the ED because she has been experiencing pain in her ear. She is diagnosed with an ear infection, and released the same day with a prescription for antibiotics and the direction to make a follow up appointment with her primary care physician in two weeks.
- A patient visits an urgent care facility when he sprains his ankle playing soccer. He is treated and released that night with a prescription for pain killers and a wrapped ankle.

General Departments in Healthcare Organizations

Healthcare organizations are large and made up of many departments. There are a number of general departments that would be found in most organizations.

Department	***Description***
Peri-Op	Peri-Operative Care (Peri-Op) provides medical services and care to a patient before, during, and after surgical procedures. Departments within Peri-Op include: • Pre-Surgical • Operating Room (OR) • Post-Anesthesia Care Unit (PACU)/Recovery
ICU	Intensive Care Units (ICU) or Critical Care Units (CCU) provide medical services for critically ill patients who need constant, intensive treatments and monitoring, often including life support. Specialized departments include: • Neonatal Intensive Care Unit (NICU) • Pediatric Intensive Care Unit (PICU) • Trauma Intensive Care Unit (TICU)
Med/Surg	Medical/Surgical (Med/Surg) provides general, non-specialized medical and surgical services to patients of all types. This includes the OR.

Department	Description
ED	An Emergency Department (ED)—sometimes also referred to as Accident and Emergency (A&E) or Emergency Room (ER)—treats a wide range of medical needs on an immediate basis, without prior appointment, that may or may not be life-threatening in nature. Departments within the ED may include: • Triage • Main ED Unit • Trauma Unit • Pediatric Unit • Behavioral Health Unit • Observation Unit • Short-Stay Unit
Therapeutic departments	Therapeutic departments provide a wide variety of therapy services to patients to help them recover from a medical condition or surgery. Departments include: • Respiratory Therapy • Physical Therapy • Occupational Therapy • Speech-Language Therapy
Ambulatory	Provides medical treatments and surgeries on an outpatient basis, where patients typically have scheduled visits or day surgeries, and are released once the visit or surgery is completed.
Tests and medications	Departments that run or analyze tests related to a patient's condition or dispense medications to treat a patient's condition. Departments include: • Radiology • Laboratory • Pharmacy

Inpatient General Departments

General departments within a healthcare organization that provide inpatient services include:

- Peri-Op.
- ICUs.
- Med/Surg.
- ED.
- Therapeutic departments.
- Tests and medications.

Outpatient General Departments

General departments within a healthcare organization that provide outpatient services include:

- Therapeutic departments.
- Ambulatory.
- Tests and medications.

Specialized Departments in Healthcare Organizations

Any medicine that treats a specific area of the body or type of medical condition is considered a specialty. There are also a number of specialized departments within an organization.

Department	***Description***
OB/GYN	Obstetrics and Gynecology (OB/GYN) provides maternity services including pre- and post-natal care. Departments within OB/GYN include: • Family Birthing Center (FBC) • Labor and Delivery (L&D)
Peds	Pediatrics (Peds) provides medical care for infants, children, and adolescents. Within Pediatrics, there are usually specialities as well, such as Pediatric Orthopedics, Pediatric Oncology, etc.
Cardiovascular	Provides specialized medical services relating to diseases or conditions of the heart and blood vessels.
Behavioral Health	Provides treatment for a wide variety of mental health issues, from depression to schizophrenia. Departments within Behavioral Health include: • Behavioral Health Unit • Behavioral Health Observation Unit
ONC	Oncology (ONC) provides treatments for cancers and blood disorders, including radiation and chemotherapy treatments.
Additional specialties	Additional specialty areas include but are not limited to: • Ophthalmology • Dermatology • Plastic Surgery • Nuclear • Urology (URO) and Dialysis • Ear, Nose, and Throat (ENT) • Rheumatology

> Some facilities may refer to their OB/GYN departments as the Stork department.

Inpatient Specialized Departments

Specialized departments within a healthcare organization that provide inpatient services include:

- OB/GYN.
- Oncology.
- Peds.
- Behavioral Health.

Outpatient Specialized Departments

Specialized departments within a healthcare organization that provide outpatient services include:

- OB/GYN.
- Oncology.
- Peds.
- Cardiovascular.
- Additional specialities.

Basic Medical Workflow

There is a general workflow, or process, that will take place when a patient visits any healthcare organization facility.

1. When a patient first arrives at a facility, the patient will be registered and admitted.
2. After the intake process, the patient will then be examined, with consultations from medical professionals from other specialties as needed, and an initial diagnosis or classification of their medical issue or condition will be made.
3. Based upon the diagnosis, disposition classification will determine when the patient will be potentially discharged,
4. Also, a treatment plan will be developed for the individual patient's needs.
5. Care will then be provided to the patient as determined by the treatment plan, with the goal of meeting the discharge date as determined by the disposition classification.
6. If the patient's treatment plan goes as planned and the patient meets the requirements, then they will be discharged from the facility.
7. Follow-up appointments or treatments will be scheduled with the necessary doctors to ensure that the patient is recovering appropriately.

IT-Based Enhancements to Medical Workflow

There are a number of IT-based enhancements with the introduction of new technology that aim to improve the workflow process and make each step easier.

IT-Based Enhancement	*Description*
Computerized data collection	Electronic data about a patient is collected and entered into a patient's medical file, and is stored within a data collection database that can be accessed by a variety of medical staff. This enhancement is used during the following workflow steps: • Registration/intake/admission • Examination and initial classification • Treatment plan and care

IT-Based Enhancement	Description
CPOE	Computerized physician order entry (CPOE) is the process of entering electronic information and instructions concerning a patient into that patient's medical files. Orders can then be communicated over a network to other medical staff or departments that are involved in processing the order. This enhancement is used during the following workflow steps: • Consultation • Disposition classification • Treatment plan and care • Discharge • Follow-up
Dictation	The process of reading aloud and recording patient data using a dictation device.This enhancement is used during the following workflow steps: • Examination and initial classification • Consultation • Disposition classification • Treatment plan and care • Discharge • Follow-up
Transcription	The process of converting dictated audio recordings of patient data, as recorded by a physician or other healthcare professional, into a text format, as done by a medical transcriptionist or via computer through voice recognition. Also includes entering patient orders currently in written format into the Electronic Medical Record (EMR) or Electronic Health Record (EHR) system. This enhancement is used during the following workflow steps: • Examination and initial classification • Consultation • Disposition classification • Treatment plan and care • Discharge • Follow-up
Digital signatures	Equivalent to a handwritten signature, a digital signature is encrypted data that acts as a person's signature on electronic documents or files. It verifies that the message or document is authentic, was created by a known sender (the signer), and was not somehow altered in transit. This enhancement is used during the following workflow steps: • Examination and initial classification • Consultation • Disposition classification • Treatment plan and care • Discharge • Follow-up

IT-Based Enhancement	Description
Electronic referrals/consults	Taking the place of handwritten letters of referral or consult, it is the process of electronically generating and sending a referral message from the referring medical professional to the one providing the referred service. This enhancement is used during the following workflow steps: • Consultation • Follow-up

ACTIVITY 2-1
Understanding Healthcare Organizations

Scenario:

Use the knowledge you gained in this topic to answer these questions about healthcare organizations.

---

1. **A 67-year-old woman falls down in her home, breaking her hip and hitting her head, cutting it open. She is rushed to the hospital, where she is treated for the head wound and has hip replacement surgery, and is recovering well. Based on the knowledge of the different departments in an organization, which of the following departments would the woman likely come in contact with throughout her treatment? (Select all that apply.)**

    a) ED

    b) Cardiovascular department

    c) Perioperative Services

    d) Radiology

    e) ICU

---

2. **True or False? A public hospital cannot be a teaching hospital.**

    __ True

    __ False

---

3. **A married couple needs to determine a healthcare plan for themselves that will suit their immediate needs and for the coming years. She was recently diagnosed with the onset of Alzheimer's disease, and he takes daily medication for diabetes management, but is otherwise mentally and physically healthy. Of the following healthcare organizations, which would make the best choice to fulfill their healthcare needs now and over time?**

    a) Nursing home

    b) Continuing care facility

    c) Intermediate care facility

    d) Home healthcare

TOPIC B

Medical Terminology, Equipment, and Software

In the previous topic, you discussed the different types of healthcare organizations. Similarly, there are numerous terms, equipment names, and software types that are specific to the healthcare industry that an IT professional working in the industry should be familiar with. In the topic, you will identify terminology, equipment, and software that are specific to the medical industry.

The industry-specific equipment, terms, and technology found in healthcare can be overwhelming. Understanding and being able to use correct terminology will allow you to effectively communicate with healthcare staff and be more successful at meeting their needs. Likewise, specific pieces of equipment and software are common to the healthcare field that are not found elsewhere. Familiarizing yourself with these things is an essential step in learning to communicate with medical professionals, and work within a healthcare IT environment.

Medical Terminology

There are a number of commonly used medical terms that you should become familiar with.

Medical Term	Definition
Imaging	Medical imaging refers to the use of various technologies to create images of the human body for use in the clinical field, such as diagnosis, treatment, and tracking of a disease or medical issue within the body.
PCP	The primary care physician (PCP) is a doctor who serves as the first contact for a patient for a variety of medical services, including physicals or well-visits, and who also serves as either the diagnosing doctor or the referring doctor when a patient presents a medical condition that he or she cannot treat.
Stat	Derived from the Latin "statim," it is used to connote immediacy or urgency.
Acuity	The acuteness, or level of severity of an illness or disease.
Code Blue/Rapid Response	Hospitals will often use their own "code" terminology ("code red," "code black") to mean different situations/response levels, but typically "code blue" is used to communicate that a patient has gone into cardiac arrest, and immediate medical attention/rapid response is needed to resuscitate the patient.
Scope of practice	The procedures, processes, or actions, as defined by state and national licensing boards, that are permitted for an individual in a particular licensing area, usually driven by criteria such as specific education and experience requirements. The scope of practice for a license is limited to what is permitted by law to be performed under that license.
Preceptor	A senior, skilled medical staff member who serves as an instructor or supervisor, providing experience and feedback, to medical students or newly hired employees still in training.

Trauma Center Levels

A *trauma center* is a facility equipped to treat patients suffering traumatic injuries. There are five levels of trauma center care.

Level	Description
Level I Trauma Center	Can provide the highest possible level of surgical care to trauma patients, with a full range of specialists and technology available 24 hours a day. It is required to have an ongoing research program and trauma education/ prevention services.
Level II Trauma Center	Can provide essential trauma care 24 hours a day with all available specialties, personnel, and equipment. Provides comprehensive trauma care and clinical assistance to a Level I facility as needed. It is differentiated from Level I because it is not required to have ongoing research programs or surgical residency.
Level III Trauma Center	Can provide treatment, surgery and intensive care to most trauma patients, but does not have all available specialists and their equipment in facility. It has transfer agreements with a Level I or II facility for the treatment of severe injuries that the Level III cannot treat.
Level IV Trauma Center	Can provide initial evaluation, stabilization, and diagnosis of a trauma patient, but then the patient must be transferred to a Level I, II or III facility for treatment and care. It is required to provide services 24 hours a day.
Level V Trauma Center	Can provide initial evaluation, stabilization, and diagnosis of a trauma patient, but then the patient must be transferred to a Level I, II or III facility for treatment and care. It is differentiated from Level IV because it is not required to have services available 24 hours a day, but must have an after-hours trauma response plan in place.

Trauma Center Certification

A hospital must receive certification to be considered a trauma center. Official designation as a trauma center is governed by individual state laws. To be designated as a trauma center, which includes the designation of the trauma level of the facility, a hospital must meet specific criteria that have been established by the American College of Surgeons and must pass an onsite review performed by the Verification Review Committee.

Controlled Substance Levels

A *controlled substance* is any drug or chemical substance that is regulated by the federal government in its production, possession, or use, including illegal and prescription drugs. There are five levels, or schedules, of controlled substances.

Schedule	Description
Schedule I Controlled Substance	The drug or substance has a high potential for abuse; the drug or substance currently has no accepted medical use in treatment in the United States; and there is a lack of accepted safety for use of the drug or substance under medical supervision. An example of a Schedule I drug is heroin.

Schedule	Description
Schedule II Controlled Substance	The drug or substance has a high potential for abuse; the drug or substance is currently accepted for medical use in treatment in the United States, with severe restrictions; and abuse of the drug or substance may lead to severe psychological or physical dependence. An example of a Schedule II drug is morphine.
Schedule III Controlled Substance	The drug or other substance has less potential for abuse than those categorized as Schedule I or II; the drug or substance is currently accepted for medical use in treatment in the United States; abuse of the drug or substance may lead to moderate or low physical dependence or high psychological dependence. An example of a Schedule III drug is pentobarbital.
Schedule IV Controlled Substance	The drug or substance has a low potential for abuse as compared to those categorized in Schedule III; the drug or substance is currently accepted for medical use in treatment in the United States; abuse of the drug or substance may lead to limited to physical or psychological dependence, especially in comparison to those categorized in Schedule III. An example of a Schedule IV drug is lorazepam.
Schedule V Controlled Substance	The drug or substance has a lower potential for abuse as compared to those categorized in Schedule IV; the drug or substance is currently accepted for medical use in treatment in the United States; abuse of the drug or substance may lead to limited to physical or psychological dependence, especially in comparison to those categorized in Schedule IV. An example of a Schedule V drug is pyrovalerone.

Types of Medical Equipment

There are numerous types of medical equipment that you may encounter in your experience and which you should be familiar with.

Type of Medical Equipment	Description
Portable X-ray machine	A mobile X-ray machine that allows X-ray technicians to bring the X-ray to the patient, instead of bringing the patient to a separate room. New technology is small enough and energy-efficient enough to transport the machine from floor to floor, and wireless capabilities to be able to push X-rays immediately for review.
MRI	A magnetic resonance imaging (MRI) machine uses high-powered magnetic fields and radio frequencies to scan and create images of the body. MRIs provide good contrast for soft tissues, making it an especially useful tool for imaging the brain, muscles, heart, other organs and cancers as compared to CT scans or X-rays.
Vital signs monitor	Portable or fixed stations that can be used to take a patient's important vital signs such as blood pressure, temperature, and blood oxygen saturation (SpO2) levels. It typically includes a vitals (or blood pressure) cuff, thermometer, and fingertip heart rate monitor.

Type of Medical Equipment	Description
EKG/ECG	An electrocardiogram (EKG or ECG) is an non-invasive procedure in which electrodes are placed on the outer surface of the skin and an electrocardiograph detects and records the electrical activity of the heart produced with each heartbeat.
EEG	Electroencephalography (EEG) is a non-invasive procedure in which electrodes are placed on the scalp to record the electrical activity of the brain produced with neural communications.
Ultrasound	An ultrasound machine uses high-frequency sound waves, which reflect or echo off of a boundary within the body, to create a two- or three-dimensional image of something within the body, such as an image of a fetus in the womb.
PET	A positron emission tomography (PET) scan is an imaging test that uses a radioactive chemical, called a radiotracer, that is injected into the bloodstream and is absorbed by the organs and tissues and a scanner that detects and records the radioactive energy given off by the radiotracer to create a three-dimensional image of the organ or tissue being studied. It can measure vital functions like blood flow and oxygen usage, and is often used to detect cancer, heart disorders, or brain disorders.
CT	A computed tomography (CT) or computerized axial tomography (CAT) scan uses a series of X-rays taken of the same area from different angles to generate a three-dimensional image of an area of the body being scanned.
Vascular/nuclear stress test	A radioactive tracer is injected into a vein, and a gamma camera detects the radiotracer as it travels to the heart, producing an image of bloodflow to and from the heart.
Blood glucometer	A glucose meter, or blood glucometer, is used to test the levels of glucose in the blood, a particularly important daily activity for those with diabetes
IV pump	An IV pump, or infusion pump, administers fluids, nutrients, or medication into a patient's circulatory system intravenously.

Medical Administrative Equipment

There are several types of specialized equipment used primarily by medical administrative staff.

Medical Administrative Equipment	Description
Card scanner	A document reader that scans card-sized documents such as a driver's license or insurance card, accurately reads the information on the card, and then records and stores an image of the card and the data using accompanying software, which can be retrieved and exported.
Hand-held barcode scanner	A hand-held device that can scan stock-keeping unit (SKU) barcodes to manage inventory for a variety of items kept on hand within a facility. Also used to scan barcodes on patient and staff facility identification (wrist bands, staff ID badges) to obtain patient information, medication verification, etc.

Medical Administrative Equipment	Description
Rx printers	As the medical world goes to electronic records, electronic prescriptions are also taking the place of handwritten prescriptions. A prescription (Rx) printer will print pharmacy-accepted and tamper-resistant prescriptions from the patient's EMR files.
Lab printers	Specialized printers and printing supplies that allow for the printing of labels, barcodes, and other materials specific for use in a lab environment.
Copiers	There are no copiers specific to use in the healthcare industry, but it is important to know that printers, copiers, and scanners are often used in facilities to print, copy, or scan in sensitive materials like medical records.
Dictation devices	Digital dictation devices are now available which record a verbal dictation of a patient's medical files in a digital format, which can then be uploaded to a patient's EMR or sent electronically to other necessary parties.

Types of Medical Software

There are numerous software applications used in the healthcare industry designed to streamline management of data and information for the facility or organization.

Type of Software	Description
Patient tracking	*Patient tracking software* allows staff to track a patient's flow of care in the system from registration, through treatment, and during and after discharge, both procedurally (where are they in the process) and physically (where are they in the facility). Patient tracking monitors and coordinates patient movements throughout the system, ensuring that a facility is utilizing its capacity and resources most efficiently and preventing delays, dissatisfaction, and potential to lose revenue.
Scheduling	Online or electronic *scheduling software* provides a start-to-finish workflow from the time a patient is scheduled through their checkout after their appointment, including insurance verification, check-in, checkout, and payment. Allows for multiple or recurring appointments to be scheduled at once. It also integrates key information or patient data at key points in the process to streamline the workflow for staff.
Order entry	*Computerized physician/provider order entry (CPOE)* systems allow for the electronic entry of all medical orders/instructions for treatment for a patient from their licensed caregiver into the software system. CPOE systems reduce the potential for error that comes with handwritten orders; aggregate all medical orders in one location for one patient; and prevent the potential for medications or procedures to negatively interact with each other down the line, notifying the ordering caregivers in advance of potential hazards.

Type of Software	Description
Practice management	*Practice management software* is an all-encompassing solution of many other IT-based pieces that streamlines the workflow processes of all activities needed to run a practice or facility while providing the ability to become a paperless office, including patient tracking, medical coding and billing, payment collection (both insurance company and co-payer), rules compliance, and reporting capabilities.
Billing/coding	*Billing and coding software* streamlines the medical billing and collections process by providing one location where charges are entered, codes can be checked, insurance claims and statements can be generated and sent, claim denials can be managed, and payments can be posted and processed.
Tracking/auditing	*Tracking and auditing software* provides a single system for tracking and managing compliance with medical claims audits that are performed by both government and commercial healthcare (insurance) organizations. Streamlines tasks and processes with dashboards, tools, and reminders to make sure that all steps in the auditing process are completed fully and on time, and prevents future errors in similar tasks.

Legacy Systems Versus EMR/EHR

In legacy medical systems, these software applications are often used as stand-alone applications, but now they are typically integrated into a single EMR/EHR system solution.

ACTIVITY 2-2

Identifying Medical Terms, Equipment, and Software

Scenario:

Use the knowledge of medical terminology, equipment, and software you gained in this topic to answer the following questions.

1. Match the medical term on the left with the correct definition on the right.

___	Acuity	a.	The level of severity of a patient's illness or disease.
___	Preceptor	b.	A medical facility equipped to treat patients suffering from life-threatening injuries.
___	Scope of practice	c.	A senior, skilled medical staff member who serves as an instructor or supervisor to medical students or new hires in training.
___	Trauma center	d.	The procedures, processes, or actions, as defined by state and national licensing boards, that are permitted for an individual in a particular licensing area, usually driven by criteria such as specific education and experience requirements.

2. Dr. Michaels and two of his colleagues are opening a private practice. They went to move to a paperless system for their patients. Which software system would make the most sense for them to implement at their office?

a) Patient tracking

b) Order entry

c) Practice management

d) Scheduling

3. **Match the type of medical imaging process with the correct description on the right.**

___	MRI	a.	A radioactive chemical, called a radiotracer, is injected into the bloodstream and is absorbed by the organs and tissues and a scanner detects and records the radioactive energy given off by the radiotracer to create a three-dimensional image.
___	EEG	b.	High-powered magnetic fields and radio frequencies are used to scan and create images of the body. Provides good contrast for soft tissues, making it an especially useful tool for imaging the brain, muscles, heart, other organs, and cancers.
___	EKG	c.	A series of X-rays taken of the same area from different angles to generate a three-dimensional image of an area of the body,
___	PET	d.	Electrodes are placed on the scalp to record the electrical activity of the brain produced with neural communications.
___	CT	e.	High-frequency sound waves are used to reflect or echo off of a boundary within the body to create a two- or three-dimensional image.
___	Ultrasound	f.	Electrodes are placed on the outer surface of the skin and a special machine detects and records the electrical activity of the heart produced with each heartbeat.

TOPIC C

Medical Coding and Billing

In the previous topic, you were introduced to some of the medical terminologies and equipment that an IT professional will need to be familiar with to function in the healthcare industry. Just as important as the equipment and devices used in the medical environment are the ways in which patient data is communicated: through the use of medical coding and billing. In this topic, you will learn more about medical coding and billing, and what related technologies you may need to support as part of your IT responsibilities.

Medical coding and billing are complex administrative functions within any healthcare organization, and with the advent of electronic medical records, they now rely nearly 100 percent on technology to function correctly. As an IT professional working in the healthcare industry, you should be prepared to deal with technologies related to this area. Acquiring this basic familiarity with these departments and the technologies they use will provide a foundation you can use to maintain and troubleshoot these systems.

Medical Coding

Definition:

Medical coding is the process of assigning a universally recognized and used medical code number to a specific clinical term, such as a medical task or service, or diagnosis or procedure. There are many accepted medical coding systems that are issued by various authorities. Different coding systems address different aspects of medical care.

Example: CPT Code for a Vaccination

Last year, Susie had to receive a tetanus shot. In her EMR, her doctor entered 90714, the Current Procedural Terminology (CPT) code for receiving a tetanus shot. Susie's insurance company recognized the code, and since it covers tetanus shots, paid for the service. Earlier this year, Susie transferred to a new doctor. When he reviewed her files, he recognized the medical code, and asked about the situation that had resulted in the need for a tetanus shot.

CPT

Current Procedural Terminology (CPT) is a list of descriptions and accompanying five-digit numeric codes used for reporting medical services and procedures, published every year by the American Medical Association.

ICD-10

The *International Statistical Classification of Diseases and Related Health Problems, 10th revision (ICD-10)* is one of several internationally endorsed medical coding classifications lists which gives a numeric code to diseases, signs and symptoms, possible complaints, abnormalities, and possible causes of injuries and diseases. The ICD-10 is published by the *World Health Organization (WHO)*.

SNOMED CT

The *Systemized Nomenclature of Medicine – Clinical Terms (SNOMED CT)* is an organized collection of numeric codes correlating to clinical information such as diseases, procedures, microorganisms, medications, and so forth that may be used in a patient's records. It was created by the College of American Pathologists (CAP) and is currently owned, maintained and distributed by the International Health Terminology Standards Development Organization (IHTSDO), a not-for-profit medical association in Denmark.

NDC ID

The U.S. Drug Listing Act of 1972 requires that all registered drug manufacturers provide the *Food and Drug Administration (FDA)* with an up-to-date list of all drugs manufactured, prepared, processed and distributed for commercial use. The act also directed the FDA to create a *National Drug Code Identification (NDC ID),*a unique, 10-digit, three-segment numeric code for each drug registered. The FDA compiles and publishes this list, the *National Drug Code Directory*, updating it on a semi-monthly basis.

E/M Codes

Evaluation and Management (E/M) Codes are five-digit codes, based on CPT codes, that are used to describe a medical professional-patient interaction, such as an office visit or a hospital, to facilitate the billing process. They were established by the United States Congress, and have been adopted by private health insurance companies as the standard for determining and communicating the types and severity of patient conditions.

Medical Billing

Definition:

Medical billing is the process of submitting and tracking claims made by healthcare providers or organizations to insurance companies on behalf on the insured patient in order to receive payment for services rendered.

Example: Billing for a Physician's Visit

Following a patient's visit to her PCP, a medical biller for the practice will determine the proper medical code corresponding to all of the services rendered to the patient (the office visit would be one code, the patient's diagnosis would be another code, any medications prescribed another code, and so on), and these codes will be transmitted to the patient's insurance company to be reviewed and processed to determine the amount the insurance company will pay based on the scope of service.

EMR/EHR Outbound Communication

There are numerous parties outside of those included in a particular EMR or EHR system that may request or require information from a patient's EMR or EHR. Patients can request a copy of their records, and external clinicians outside the practice, insurance companies, or others may request information from a patient's records. Obviously, patient health information is sensitive material, and there are required processes in place to prevent just anyone from requesting or being able to obtain information from a patient's EMR or EHR.

ROI Departments

Most large healthcare organizations will likely have dedicated staff to handling requests for EMR or EHR information in a *Release of Information (ROI) department.* Forms must be completed to request the information from the records (patient or other organization), and forms must be completed to authorize the release of the information from the records (typically, the patient or the patient's designee, if necessary). ROI staff will process and track the request, ensuring that it has the required signatures, that the records are being securely sent to the requesting party, and recording that the request and response were completed. Under HIPAA, a patient does not have to be notified that a third-party requested information from their personal health information, but record of all disclosures of a patient's health information is required, and this list can be requested by the patient.

Billing Clearinghouse

A *billing clearinghouse* acts as the intermediary between a medical biller at the healthcare practice and the insurance company, making sure the claim sent by the practice is accurate before sending it on to the insurance company. The billing clearinghouse scrubs each claim to check for errors, and once it is accepted without error, securely transmits the claims file to the insurance company.

The billing clearinghouse plays a crucial role in the billing process. There are millions of providers submitting numerous insurance claims for their millions of patients—sometimes even submitting multiple claims for one patient and one visit. The billing clearinghouse receives all of these claims and acts as the middle man between the providers and the insurance companies, taking on the arduous task of ensuring that each claim is correct before being processed. This can involve going back and forth between provider and clearinghouse to ensure that the claim is accurate.

ACTIVITY 2-3

Understanding Medical Billing and Coding

Scenario:

Use the knowledge of medical billing and coding you gained in this topic to answer the following questions.

1. **Of the following statements, which most accurately explains the importance of medical billing and coding in the healthcare industry?**
   a) Medical professionals need to get paid appropriately for the services they provide.
   b) There are so many different types of systems using various codes, there needs to be some consistent system for patient data and payment purposes.
   c) Patients need to be able to feel comfortable that their information can be transferred between professionals with no mistakes.
   d) Medical professionals need to be able to quickly and efficiently record and store pertinent patient information.

2. **Match the type of medical coding systems to the correct description.**

___	ICD-10	a.	Numeric codes used to describe a medical professional-patient interaction.
___	SNOMED CT	b.	Classification list of numeric codes used to describe diseases, signs and symptoms, etc.
___	NDC ID	c.	A unique numeric code used to identify registered drugs.
___	E/M Codes	d.	An organized collection of numeric codes correlating to clinical information.

3. **Which of the following describes the complete medical coding and billing process most accurately?**
   a) The codes for services rendered are determined. The claim is generated. The billing clearinghouse scrubs the claim. The claim is submitted to the insurance company. The insurance company accepts or rejects the claim.
   b) The codes for services rendered are determined. The claim is generated. The claim is submitted to the insurance company. The insurance company accepts or rejects the claim.
   c) The codes for services rendered are determined. The billing clearinghouse scrubs the claim. The claim is submitted to the insurance company. The insurance company accepts or rejects the claim.
   d) The codes for services rendered are determined. The claim is generated. The billing clearinghouse scrubs the claim. The claim is submitted to the insurance company. The insurance company automatically accepts the claim.

TOPIC D

Medical Computer Interfaces

In the previous topics, you have learned about the numerous systems and applications that have been introduced to the healthcare industry as more organizations move towards being entirely electronic. Yet, these various systems all need to be able to communicate between one another to send and receive important patient information. In this topic, you will learn about the interfaces that have been developed to allow communication between systems.

As more healthcare organizations move towards functioning entirely electronically, a multitude of systems and applications have been introduced. The problem is, how do we ensure that all of these various systems can communicate seamlessly between one another, especially when it concerns information as sensitive and important as a person's health? With all of the various types of systems, interfaces specific to the healthcare industry have been developed to ensure that systems can communicate with one another. Part of your role as a healthcare IT technician may be to implement or troubleshoot these interfaces.

Medical Interfaces

Definition:

Medical interfaces are software systems solutions developed using specific industry standards and rules that allow all the separate medical systems to communicate as seamlessly as possible with one another.

Example: Medical Interfaces for a Lab Test

A patient's PCP orders a series of blood work. The order is placed electronically. Unfortunately, the doctor's office and the lab use two different software systems. Fortunately, the lab's system can understand the order being sent, and the doctor's office can decipher the results returned, because the two systems communicate through an interface that uses standard messaging systems to operate seamlessly between different applications.

HL7

HL7 specifications are healthcare industry standards and a framework concerning the exchange and integration of patients' electronic information between software systems, as developed by the voluntary, not-for-profit consortium called Health Level Seven. Vendors developing interfaces adhere to these standards, ensuring that the disparate software applications used by healthcare organizations and the interfaces that communicate between them are all speaking the same electronic language to accurately exchange patient medical data.

Standard Components of HL7

Software applications communicate with one another using HL7 messages, and HL7 messages are made up of segments, a group of fields that contain data. Each segment is a unique, three-character code that relays a specific piece of patient medical data. There are close to 200 segments used in HL7.

HL7 Segments

This table shows some of the most commonly used HL7 segments.

HL7 Segment	*Relayed Information*
AL1	Patient Allergy Information
BLG	Billing
DG1	Diagnosis
EVN	Event Type
FT1	Financial Transaction
GT1	Guarantor
IN1	Insurance
MSH	Message Header
NK1	Next of Kin/Associated Parties
NTE	Notes and Comments
OBR	Observation Request
OBX	Observation Result
ORC	Common Order
ROL	Provider Type
PID	Patient Identification
SCH	Scheduling Activity Information

For a complete list of all HL7 segments, visit **www.interfaceware.com/hl7-standard/hl7-segments.html**.

CCR

A *Continuity of Care Record (CCR)* is a health record standard that was developed by a number of American healthcare organizations as a means of creating summary documents containing the most relevant and pertinent information about a patient, such as insurance information, recent diagnoses, current medications being taken, known allergies, and so forth. CCRs can be shared electronically between medical caregivers regardless of their respective EMR or EHR software applications.

CCD

A *Continuity of Care Document (CCD)* is a health record standard similar to the CCR, designed to provide guidelines for creating summary documents containing the most pertinent patient information, which can be shared electronically between medical caregivers regardless of their respective EMR or EHR system. CCD can be viewed as a "next generation" of the CCR, as it was developed with representation from both HL7 and the American Society for Testing and Materials International (ASTM), which was a key player in the development of the CCR. It is a more robust implementation of CCR, combining the interoperability of HL7 technologies with the consistency of CCR information exchange amongst organizations.

PACS

A *Picture Archiving and Communications System (PACS)* is an application system where medical images of almost all kinds, including MRIs, CT scans, ultrasounds, and mammograms can be stored and retrieved electronically by various members of a healthcare organization. PACS is used as the platform for the integration of medical images with other medical software systems, so that all patient medical information can be viewed within a single-source location, like that patient's electronic medical record. These images can also be accessed by doctors at other facilities or accessed remotely in cases where the immediate view of an image is necessary.

e-Prescribing

Definition:

If available as part of their medical software, medical professionals can use *e-prescribing,* which is the transmission of a patient's prescription for medication electronically from the prescriber's computer to the pharmacy's computer. The pharmacist must validate the prescription before dispensing the medication to the patient.

Example:

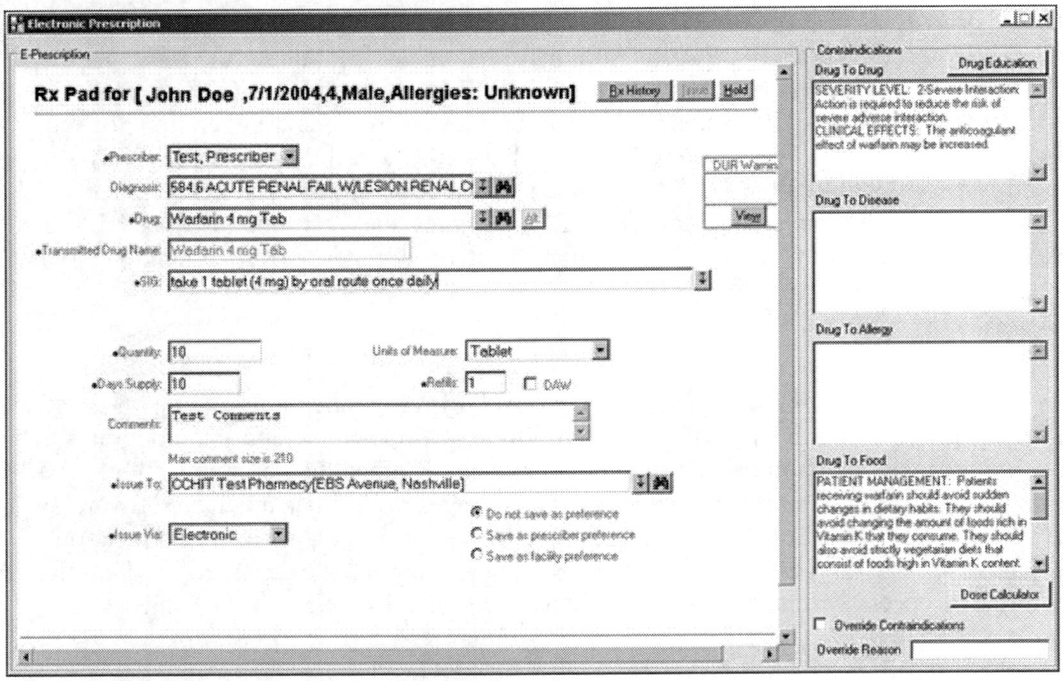

Figure 2-1: *An e-prescription.*

Medication Reconciliation

During *medication reconciliation,* a list of a patient's prescription orders is compared to a list of those that the patient is currently taking in order to avoid any possible medication errors such as duplicated prescriptions, errors in dosage, or potentially hazardous drug interactions.

Medication reconciliation should be completed at every transition point of a patient's healthcare plan, whether between doctors or between facilities. The complete list of a patient's medications should be updated and shared with all necessary persons after each reconciliation is completed.

The Medication Reconciliation Process

The medication reconciliation process includes: developing a list of medications currently prescribed or that will be prescribed for a patient; developing and reviewing a list of medications currently being taken by the patient (with the help of the patient or someone close to the patient); comparing the two lists for redundancies, interactions, dosage errors, and more; and then making important clinical decisions based on the comparison, which may include discontinuing non-active prescriptions, renewing expired prescriptions, changing dosages of existing medications, and prescribing new medications.

Bedside Medication Verification

Bedside medication verification is a checks-and-balances system that ensures that a patient is receiving the correct medication, the correct dose of medication, at the correct time, from an authorized caregiver by requiring that barcodes be scanned and information verified prior to the medication being administered.

The Bedside Medication Verification Process

Depending on the system, before administering any medication, two to three barcodes must be scanned:

1. If required, the ID of the person administering the medication, ensuring that the person is authorized to dispense the medication and that another staff member has not done so already.
2. The patient's wristband, identifying the patient.
3. The medicine label of the drug being administered, to confirm that it is the proper medication and dosage for that particular patient.

When these have been verified, the medication can then be administered to the patient.

Allergy Interactions

Any adverse reaction to a medication is referred to as a *drug allergy* or *drug reaction*. Adverse reactions from a drug allergy can range from mild and irritating like skin rashes, to potentially life-threatening like anaphylaxis. The reaction is caused by the immune system not recognizing the drug as helpful in the body, but rather overreacting to the drug as if it were attacking the body.

Formulary Checking

Formulary checking is the automatic process of checking a prescription for medication against a patient's known allergies for possible drug-allergy reactions, and against current medications for possible adverse drug-drug interactions, or contraindications. Formulary checking occurs immediately when the new drug is prescribed in the e-prescription system. Once the prescription is entered into the EMR or EHR system, a basic formulary check is run automatically to determine if there is any potential for negative interaction. If one is flagged, the prescriber or pharmacist is notified and must make the final decision to override the notification and fill the prescription or decide on another course of action. Ultimately, the pharmacist is responsible for performing additional checking and validating the drug order before dispensing.

> A drug-to-drug interaction, also known as a contraindication, is a condition or factor that serves as a reason to withhold a specific medical treatment.

ACTIVITY 2-4

Understanding Medical Interfaces

Scenario:

Use the knowledge of medical interfaces you gained in this topic to answer the following questions.

---

1. **Match the prescription-related term on the left with the correct description on the right.**

___	Medication reconciliation	a.	The automatic process of checking a prescription for medication against a patient's known allergies (drug-allergy) and current medications for possible adverse interactions (drug-drug) immediately when it is prescribed in the e-prescription system.
___	Bedside medication verification	b.	A checks-and-balances system that ensures that a patient is receiving the correct medication, the correct dose of medication, at the correct time, from an authorized caregiver by requiring verification of patient, medication, and possibly dispensing personnel prior to the medication being dispensed.
___	Formulary checking	c.	A process that involves comparing a list of a patient's medication orders to a list of those that the patient has been taking to avoid any possible medication errors such as duplicated prescriptions, errors in dosage, or potentially hazardous drug interactions.

---

2. **Which of the following steps would potentially take place during bedside medication verification? (Select all that apply.)**

   a) The patient's wristband is scanned.

   b) The ID of the dispensary personnel is scanned.

   c) The barcode on the medication label is scanned.

   d) The ID of the administering personnel is scanned.

   e) The ID of the provider who prescribed the medication is scanned.

---

3. **Match the interface-related term on the left with the correct description on the right.**

___ HL7	a. A health record standard that was developed as a means of creating summary documents containing the most relevant and pertinent information about a patient that can be shared electronically between medical caregivers, regardless of their respective EMR or EHR software applications.
___ PACS	b. A health record standard designed to provide guidelines for creating summary documents containing the most pertinent patient information, which can be shared electronically between medical caregivers regardless of their respective EMR or EHR system, but uses standards from both HL7 and ASTM.
___ CCD	c. An application system where medical images of almost all kinds, including MRIs, CAT scans, ultrasounds, mammograms, etc., can be stored and retrieved electronically.
___ CCR	d. Healthcare industry standards and a framework concerning the exchange and integration of a patients's electronic information between software systems.

Lesson 2 Follow-up

In this lesson, you learned about the medical environment including its organization, stakeholders, and the most significant technologies. Having an understanding of how the medical environment is structured and familiarity with essential jargon will allow you as a healthcare IT technician to meet the challenges of this unfamiliar environment.

1. **How does the information presented in this lesson directly affect your responsibilities as an IT professional in the healthcare industry?**

2. **Why do you think it is important to have an understanding of the medical environment overall?**

3 Using IT in the Medical Workplace

Lesson Time: 3 hour(s)

Lesson Objectives:

In this lesson, you will leverage core medical concepts to describe the use of IT in the medical workplace.

You will:

- Describe the need for and use of roles and responsibilities in healthcare IT.
- Communicate effectively with other IT staff and healthcare staff while using technology appropriately and respecting all applicable rules, roles, and regulations.
- Identify the legal best practices, requirements, and documentation used in the medical environment.
- Explain the process of medical document imaging.
- Identify the techniques used to properly manage sanitation.

Introduction

Earlier in the course, the focus had been primarily on the healthcare industry and environment, including regulations and standards that govern a medical environment. With all this in mind, you will now focus on how technology fits into the everyday medical workplace.

Working with IT in any workplace has unique challenges, but the medical workplace is particularly fraught with challenges. Understanding the practical implications of technologies and how they are applied to healthcare business problems builds upon your understanding of the healthcare environment to enable you so successfully solve business problems in healthcare using IT.

TOPIC A
Roles and Responsibilities

Earlier in the course, you identified various medical departments, common terminology used, and other medical systems commonly found in a medical environment. The next logical step is to identify all the common roles and responsibilities of the people who work in those areas. In this topic, you will describe the roles and responsibilities of those who work in the healthcare field.

To properly support any type of medical office, you must be able to identify key roles and responsibilities that need to access Electronic Medical Record (EMR) or Electronic Health Record (EHR) systems. This enables you to provide the right level of support quickly and efficiently when issues arise.

Information Sensitivity and Clearance

Any medical office setting or hospital is responsible for keeping all patient records and files private. Because of the sensitivity of the data, strict clearance guidelines are established to dictate who can access and read the contents of any patient record. In the United States, government law states that only the healthcare provider and the patient can read the contents of the health record, unless authorized by the patient.

Sensitivity Labels

Access to patient data within the EHR system can be managed using sensitivity labels. A *sensitivity label* determines the clearance for an information zone within the EMR system.

Break Glass Access

Definition:

Break glass access is temporary and specific emergency access to specifically locked Personal Health Information (PHI) data in order to gain access to information which enables task completion. This action is common in record keeping, situations that require a release of information, and in emergency situations. When a situation requires break glass access, there is usually a warning presented to the user asking if access to data is necessary.

Example: ED Access

A doctor or nurse caring for a patient within the Emergency Department (ED) may use a break glass access to view a patient record to verify that there is no previous psychological diagnosis, or HIV status that needs to be considered in order to provide the right level of care.

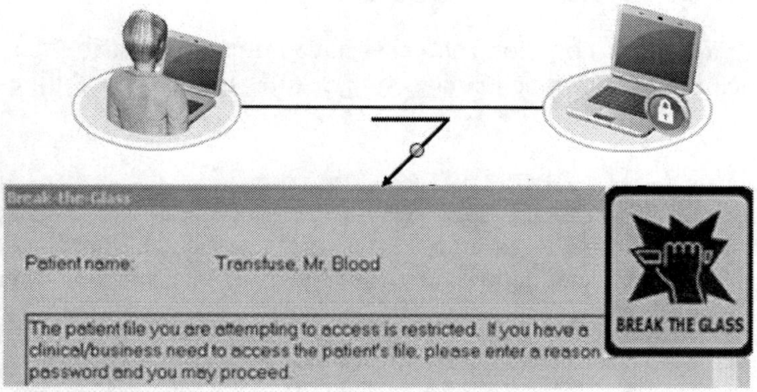

Figure 3-1: *Break the glass access.*

Medical Personnel

Within the EHR or EMR system, access roles and responsibilities are assigned according to Health Insurance Portability and Accountability Act (HIPAA) regulations. Most EMR and EHR systems will have predefined profiles available in the system that can be assigned to clinical roles within your environment:

- A medical doctor (MD).
- A registered nurse (RN).
- A physician's assistant (PA).
- A patient care technician (PCT).
- A medical assistant (MA).
- A licensed practical nurse (LPN).
- And, a dental assistant (DA).

Medical Office Staff and Business Personnel

Medical office staff and other business clients may have limited access to EMR or EHR system data, depending on their specific role. Within an medical office or hospital there are a variety of common roles you may encounter including:

- A nursing unit clerk/secretary (NUC).
- A unit administrator (UA).
- A project manager (PM).
- A practice manager (PM).
- An office manager.
- And, other business personnel and staff members.

> Keep in mind that the PM acronym can refer to both a project manager and practice manager.

IT and Other Technical Roles

Within the IT field, there are many common roles that have unique responsibilities within an IT infrastructure. Healthcare IT environments have similar roles and responsibilities.

Role	Responsibility
Security administrator	Responsible for ensuring that an organization's information security policies are being followed by employees and that sufficient controls are in place to prevent unauthorized access to data, systems, and facilities.
Network administrator	Responsible for the network infrastructure and components within an organization. Responsibilities include the setup, monitoring, management, updating, and optimizing of network hardware components, Local Area Networks (LANs), Wide Area Networks (WANs), and wireless networks.
Systems administrator	Responsible for the maintenance of an organization's hardware systems, networks, and server systems. This role may be an individual or a team of administrators, depending on the needs and size of a business.
Database administrator	Also referred to as a *DBA*, is responsible for designing, implementing, maintaining, and repairing databases. This person is also responsible for the security and maintenance of an organization's database system and all the data stored on the systems.
Desktop support	Responsible for assisting end users and attempting to restore normal service to users as quickly as possible. Desktop support typically deals with basic computer issues, such as hardware malfunction, networking issues, application problems, access requests, and new hardware requests.

Business Associates, Contractors, and Third Parties

In many cases, there may be a need for other business associates and contractors to access data within the EHR or EMR system. These individuals are required to sign HIPAA documentation, so they can have limited access to sensitive information within the system. In these cases, there may be strict guidelines issued as to what access roles and rights to data they can have. As the IT technician, you must be aware of the business contracts and agreements that exist when there are contractors involved in everyday processes and procedures. For example, you may be working with an IT outsourcing firm, and visit a number of different medical practices within a given day. In this case, you would most likely be required to sign a business agreement contract for each practice, ensuring that PHI is secured.

Working Within a Medical Team

As an IT technician in the healthcare environment, you must recognize the various roles that you will be supporting and working with. As you work with various medical teams:

- Understand what the overall system does.
- Understand what the various roles and responsibilities are within that system.
- Recognize that technology may be challenging for some medical staff.
- Support medical staff in changing workflows due to systems updates or changes.
- And, be aware of the acronym use between both technical staff and medical staff.

The Treatment Team

Any of the clinical roles can be a member of the treatment team. The *treatment team* is made up of a number of clinicians who have been assigned to work with a specific patient at any given time, such as an MD, an RN, and a PA. Team members are assigned and tracked within the EMR/EHR system, and can be updated and changed as clinician work shifts are changed.

ACTIVITY 3-1

Examining Roles and Responsibilities

Scenario:

In this activity, you will examine roles and responsibilities that interact with the EMR or EHR system on a daily basis.

---

1. **One of the medical facilities you support has contacted you because they cannot connect the EMR/EHR system to access the patient billing web-based application. When you arrive at the office and check out the situation, you determine that she can connect to the Internet, but not the billing application. You determine that the issue has to do with the EMR/EHR in-house server. Who should you contact for server issues?**
   - a) Security administrator
   - b) Network administrator
   - c) DBA
   - d) Systems administrator

---

2. **When is break glass access necessary in a medical setting?**

---

3. **In the hospital where you work as an IT support technician, there has been a breach in security within the ED. Someone has reported that a laptop has been stolen. The laptop was a shared device for updating and tracking all ED patient information. What medical roles will this impact?**

TOPIC B

Manage Communication and Ethics Issues

In the previous topic, you identified different medical roles you may encounter while supporting IT within a medical facility. Now that you know who you will be working with, you can focus on using good communication skills and conducting yourself in a professional way while on the job at any medical environment. In this topic, you will manage communication and ethics issues.

Communicating and interacting with non-IT professionals can be challenging, and even more so in a medical environment where time is short and jargon abounds. Because of this, it is vital to your effectiveness as an IT professional that you are aware of the hurdles that may arise, and how to overcome them.

Communication Skills

Using the proper communication skills when dealing with clients and colleagues provides a professional environment that is conducive to effective communication with doctors, nurses, and other medical staff within the healthcare environment.

Communication Skill	Description
Verbal communication	• Use clear, concise, and direct statements. This will help you get to the crux of the matter more quickly, and it will help the clinician understand what you are saying. • Avoid using IT jargon, abbreviations, acronyms, and slang. Many clinicians and office staff will not have the same level of technical knowledge as you and your colleagues, and using terminology that is beyond their level of knowledge can confuse or upset them. • Use timing to set the pace of a conversation. A pause may be more valuable than an immediate answer, as it allows you time to formulate your response. If a situation escalates and the person you are interacting with becomes agitated, you may ask him or her to slow down so that you can get all the information.

Communication Skill	Description
Non-verbal communication	• Be aware of the non-verbal clues you use, whether you are talking or listening. Body language communicates more than actual words. Studies show that up to 70 percent of a message is conveyed through actions. Even when you are talking on the phone, non-verbal characteristics—such as tone of voice—will add meaning to your message and help you interpret the concerns of the clinical staff. • Use the proper level of eye contact. You and the person you are interacting with will make, maintain, and break eye contact as you talk with each other. When attention is directed to the problem at hand, eye contact may be minimal. Avoid staring directly at the clincian—a form of invading personal space—or letting your gaze wander, which indicates disinterest, or even worse, inappropriate interest. • Use gestures and facial expressions to reinforce the spoken message. Broad, friendly gestures indicate being open to the conversation, while sharp or jabbing gestures usually mean anger. The variety, intensity, and meaning of facial expressions are almost endless. You and the clinician you are working with read each other's faces to gain insight into the spoken words. • Use non-verbal encouragement to gather information. Encourage the person you are interacting with to continue with "Mm-hmm" and a slight nod of your head. You convey that you are listening and want to know more. • Be aware of physical positioning and posture. Respect the person's personal space. Depending on the circumstances, you may be from 1.5 to 4 feet away from the person you are interacting with. If this clinician or staff member backs up, you are too close. You may be working in close quarters; ask permission before you move into a person's personal space—for example, sitting in the office chair. Messages are conveyed by body position. Slouching indicates "I am bored with this conversation." Holding one's arms across the chest says "I am closed off to what you are saying." Watch your body's signals, as well as those of the clinician you are working with. • Be aware of the effect of tone of voice. The tone of voice indicates many internal moods: excitement, boredom, sarcasm, fear, or uncertainty. A rise in your voice at the end of a sentence makes it sound like a question, implying lack of assurance instead of competence. Listen to the clinician's tone. Volume—loudness or softness—colors the spoken message. If the person's agitation escalates, try lowering your volume to re-establish a sense of calm. • Use the appropriate level of physical contact. A firm handshake is appreciated and may be expected in some business dealings. Other forms of touching are generally unnecessary, inappropriate, and risky.

Communication Skill	Description
Listening skills	• Listen to the clinician or staff member. If you do not, you run the risk of missing some important information that can help you solve the problem. • Allow the clinician or staff member to complete statements—avoid interrupting. This will convey the message that you respect them and want to hear what he or she is saying. • Employ passive listening techniques. Your message is: "I am listening. Tell me more." You are alert, attentive, and accepting, but do not participate actively in the conversation. Your silence may help the individual to collect his or her thoughts, especially if he or she is upset or angry. Listen for factual data and be alert for feelings and attitudes, which are conveyed non-verbally. It may be difficult to keep from jumping in with a question or a "Yes, but..." Resist the temptation by writing down your thoughts to refer to later. • Employ active listening techniques. When the clinician or staff member is describing the problem, listen actively to elicit as much information as you can. Clarify user statements by asking pertinent questions.

Technical Communication Methods

When supporting a medical office or hospital, there are a number of methods to use for communication. Depending on the situation, one method may be more effective than others.

Method	Description
Email	*Email* allows a user to send an electronic message to another user or group of users. This method is useful when you need to communicate with one or more contacts about system updates, installations, or issues.
IM and secure chat	*Instant messaging (IM)* is a type of communication service which involves a private dialogue between two persons via instant-text-based messages over the Internet. *Secure chat* is an instant messaging service that uses strong encryption to send and receive secure messages. IM is an efficient method of communication, because it is done in real-time and can enable you to communicate on an individual basis quickly.
EMR system	The EMR system may have built-in workflow functionality that would notify personnel when a process or procedure is completed. This process can be used to communicate when a task is complete, or has moved to the next phase.
Fax	A fax is typically used to send an electronic copy of a hardcopy document quickly. This type of communication method is used commonly to send medical reports, patient prescriptions, and doctor referrals between offices.
Secure FTP	*Secure File Transfer Protocol (Secure FTP)* is a secure version of FTP that uses a Secure Shell (SSH) tunnel as an encryption method to transfer, access, and manage files. Secure FTP is used primarily on Microsoft® Windows® systems.

Method	***Description***
Phone	The phone is a traditional way of communicating and is used primarily in a medical setting to quickly resolve patient issues. Most often the phone system is used to manage appointments and communicate with patients about medical issues.
VoIP	*Voice over IP (VoIP)* is an implementation in which voice signals are transmitted over IP networks. The phone can be an IP telephone unit, a VoIP interface at a Private Branch Exchange (PBX) or a softphone (a software application such as Skype), which enables the originating device to access the IP network and place and receive telephone calls.
Collaborative software	*Collaborative software* refers to applications that enables sharing of files, wikis, and blogs within a healthcare environment. For example, Microsoft® SharePoint®.

Professional Conduct

Acting in a professional manner when dealing with colleagues and clients provides a work environment where expectations are met and work is completed as expected.

Facet	***Description***
Appearance	Exhibit a professional appearance while in the medical environment. Any medical facility requires that you present a neat, clean, business-like appearance.

Facet	Description
Respect	Be respectful and sensitive of the medical environment in which you are working. • Maintain a positive attitude when talking with clinicians and other staff members. Arguing or getting defensive with individuals will make it harder for you to solve problems and fix issues. • Be culturally sensitive. This is especially important within a medical environment. Always be conscious of who you are working with, and how your actions can be portrayed. • Never minimize a problem. What seems simple to you could be a mission-critical problem to the clinician. • Never insult a clinician, or any other staff member. No matter how frustrating a situation might become, rudeness is never the answer. • When dealing with clinicians and medical staff, avoid distractions and interruptions. Repeatedly answering a mobile phone, talking to coworkers, or attending to any other personal distractions while you are supposed to be supporting medical staff sends the message that the problem is unimportant to you. • When dealing with a difficult person or situation, avoid arguing, being judgmental, or being defensive. Never minimize a problem. • Be sure to keep your work area at any of the medical office sites neat. Do not pile materials on staff member's books and files. When onsite at a medical office or hospital, ask where to dispose of materials. • Be on time. Tardiness can give a negative impression of you. If you are going to be late, always call and communicate with the medical staff. • Be respectful of the property at the medical site. Always ask permission before entering an office, workspace, or hospital room, using the telephone, sitting down at a computer, or adjusting the workspace.
Accountability	Be accountable. Do not misrepresent your credentials, competence, or training. Take responsibility for your actions, and admit your mistakes. In questions of conflict of interest between your company and the medical staff, refer to your supervisor or follow your company's procedure.
Confidentiality	Be circumspect. Treat any information located on a desktop, a computer, or a printer that pertains to patients or medical staff as confidential.
Ethics	Practice ethical conduct. You have an obligation to take responsibility for ethical conduct within your delivery of service. The issues involved are complex and ever-changing in the medical field. An unethical practice may become so routine that it is falsely assumed to be acceptable behavior. Learn your medical office or hospital policies and adhere to them.
Honesty	Be forthright with clinicians and staff members about what is occurring and the actions you will take. Clients have a right to understand the process you are following and how it will affect them.
Prioritizing	Set priorities. You will often need to set priorities and make judgment calls. You will recommend whether your clinician should repair or replace equipment. You will rank the urgency of the needs. Base your decisions on common courtesy, fundamental fairness, and keeping promises. Be familiar with your medical office or hospital policies and follow them.

Facet	Description
Expectations	You should set expectations with the medical staff up front. Set a timeline and a communication plan that both you and the staff agree on at the start of the relationship. Always communicate repair and replacement options, and provide the proper documentation needed for the services provided. Always follow up and get feedback on the work completed. This information allows you to improve customer satisfaction with future projects. When working with project managers on assignments, it is crucial to conform to any requirements before, during, and after work completed, to make sure that all expectations have been met for a project.

Adapting to Varying Medical Environments

Working within a medical environment can be challenging depending on the office, hospital, nursing home, or outpatient care center. As the IT technician, you must be aware and understand that you may be exposed to clinical areas where patients are being treated, where emergency medical care is given, and in some cases trauma centers. Before entering any medical setting or room, you must adapt the appropriate procedural behavior according to the situation or environment.

Situational Awareness

In some cases, you may not be comfortable with the varied circumstances in a medical environment. In these cases it is important to acknowledge your limitations, and know how to express your feelings. If a situation or environment brings on a strong physical feeling of being uncomfortable, then you must recognize this and take action to alleviate the negative feelings and remove yourself from the situation or environment.

Common Medical Environments

There are a number of common medical environments within a healthcare organization. These common areas may demand specific safety and operating procedures.

Medical Environment	Description
Imaging Center	Area where all medical imaging procedures are conducted, such as magnetic resonance imaging (MRI) scans, computed tomography (CT) scans, ultrasounds, and so forth.
Recovery Room	Area where patients are housed after a surgical procedure or any procedure requiring anaesthesia. Patients are closely monitored for any indications of post-operative complications.
Examination Room	A private room where a patient is examined and diagnosed by a medical practitioner.
Float Room	Any room used to temporarily house patients when they are in transition between their patient room and another location, such as before or after tests or surgeries. A Float Room may also be called a holding bay, temp room, or prep room.
Operating Room (OR)	Area where surgical procedures are performed in a sterile environment.

Medical Environment	Description
Isolation Room	Areas within a medical facility designed to prevent the spread of air-borne infections through the use of negative pressurization control of the air inside and outside the room. Patients with highly infectious diseases, like tuberculosis, will be isolated in these pressure controlled environments to prevent the spread of the infection to other patients and staff.
Procedure Room	Area where minor procedures are performed, including minor surgeries not requiring anaesthesia and post-operative care.
Emergency Room (ER)	Area of the facility where needing immediate medical treatment arrive and are provided with initial care for their medical illness or injury, before being admitted for further treatment by another department.

Manage Communication and Ethics Issues

Working within a healthcare environment can be challenging due to the nature of the services, and care given to patients. Proper communication and ethics can be crucial to providing support while being respectful of your surroundings.

Guidelines

To properly manage communication and ethics issues:

- Use good communication skills when conversing with medical and office staff.
- Actively listen to clients when they are communicating an issue or problem.
- Conduct yourself in a professional way.
- Be aware of your environment, and adjust your behavior accordingly.
- If working on an assigned IT project, make sure to work within the guidelines and standards set forth by the project manager.

Example:

You are an IT support technician who has been called down to the ED to help one of the RNs who is having trouble accessing a patient's file within the EMR system. Before you go down to the ED, you prepare yourself mentally and realize that you may be exposed to things that may make you feel uncomfortable. When you arrive, the RN is visibly frustrated with the computer system. You calmly ask her to explain the steps she has taken, and you just listen and nod as she steps through the process. Once she is done, you ask her if you can access the system, so you can fix the problem.

DISCOVERY ACTIVITY 3-2

Managing Communication and Ethics

Scenario:

In this activity, you will manage communication and ethics issues within a medical environment.

---

1. Match each communication skill or behavior with the appropriate example.

___	Verbal communication	a.	Allow the user to complete statements without interruption.
___	Non-verbal communication	b.	Project professionalism by being neat and clean.
___	Listening skills	c.	Do not use information gained during a service call for your personal benefit.
___	Respect	d.	Keep sensitive client information to yourself.
___	Ethical behavior	e.	Ask permission before sitting down in a user's chair or touching a user's computer.
___	Confidentiality	f.	Use clear, concise, and direct statements.
___	Appearance	g.	Maintain the proper amount of eye contact.

---

2. Which are examples of displaying respect during a service call?

a) Asking permission before changing display settings

b) Asking "What happened just before you noticed the problem?"

c) Sitting in a user's chair without permission

d) Silencing your pager or mobile phone

---

3. You have been informed that starting next week, you will be supporting a new medical facility with their EMR/EHR implementation. You will be onsite all day for a whole week helping the front-end office staff with setting up and configuring their workstations. Your supervisor has warned you that the environment may be uncomfortable and unsettling due to the medical facility with a low-income provider and its location being in a known problem area of the city, where drugs are a constant problem. How should you prepare yourself for working in this type of setting?

TOPIC C

Legal Best Practices, Requirements, and Documentation

In the last topic, you identified the roles working within a medical environment, and what communication methods can be used while supporting those roles. Now that you are aware of people and communication issues, you can focus on the legal issues you should be familiar with and how they affect procedures and policies. In this topic, you will describe legal best practices, requirements, and documentation.

There are a large number of required documents, approvals, and signatures involved in healthcare documentation. Awareness of which documents are the most important and the legal requirements surrounding them can help you and your provider avoid potential miscommunications or even legal liabilities.

Record Keeping and Documentation

There are a number of regulatory rules and general guidelines on medical record keeping and documentation. Patient record retention procedures vary depending on the type of medical facility. Common reasons for retaining records are:

- Patient progress and management documentation.
- Patient record sharing between healthcare providers.
- And, documentation support for possible legal evaluations.

Time of Storage

The time of storage for any medical record is based on a number of different factors:

- State and federal laws.
- Case laws.
- Medical board and association policies.
- And, patient age.

State and Federal Record Retention Laws

In most cases, record retention laws and regulations. The time of storage varies among regulating agencies. For example, Medicare, the Occupational Safety and Health Administration (OSHA), and HIPAA may each have their own requirements for record retention. Regulations may differ depending on factors such as the age of the patient, whether the patient is deceased, whether the patient is covered by Medicare or Medicaid, and so forth. Records should be kept for the longest time required by any of the applicable laws, regulations, or policies.

Important Medical Records

Any record that contains specific clinical care that was given to a patient must be kept. Types of records can include any doctor notes; nurse notes; lab testing results; medications administered or prescribed; and all media such as X-rays, graphs, and charts. In certain states, healthcare providers may be required to also retain all billing information and any records that have been transferred from another provider.

Working with PHI

In order to keep personal health information safe within a healthcare environment, there are a number of practices used to ensure that information is not exposed or shared with unauthorized individuals.

Practice	*Description*
Computer placement	Proper placement of computers within a medical office can prevent exposure to sensitive data by preventing unauthorized individuals from viewing a computer screen. Simple planning and proper equipment placement prevents the data displayed on computer screens from being viewed.
Privacy screens	Privacy screens should be used to block any general access to patients while they are being treated. Screens can also be used to block the view of computers, patient files and records, and billing areas.
Printer placement	Any printer that is used for printing patient records, prescriptions, billing information, immunization reports, and medication lists should be in a secured section of the office and only accessible by authorized users.
Screensavers	Screensavers should be used when a system has been idle for a certain amount of time. The guidelines on when they should be used are specific to the office, but when systems are in view by individuals other than authorized users, guidelines should be in place. This feature is useful to block information from view, but once the mouse or keyboard is activated, the computer is accessible by anyone.
Time lockout	Computer systems should be configured to lock when there has been no activity within a given time. Clinicians should lock out of all computers before they walk away, especially when in an Examination Room with a patient. The time lockout feature is similar to the screensaver in that it prevents unauthorized users from viewing any information displayed, but once locked, you must enter a password to access any information. If clinicians forget to log out, then a time lockout will lock a computer automatically.

Disposal of PHI

PHI information that meets expiration requirements must be disposed of using an approved secure disposal method.

Method	Description
Secure shredding/ sanitizing	A method used to securely remove data from hard drives and other electronic storage devices. Secure shredding utilities completely remove data and any data remnants from a device. There are two common methods used in sanitizing devices: *Data wiping* is a method used to remove any sensitive data from a device and permanently delete it. *Data sanitization* is the method used to repeatedly delete and overwrite any traces or bits of sensitive data that may remain on a device after data wiping has been done.
Degaussing	A method used to remove data from magnetic media. Degaussing changes the magnetic alignment of data, so that it cannot be recovered.
Physical disposal	Paper shredders are used to dispose of hard copy materials, such as receipts, bills, and patient records that have been imaged and entered into the EMR system. For security purposes, you must shred or burn sensitive documents and bulk erase magnetic media such as disks or tapes before discarding them. Crack or break optical disks. This helps prevent attackers from obtaining sensitive information from discarded hardware and media.

PHI Media

Any bits of electronic data left on a computer, device, or media can potentially be stolen and used to harm the patient or healthcare provider. Examples of physical media that may contain PHI data include:

- Paper charts.
- Tapes.
- DVDs/CDs.
- Hard drives.
- Fax machine hard drives.
- Copier hard drives.
- External hard drives.
- Thumb drives.
- Smartphones.
- Tablets.

Liability

Definition:

Liability is the condition of being actually or potentially subject to a legal obligation based on one's actions or omissions. A medical practitioner can be held liable for malpractice when there was a specific duty owed, but the duty was breached, and the breach caused an injury or additional damages. When these factors are present, the practitioner and the hospital are liable for the results.

Example: Liability in a Surgical Procedure

A patient going in for surgery is given an anesthetic. The anesthesiologist overlooked a previous treatment complication, and as a result the patient suffers liver damage and possible life-threatening complications. In this case the anesthesiologist is held liable because he or she overlooked key information in the EMR. The hospital and all treatment team members may also be held liable.

Liability Waivers

Definition:

A *liability waiver* is a legal document that may be signed by a patient (or those acting legally on behalf of a patient) to acknowledge the risks involved in a specific medical procedure or medication. By doing so, the signer potentially removes legal liability from the hospital and medical practitioner. However, liability waivers may not be enforceable, depending on the specific state law, public policy, juries, and the language of the waiver.

Example:

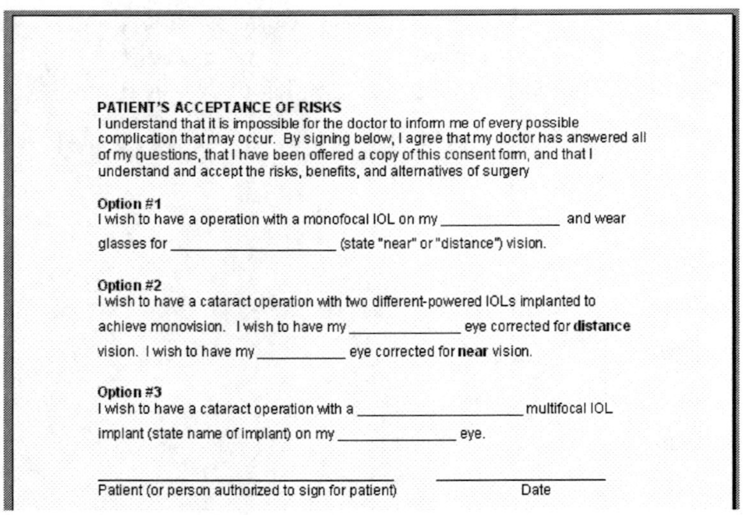

PATIENT'S ACCEPTANCE OF RISKS
I understand that it is impossible for the doctor to inform me of every possible complication that may occur. By signing below, I agree that my doctor has answered all of my questions, that I have been offered a copy of this consent form, and that I understand and accept the risks, benefits, and alternatives of surgery

Option #1
I wish to have a operation with a monofocal IOL on my ______________ and wear glasses for __________________ (state "near" or "distance") vision.

Option #2
I wish to have a cataract operation with two different-powered IOLs implanted to achieve monovision. I wish to have my ____________ eye corrected for **distance** vision. I wish to have my __________ eye corrected for **near** vision.

Option #3
I wish to have a cataract operation with a __________________ multifocal IOL implant (state name of implant) on my _____________ eye.

______________________________ ____________________
Patient (or person authorized to sign for patient) Date

Figure 3-2: *A sample liability waiver.*

BAAs

Definition:

A *business associate agreement (BAA)* is a document that defines the authorized uses of PHI, and how the information is to be used and managed. The agreement also includes actions to be taken in the event of a breach of PHI. BAAs are commonly used by medical service providers when they hire additional suppliers and service providers. When the service provided by any of these suppliers includes access to PHI, a BAA is required to ensure that information is secure from unauthorized access.

Example:

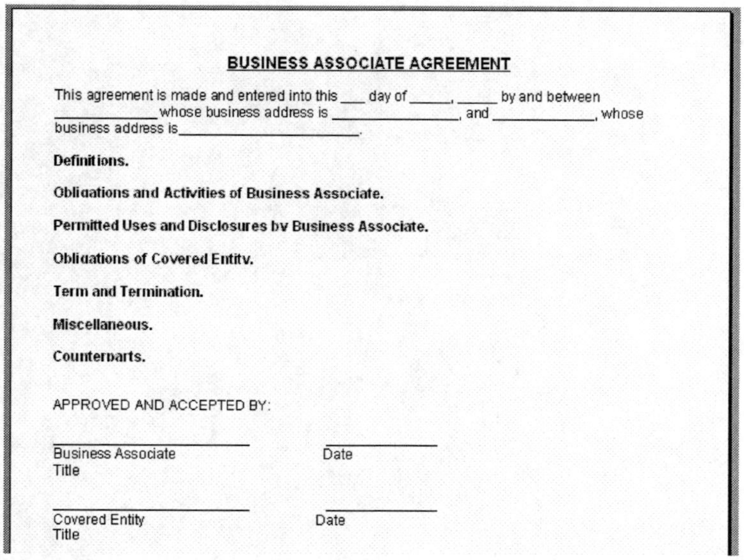

BUSINESS ASSOCIATE AGREEMENT

This agreement is made and entered into this ___ day of _____, _____ by and between __________ whose business address is ______________, and ___________, whose business address is__________________.

Definitions.

Obliaations and Activities of Business Associate.

Permitted Uses and Disclosures bv Business Associate.

Obliaations of Covered Entitv.

Term and Termination.

Miscellaneous.

Counterparts.

APPROVED AND ACCEPTED BY:

Business Associate Date
Title

Covered Entity Date
Title

Figure 3-3: *A sample BAA.*

Third-Party Interactions

Third-party vendors are used in many different capacities within the medical field. Because of this, agreements must be established and signed by both parties before services are rendered. There are two common agreements used.

Agreement	*Description*
Service-level agreement (SLA)	A contractual agreement between a service provider and a customer that stipulates the precise services and support options the vendor must provide. It also includes the terms for penalties in case of service failures, and, for technology vendors, includes guaranteed performance levels, such as uptime ratings, as well as descriptions of the hardware and software included in the service.
Memorandum of understanding (MOU)	A document that lists agreed upon actions between two parties. It can be used to identify and define common actions, processes, and procedures, and in some cases can hold the same binding power of a contractual agreement.

Third-Party Medical Billing

With the increase in medical practice size and the number of patients covered by an individual doctor, the medical billing process has become more complicated and tedious. Third-party services, known as medical billing services, are sometimes used to manage all aspects of the medical billing process and increases efficiencies across all areas of healthcare.

ACTIVITY 3-3

Examining Legal Best Practices

Scenario:

In this activity, you will examine the legal best practices, requirements, and documentation that you may encounter while supporting medical personnel.

1. **One of the medical offices that you support is in the process of transitioning from a traditional paper file-based system to an electronic EMR/EHR system. There are a number of patient files that have not been accessed in over a year. What time of storage factors should be considered when deciding whether to enter the files into the system?**

2. **True or False? One of the doctors in the medical practice where you work has been accused of malpractice by a patient. The patient is claiming that the doctor prescribed him a medication that he was allergic to, even though the medication is documented as being problematic in his file. The patient has suffered severe asthma symptoms and has been hospitalized because of the reaction to the medication. In this scenario, the doctor potentially could be held liable for the outcome of this patient's health.**

   __ True

   __ False

3. **What is the correct description for each agreement document?**

___	BAA	a. Lists all agreed upon actions and services between two parties.
___	SLA	b. An agreement between a service provider and a customer that stipulates the precise services and support options the vendor must provide.
___	MOU	c. Defines the authorized uses of PHI.

4. **The hospital where you work has just re-configured the main entrance and reception area to make it more accessible to wheelchairs and walkers. In doing this, you discover that the reception computer displays can now be seen by anyone sitting in the waiting area. What PHI practice would you suggest in this scenario to prevent anyone from seeing sensitive information on those computers?**

TOPIC D
Medical Document Imaging

In the last topic, you identified the technologies that make up an EMR or EHR system, and now you are ready to discover how document imaging feeds directly into that system. In this topic, you will describe how document imaging fits into the EMR or EHR system.

Even with the advent of EMR, document scanning is still a large part of many healthcare IT systems. Understanding the essential elements of document imaging will allow you to provide the right level of support for all day-to-day activities.

Document Imaging

Definition:

Document imaging is the electronic copying of hard copy documents to digital form. Documents are scanned and stored in the EMR or EHR system in a number of different ways. The scanning and storing process can be done at any point of an EHR or EMR implementation. Some medical facilities will scan and store historical records during the system implementation, and some will wait until the system is completely implemented to scan and store records. The imaging process can be tedious and complex because of the number of handwritten notes, patient records, and files that need to be converted to digital form.

Example:

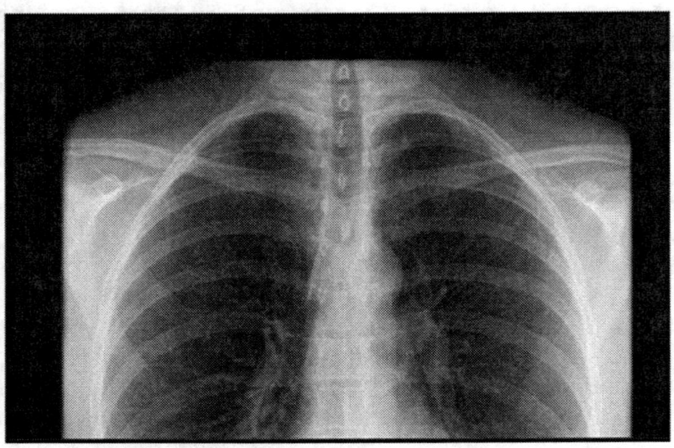

Figure 3-4: *A scanned chest X-ray.*

Ongoing Scanning

The process of scanning medical documents for storage within the EMR/EHR system is an ongoing process. In many cases, the physical outputs from other medical applications must be scanned, attached to a patient's electronic record, then stored within the system.

Image File Types

Once the documents are scanned, they must conform to the file type supported by the EMR or EHR system. There are a number of file types that can be used when creating imaging files.

File Type	Characteristics
TIFF	Tagged Image File Format (TIFF) characteristics include: • High-quality images and supports multiple images in a single file. • Allows large file sizes. • High resolution capabilities. • Allows a wide range of compression schemes, including two-dimensional (2D).
PDF	Portable Document Format (PDF) characteristics include: • An open standard for exchanging documents. • Typically includes both vector and bitmap images.
JPG/JPEG	Joint Photographic Experts Group (JPEG) characteristics include: • Highly compatible file format commonly used for high quality images. • Lower resolution capabilities. • Limited to smaller file sizes. • Compression is limited to lossy, which means that some data is lost when the file is compressed.
GIF	Graphics Interchange Format (GIF) characteristics include: • A bitmap image format. • Supports transparency and animation. • Lower resolution capabilities • Compression is lossless, which means that quality and data is not jeopardized when compressed.

Resolution Considerations

The resolution capabilities for each file type must be considered when saving images and storing them in the EMR/EHR system. For example, if you are storing a patient's electronic X-ray, a high resolution may be required, such as the TIFF file format, instead of a JPG, that uses a lower resolution. The crux of the issue is that the higher resolution file formats will need more space than lower resolution formats. These points must be considered when determining what file formats are used for scanned medical files.

OCR

Optical character recognition (OCR) is the process of transforming handwritten, scanned images of text or typed text into machine-encoded text. This process is often used to convert hardcopy patient records into files that are compatible with the EMR or EHR system.

The EMR/EHR Scanning Process

EMR and EHR systems require that patient records get scanned and saved within the system. The EMR scanning process includes many different phases.

Phase	Description
Preparation and transport	Hardcopy documents must be prepared for the scanning device. This usually involves removing staples, tape, and creases from the documents, so that they can be fed into the scanner without issues. Once the documents have been prepped, they are either fed manually into a scanner/copier machine, or may need to be placed on a flatbed scanner.
Scanning	The scanning phase involves creating the digital copies of the hardcopy documents. Scans can be either black and white or color, depending on the requirements of the EMR/EHR system.
Output	The output from the scan is then saved and moved to the appropriate location depending on the process for a specific medical facility. At this point in the process, additional information such as the scan date and time may be added.
Indexing/metadata	Once the scanned images are saved to the appropriate location, they are then re-named and indexed for ease of use within the system. At this point, the patient's unique patient identifier is associated with the record and *metadata* is also applied to each document to allow for quick searching and file location within the system. This information can include key search terms, and the subject matter, author, and other identifying attributes that get attached directly to a patient's record.
Storage and retrieval	Once the scanned files are complete with necessary information applied, they can be stored within the EMR/EHR system. Storage methods and requirements are specific to each medical facility, and what the migration, backup, and duration requirements are applied. Once the documents have been stored properly, they can be retrieved by users logged in to the EMR/EHR system, using the unique identifiers and metadata keywords applied during the indexing phase.

ACTIVITY 3-4

Examining Medical Document Imaging

Scenario:

In this activity, you will examine the medical document imaging process.

1. **Sam, the office manager for a large medical practice, is in charge of getting all patient files from hardcopy to digital copies to store in the EMR system. He is currently in the process of adding keywords to each scanned file so that the files can be found quickly during a search. What phase of the process is this?**

   a) Preparation and transport

   b) Scanning

   c) Output

   d) Indexing

   e) Storage and retrieval

2. **What part of the EMR/EHR scanning process is the most challenging?**

3. **What are some of the system implications of scanning and storing hard copy medical files?**

TOPIC E

Sanitation Management

Now that you have been through the medical records process, you are ready to venture into a more medical-specific area of the healthcare environment. General sanitation is important because it affects everyone. In this topic, you will identify the sanitation requirements and best practices.

Sanitation in medical environments is vital for both patients and staff, even if that staff never interacts directly with a patient. Knowing when and how to properly sanitize both personnel and equipment can save you and others unnecessary illness and help improve patient outcomes.

When to Use Sanitation Techniques

Sanitation is a main concern for anyone working in the medical field. Problem areas include shared keyboards, mice, printers, and copier machines. Because IT technicians will most likely be touching computer equipment and systems, it is important to recognize the areas that may contain a higher level of pathogens and other infectious germs. Shared equipment will always be problematic. Because of this, IT equipment and equipment located in isolation areas must be cleaned regularly.

Proper Sanitation Techniques

Following the proper sanitation steps while working in a medical facility can prevent many different illnesses and diseases:

- Follow proper hand washing guidelines according to the Centers for Disease Control (CDC).
- When required, wear protective gear such as gloves, aprons, and face masks.
- Disinfect and clean shared computer equipment regularly, such as keyboards, laptops, mice, printers, and fax machines.
- Follow specific sanitation guidelines and procedures for the room or area that you are working in.
- Follow specific hospital guidelines.

The Infection Control Office

The infection control office is responsible for ensuring that the guidelines issued by the Joint Commission are enforced within the hospital environment.

IT Equipment Sanitation

IT equipment within a medical environment is often shared among a number of professionals. In these cases, the risk of spreading disease is higher than in other settings. Equipment that carries the most germs and bacteria are keyboards, mice, laptops, printers, and fax machines. Because of this, IT technicians and all other personnel must enforce daily cleaning and disinfecting of all shared IT equipment.

HA vs. CA

Within a hospital environment, infectious diseases are classified into two levels: Hospital Acquired (HA) and Community Acquired (CA). HA refers to any infectious disease that originated within the hospital environment, and CA refers to any infectious disease that originated outside the hospital environment.

ACTIVITY 3-5
Examining Sanitation

Scenario:
In this activity, you will examine sanitation techniques and guidelines.

---

1. **As an IT technician working in various medical environments, what are some steps you can take to prevent the spread of disease and illness while working with IT and medical equipment?**

---

2. **True or False? Shared computer equipment within a medical facility is at a high risk for spreading disease to medical staff.**

   __ True

   __ False

---

3. **How can you mitigate the risk of spreading diseases through shared IT equipment in a medical facility?**

Lesson 3 Follow-up

In this lesson, you discovered how technology is implemented within a medical environment, and more specifically, how the roles of medical staff interact with the technology components within that system.

1. **Given the nature of PHI data, how do you anticipate that you have to change your practices?**

2. **How do you think your IT practices will change when working in a medical setting?**

4 Healthcare IT Technical Components

Lesson Time: 3 hour(s), 30 minutes

Lesson Objectives:

In this lesson, you will describe the essential elements of computing including hardware, software, networking, and change control.

You will:

- Apply core IT concepts as a foundation for healthcare IT tech support best practices.
- Describe core networking components.
- Install and manage servers and software.
- Support hardware components.

Introduction

In the previous lessons, the focus has been on healthcare systems, technologies, and environments. Now you can cycle back to examine the core technical components of information technology that remain relevant within healthcare IT. In this lesson, you will review the essential elements of computing, which include hardware, software, and networking processes and procedures.

While many of the basics of computing and networking remain stable, technology is constantly evolving. As an IT technician within the healthcare environment, it is important to understand the technical components of any computer or network so that as procedures and processes change to meet the needs of the medical community, the technology can remain supportive and can adapt to any changes that may occur.

TOPIC A

Computing Essentials

Up to this point in the course, the focus has been on healthcare-specific components and technology. In this topic, you will take a step back to review the basics of computer technology and how basic devices and connections make up a network. In this topic, you will apply core information technology concepts as a foundation for healthcare IT technical support best practices.

A strong foundation in computing essentials is the keystone for any IT technician's troubleshooting ability. As an IT professional in any industry, you will need to understand the basics of computer technology and network systems. Knowing these essentials will make you an important resource to any company, but will certainly be a strong base of knowledge and skills as you look to transition into the healthcare industry as an IT professional. This topic ensures you have the knowledge necessary to be successful in your IT endeavors.

Essential Components of Computers

Computers must have certain components installed and configured to be functional. The essential components include:

- A system unit, the main component of a personal computer, which includes the other devices necessary for the computer to function.
- A display device that enables users to view the text and graphical data output from a computer.
- And, an input device that enables users to enter data or instructions into a computer.

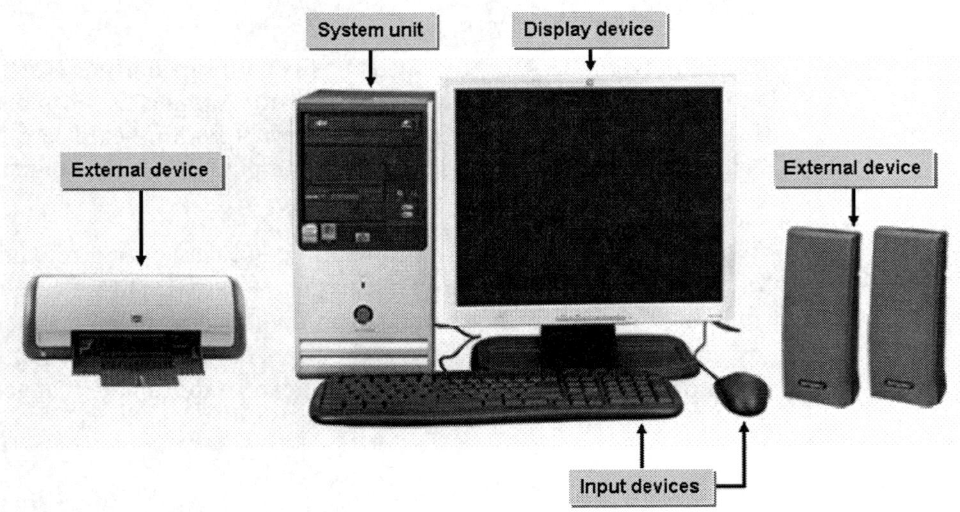

Figure 4-1: *A basic computer setup.*

Operating Systems

The operating system is a component of the system unit and provides the graphical user interface (GUI) for users. There are a number of different operating systems that you may encounter within the healthcare system. The most common operating system is Microsoft Windows. Microsoft® Windows® comes in several different versions and revision levels for use on personal computers, tablets, smartphones, and network servers. Other systems can include Mac OS® versions, and possibly Linux and Unix systems. As smartphones become more available and commonly used, mobile operating systems are increasing, including Apple iOS®, Google Android™, and BlackBerry OS®.

Human Interface Devices

Definition:

Human interface devices are hardware components that enable users to interact with computers. Interface devices allow users to read, enter, and manage data within a computer system. Within the healthcare environment, there are could be a number of devices that you need to support and troubleshoot.

Example:

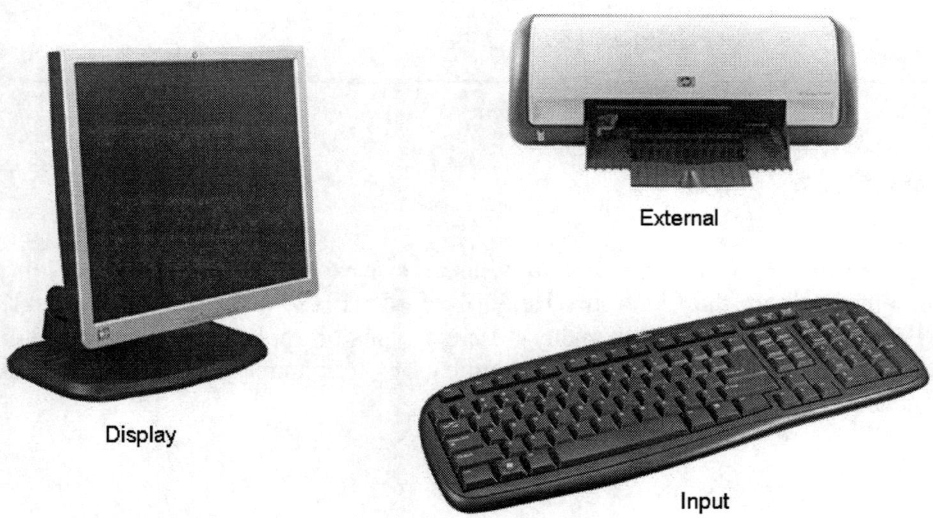

Figure 4-2: *Human interface components.*

Human Interface Device Types

There are three main human interface device types.

Human Interface Device	***Description***
Input	Personal computer components that enable users to enter data or instructions into a computer. The most common input devices are keyboards, computer mice, microphones and touch screens. An input device can connect to the system unit via a cable or a wireless connection.

Human Interface Device	Description
Display	Personal computer components that enable users to view the text and graphical data output from a computer. Display devices commonly connect to the system unit via a cable, and they have controls to adjust the settings for the device. They vary in size and shape, as well as the technologies used.
External	A personal computer's functionality can be enhanced by connecting different types of external devices to the system unit. Often called peripheral devices, external devices typically provide alternative input or output methods or additional data storage. External devices are connected to the system unit via a cable or a wireless connection. Some have their own power source and some draw power from the system. There are many types of external devices: • Microphones • Digital cameras • Scanners • Speakers • Printers • Network devices • External drives

Applications

Definition:

Applications are software components that allow users to perform specific tasks and job functions on a computer. Within the Electronic Health Records (EHR) or Electronic Medical Records (EMR) environment, there are many different types of applications used depending on the job function. Healthcare professionals use applications to manage billing, patient data, appointment scheduling, and medical records.

Example:

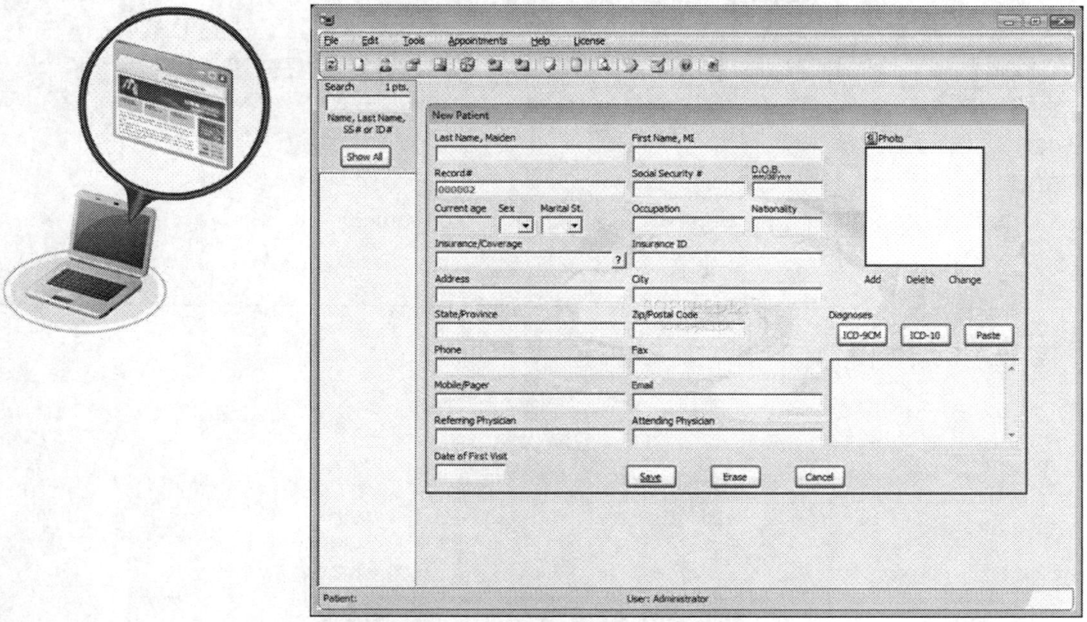

Figure 4-3: *A medical record application.*

Documentation

When setting up and configuring any computer system or technical environment, it is essential to document the process, as well as the components and how they are configured. Proper documentation of all hardware, software configuration and licensing, connections, application configuration and licensing, and systems configuration will help you troubleshoot issues and problems when they arise.

ACTIVITY 4-1

Identifying Personal Computer Components

Scenario:

In this activity, you will identify personal computer components.

---

1. **Identify the computer components in the graphic.**

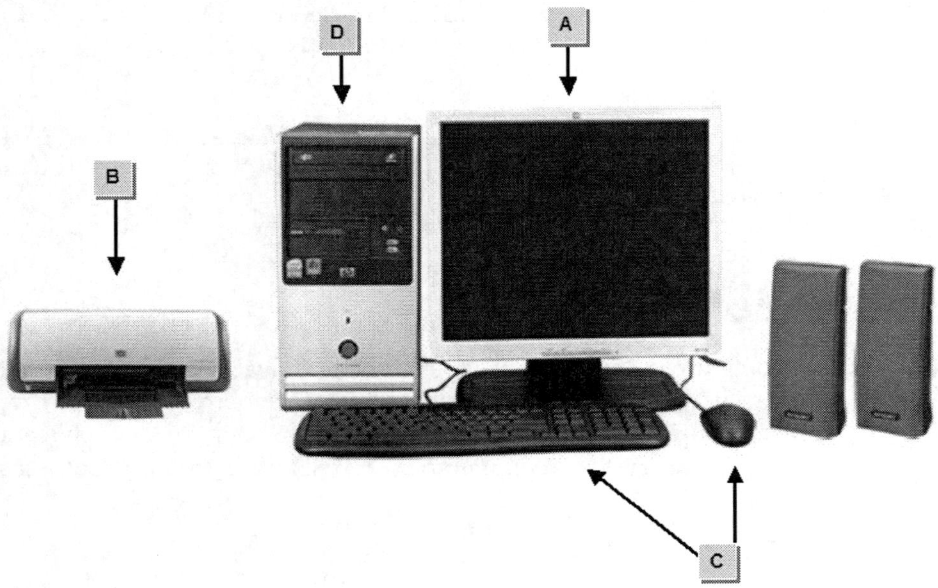

___	B	a.	System unit
___	D	b.	Display device
___	C	c.	Input device
___	A	d.	External device

---

2. **Match each external device with its function.**

___	Microphone	a.	Provides audio output
___	Speaker	b.	Provides graphical input
___	Scanner	c.	Provides text and graphical output
___	Printer	d.	Provides audio input
___	External drive	e.	Provides additional data storage

3. **What are the main categories of personal computer components?**
   a) System unit
   b) Display device
   c) Input devices
   d) Network devices

TOPIC B
Networking

In the previous topic, you identified the basic components that make up a computing environment. In this topic, you will expand on that knowledge by identifying how those components are used in a basic computer network. In this topic, you will describe core networking components.

Computer networking is at the center of nearly every IT environment. Understanding the core components of a network and how they interact is an essential part of every IT technician's toolbox. With this information, you can better serve any type of healthcare computing environment.

Network Protocols

Networking protocols enable data transfer over a physical or wireless connection. Networks utilize a number of common protocols.

Protocol	***Description***
TCP/IP	*Transmission Control Protocol/Internet Protocol (TCP/IP)* is a non-proprietary, routable network protocol suite that enables computers to communicate over all types of networks. TCP/IP is the native protocol of the Internet and is required for Internet connectivity.
DNS	The *Domain Name System (DNS)* is the primary name resolution service on the Internet and private IP networks. DNS is a hierarchal system of databases that map computer names to their associated IP addresses. DNS servers store, maintain, and update databases and respond to DNS client name resolution requests to translate host names to IP addresses. The DNS servers on the Internet work together to provide global name resolution for all Internet hosts.
DHCP	*Dynamic Host Configuration Protocol (DHCP)* is a protocol used to automatically assign IP addressing information to IP network computers. Except for a few systems that have manually assigned static IP addresses, most IP systems obtain addressing information dynamically from a central DHCP server or a router configured to provide DHCP functions. Therefore, a DHCP service is a critical component of an IP implementation in most medical environments.
FTP	*File Transfer Protocol (FTP)* enables the transfer of files between a user's workstation and a remote host. A user can access the directory structure on a remote host, change directories, search and rename files and directories, and download and upload files.
802.11	Many healthcare providers rely heavily on wireless computing devices for communication and record-keeping within their practices, and so there are various IEEE *802.11* standards that you may encounter in wireless networking implementations in your role as a healthcare IT professional. Each of the approved standards in the 802.11 family has different characteristics.
RDP	*Remote Desktop Protocol (RDP)* enables a computer to connect to another computer from a remote location as if you were in front of it. Depending on the permissions you define, you will have full access to all resources, including printers, storage devices, and the network to which the machine is attached.

Protocol	Description
RDC	*Remote Desktop Client (RDC)* is a client application that allows a user to log on remotely to a networked computer from another computer or mobile device, and presents the desktop interface of the base device on the remote device, allowing for access and control of the base device by the remote device. Clients exist for most operating systems, including Windows, Linux, Unix, Mac OS X, Android, and other operating systems.

802.11 Standards

The 802.11 protocols each have a specific set of functions.

Wireless Protocol	Description
802.11	A family of specifications developed by the IEEE for wireless Local Area Network (LAN) communications between wireless devices or between wireless devices and a base station. The standard is supported by various working groups, known collectively as 802.11x. It specifies wireless data transfer rates of up to 2 megabits per second (Mbps) in the 2.4 gigahertz (GHz) frequency band.
802.11a	The approved specification for a fast, secure, but relatively expensive wireless protocol. 802.11a supports speeds up to 54 Mbps in the 5 GHz frequency band. Unfortunately, that speed has a limited range of only 60 feet, which, depending on how you arrange your access points, could severely limit user mobility.
802.11b	Also called Wi-Fi, short for "wired fidelity," 802.11b is probably the most common and certainly the least expensive wireless network protocol. 802.11b provides for an 11 Mbps transfer rate in the 2.4 GHz frequency. (Some vendors, such as D-Link, have increased the rate on their devices to 22 Mbps.) 802.11b has a range up to 1,000 feet in an open area and a range of 200 to 400 feet in an enclosed space (where walls might hamper the signal). It is backwards compatible with 802.11, but is not interoperable with 802.11a.
802.11g	The specification for wireless data throughput at the rate of up to 54 Mbps in the 2.4 GHz band. It is compatible with 802.11b and may operate at a much faster speed.
802.11n	A recent specification for wireless data throughput. Even before approval, many "Draft N" or "Pre-N" products were already being produced and sold, which were compliant with the specification. The specification increased speeds dramatically, with data throughput up to 600 Mbps in the 2.4 GHz or 5 GHz ranges.

Remote Control Applications

Remote control networking solutions include Windows® Remote Desktop and Remote Assistance, Symantec pcAnywhere, GoToMyPC™, LogMeIn, WebEx™ PCNow, various VNC® clients and servers, Citrix XenApp, and Apple® Remote Desktop. These enable a technician to provide support and assistance over the network.

Network Devices

Different types of internetwork devices provide different levels of connectivity and security between network interconnections and network segments within a healthcare computing environment.

Device	***Description***
NIC	A *Network Interface Card (NIC)* is a device that provides network connectivity capabilities for computer systems. In most cases, this device or card is built into a computer system by the manufacturer to enable quick Ethernet access.
Switch	A *switch* is a device that has multiple network ports and combines multiple physical network segments into a single logical network. It controls network traffic on the logical network by creating dedicated, or "switched," connections that contain only the two hosts involved in a transmission. Standard switches generally forward broadcasts to all ports on the switch, but will send individual packets to the specific destination host based on the unique physical address assigned to each network adapter. Some switches can perform routing functions based on protocol addresses.
AP	An *access point (AP)* is a hardware device that acts as a wireless communication hub to provide secured wireless access and security and to extend the physical range of a wireless LAN.
Router	A *router* is a device that connects multiple networks that use the same protocol. Routers can examine the protocol-based addressing information in the network packets and determine the most efficient path for data to take. They can also filter network traffic based on other criteria. Most routers will not forward broadcast network traffic. Port forwarding on a router allows remote devices to connect to a computer, device, or service that is networked on a private LAN.
Firewall	A *firewall* is any software or hardware device that protects a system or network by blocking unwanted network traffic. Firewalls generally are configured to stop suspicious or unsolicited incoming traffic, but permit most types of outgoing traffic. Information about the incoming or outgoing connections can be saved to a log, and used for network monitoring or hardening purposes.
Internet modem	An *Internet modem* is a network device that modulates digital information onto an analog signal at one end, and demodulates the analog signal back to digital data, used for dial-up Internet connections. Depending on the type of connection used, you will use either a cable modem, a digital subscriber line (DSL) modem, a wireless modem, a voice modem, or a radio modem. A laptop modem can be an internal device, or can be added to a system using a PC Card or an ExpressCard.
DC	A *Domain Controller (DC)* is a Windows Server® computer that runs the Active Directory service. Active Directory is a directory service that acts as a central location for network administration, user management, and security. Directory information is automatically replicated between the DCs in a given forest.
Print server	A *print server* is a device or service that distributes and manages print jobs sent from client computers. The print server is connected to either a wired or wireless network and sends print jobs to the designated printers within the network.

Device	Description
Fax server	A *fax server* is a device that manages all fax messages that are sent and received within a network. Some fax servers are equipped to convert electronic messages to a fax format and then forward them on to the designated recipient.

Network Cable Types

There are different types of cable that may be used in networking computers together in a healthcare environment.

Cable Type	Description
Twisted pair	Multiple insulated conductors are twisted around each other in pairs and clad in a protective and insulating outer jacket. There may be multiple pairs depending on the type and size of cabling. Shielding can be added around the bundle of twisted pairs to reduce electronic interference. Twisted pair cable comes in two basic types: unshielded twisted pair (UTP) and shielded twisted pair (STP). As the name implies, STP includes shielding, typically a foil wrapper, around its conductors to improve the cable's resistance to interference and noise. It tends to be more expensive than UTP and is installed only when needed. Most hospitals will use the fastest, highest capacity cabling possible, usually UTP Cat5, or Cat6 cables. 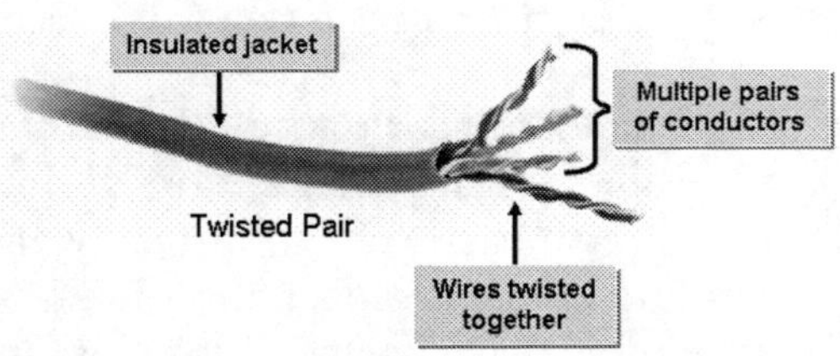
Coaxial	Also called coax, is a legacy (older) type of copper cable that features a central conductor surrounded by braided or foil shielding. An insulator separates the conductor and shield, and the entire package is wrapped in an insulating layer called a jacket. The data signal is transmitted over the central conductor. The outer shielding serves to reduce electromagnetic interference. Coaxial cable may still be found in older network installations. 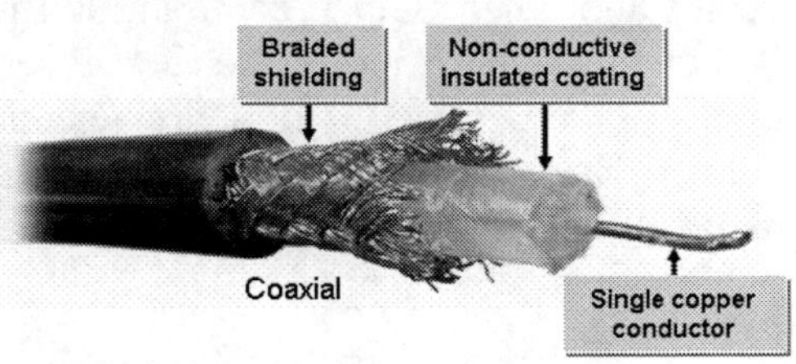

Cable Type	Description
Fiber	A type of network cable in which the core is one or more glass or plastic strands. The core is between 5 and 100 microns thick and is surrounded by cladding, which reflects light back to the core in patterns determined by the transmission mode. A buffer, often made of plastic, surrounds the cladding and core. To add strength (or "pull strength") to the cable, strands of Kevlar® surround the buffer. An outer jacket, sometimes called armor, wraps and protects the whole assembly. Light pulses from a laser or high-intensity LED are passed through the core to carry the signal. The cladding reflects the light back into the core, increasing the distance the signal can travel without being regenerated. Fiber optic transmissions are fast and reliable over extremely long distances. Due to the traffic, volume, and size of data being transmitted, like imaging files, most hospitals will use fiber optic cables. Because they are also impervious to electromagnetic interference, fiber optic cables are appropriate for use in medical environments where radiology equipment may be used. 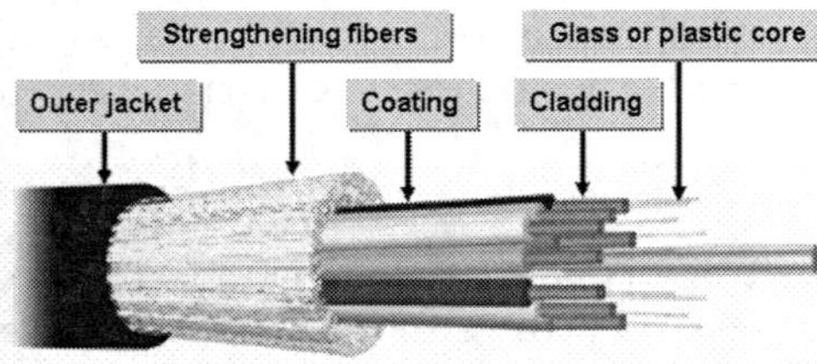 Fiber

Distributing IP Addresses

Transmission Control Protocol/Internet Protocol (TCP/IP) addresses can be distributed statically or provided dynamically by using DHCP. Configuring TCP/IP statically on a network requires an administrator to visit each node to manually enter IP address information for that node. If the node moves to a different subnet, the administrator must manually reconfigure the node's TCP/IP information for its new network location. In a large network, configuring TCP/IP statically on each node can be very time consuming, and can be prone to errors that disrupt communication.

DHCP Address Distribution

Dynamic Host Configuration Protocol (DHCP) is a network service that provides automatic assignment of IP addresses and other TCP/IP configuration information on network nodes that are configured as DHCP clients. DHCP requires a DHCP server configured with at least one DHCP scope. The scope contains a range of IP addresses and a subnet mask, and can contain other options, such as a default gateway address. When the scope is enabled, it automatically leases TCP/IP information to DHCP clients for a defined lease period.

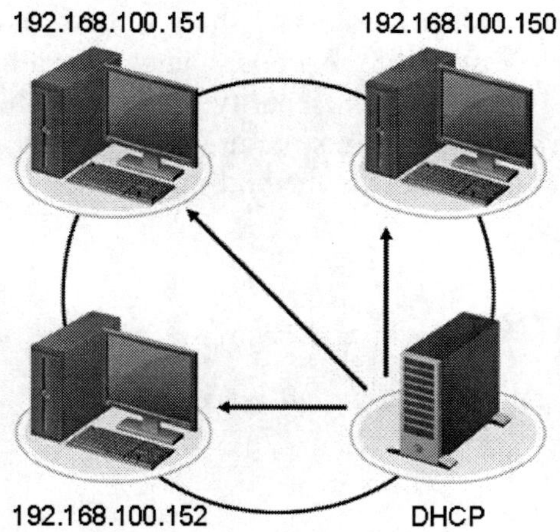

Figure 4-4: *A DHCP server dynamically assigns IP addresses to clients.*

Common Network Models

There are various network models you will find in medical environments.

Model	Description
Centralized	A network in which a *host computer*—a powerful, centralized computer system, such as a *mainframe* computer—controls all network communication and performs data processing and storage on behalf of clients and other network devices. On a host-based network, the host computer does all the computing tasks and returns the resultant data to the end user's computer. Users connect to the host via dedicated terminals or terminal emulators. Centralized networks provide high performance and centralized management, but they are also expensive to implement. A centralized network is most commonly found in legacy systems in the medical environment.
Client-server	A network in which computer functionality is divided into two roles: a server computer, which provides services and controls network operations, and a client computer, which uses the services provided by the servers. Typically, there is at least one server providing central authentication services. Servers also provide access to shared files, printers, hardware, and applications. In client/server networks, processing power, management services, and administrative functions can be concentrated where needed, while clients can still perform many basic end-user tasks on their own In more modern EMR implementations, client-server networks are the most commonly used.
Ad hoc	A type of network that is established spontaneously through a peer-to-peer wireless connection. Ad hoc networks will occur between mobile devices, hotspot machines, etc.
Mixed mode	A network that incorporates elements from more than one standard network model.

Ad Hoc vs. Infrastructure

There are advantages and disadvantages for establishing a network connection using an ad hoc method, or by using existing infrastructure. Ad hoc connections allow you to quickly connect two devices wirelessly, but without the right security settings established, this can result in wireless attacks. On the other hand, the infrastructure method uses already secured wireless access points to establish a connection. This method may not be as quick to set up, but is more secure for file and data sharing.

Types of Networks

Networks can be categorized into three different types.

Type	*Description*
WAN	A *Wide Area Network (WAN)* spans multiple geographic locations, including metropolitan areas, geographic regions, or entire nations. WANs typically connect multiple LANs and other networks using long-range transmission media. The result is that users and computers in one location can communicate with users and computers in other locations. WANs can be private, as in the case of those built and maintained by large, multinational corporations, or they can be public, such as those created and maintained by Internet service providers or the Internet itself.
LAN	A *Local Area Network (LAN)* implementation in which nodes use a wireless network card to connect to other stations. Typically used in a single building of an organization, in a home, or in a hotspot such as a coffee shop. Usually limited to 100 meters.
PAN	A *Personal Area Network (PAN)* connects wireless devices in very close proximity but not through a Wireless Access Point (WAP). Seen most often in small or home offices.

Command Line Tools for Networking

There are a number of useful command line tools you can use when setting up or troubleshooting basic networking environments.

Tool	*Use*
Ping	Verifies the network connectivity of a computer. Ping checks the host name, the IP address, and that the remote system can be reached.
Ipconfig	Displays the connection-specific DNS suffix, IP address, subnet mask, and default gateway. Must be run from a command line. To display additional information about the IP configuration, use the `Ipconfig /all` parameter with the command.
Tracert	Determines the route data takes to get to a particular destination over an IP network. The *Internet Control Message Protocol (ICMP)* sends out Time Exceeded messages to each router to trace the route. Each time a packet is sent, the *Time to Live (TTL)* value is reduced before the packet is forwarded. This allows TTL to count how many hops it is to the destination.

The Command Prompt Utility

Windows provides a command prompt interface that enables you to enter text-based commands or run command-line tools. On Windows 7, you can run the command prompt utility by choosing **Start→All Programs→Accessories→Command Prompt.**

Ipconfig Commands for DHCP

The Windows ipconfig utility provides switches that enable you to manage dynamic address leases:

- `ipconfig /release` forces the release of an IP address of a DHCP assigned network connection.
- `ipconfig /renew` requests the renewal of an IP address for a DHCP assigned network connection.

ACTIVITY 4-2

Assigning IP Addresses Manually

> This is a simulated activity that is available on the CD that shipped with this course. You can run this simulation on any Windows computer. The activity simulation can be launched either directly from the CD by clicking the **Interactives** link and navigating to the appropriate one, or from the installed data file location by opening the C:\HCIT\Simulations\Lesson 4\Assigning IP Addresses Manually folder and double-clicking the executable (.exe) file.

Scenario:

You are an IT technician for a small practice with leased addresses from their ISP in the range of 192.168.1.25 to 192.168.1.95. The subnet mask is 255.255.255.0, and the IP address of the DNS server is 192.168.1.200. The DNS server is also the default gateway on the network. You have been assigned with a task of configuring their computers to use the IP addresses provided to them by their ISP.

---

1. Assign IP addresses manually.

   a. Browse to the C:\HCIT\Simulations\Lesson 4\Assigning IP Addresses Manually folder.

   b. Double-click the Assigning IP Addresses Manually executable file.

   c. In the **Open File - Security Warning** message box, click **Run.**

   d. Follow the on-screen steps for the simulation.

   e. Close the C:\HCIT\Simulations\Lesson 4\Assigning IP Addresses Manually folder.

ACTIVITY 4-3

Assigning IP Addresses with DHCP

This is a simulated activity that is available on the CD that shipped with this course. You can run this simulation on any Windows computer. The activity simulation can be launched either directly from the CD by clicking the **Interactives** link and navigating to the appropriate one, or from the installed data file location by opening the C:\HCIT\Simulations\Lesson 4\Assigning IP Addresses with DHCP folder and double-clicking the executable (.exe) file.

Scenario:

Your practice has been experiencing problems with the DHCP server and it has been offline for several hours. You have just been notified that the server is back up and you can change the addressing back to DCHP leased addresses.

---

1. Assign IP addresses with DHCP.

a. Browse to the C:\HCIT\Simulations\Lesson 4\Assigning IP Addresses with DHCP folder.

b. Double-click the Assigning IP Addresses with DHCP executable file.

c. In the **Open File - Security Warning** message box, click **Run.**

d. Follow the on-screen steps for the simulation.

e. Close the C:\HCIT\Simulations\Lesson 4\Assigning IP Addresses with DHCP folder.

ACTIVITY 4-4

Examining Networking Concepts

Scenario:

In this activity, you will examine the network technology used in medical environments.

1. **On your network, users connect from individual workstations to access the EMR/EHR system running within a data center. Your network uses which network model?**

   a) Ad-hoc

   b) Mixed mode

   c) Client/server

   d) Centralized

2. **You have been called to one of the outpatient care centers because the office staff cannot connect to the Internet. Once you arrive, you verify that the DHCP server is functional, but in the TCP/IP properties of the workstation, an IP address has been assigned statically. What is the issue, and how would you go about fixing it?**

3. **True or False? Once you have changed the TCP/IP settings to match the Internet connection setup method, you can use the ipconfig command line tool to verify that the computer is receiving a valid IP address.**

   __ True

   __ False

4. **What utility would you typically use to verify that the system can communicate with other computers?**

   a) ipconfig/all

   b) Ping

   c) Tracert

   d) FTP

TOPIC C

Manage Servers and Software

In the previous topics, you identified the components that make up a basic computer setup as well as a network. Now that you know what the components are, its time to see how the devices are used within an EMR or EHR environment, and how servers and software fit into the overall system.

Servers and software are some of the elements of the EMR or EHR solution that users interact with the most. They can also be the most problematic. Having a strong foundation in how these components interact will give you a leg-up when it comes time to troubleshoot problems.

Programming Languages

Programming languages are used by developers to create applications, web pages, and applications for a wide range of computing devices. There are many different languages available.

Language	***Description***
XML	*eXtensible Markup Language (XML)* is a widely adopted markup language used in many documents, websites, and web applications.
SQL	*Structured Query Language (SQL)* is a programming and query language common to many large-scale database systems.
HTML	*Hypertext Markup Language (HTML)* is the a main standard that controls how web pages on Internet sites are formatted and displayed.
Flash	*Flash* is an Adobe® platform that allows developers to create animations, videos and other interactive components using the ActionScript® programming language. Components built in to Adobe Flash play in the Adobe Flash player on a variety of computer systems and mobile devices.
PHP	*PHP* is a server-side programming language used to develop dynamic web pages by embedding its code into HTML pages.
ASP	*Active Server Pages (ASP)* is a server-side programming language developed by Microsoft to provide a method to create dynamic web pages.

APIs

Definition:

An *Application Programming Interface (API)* is application code that enables various applications to communicate with each other. APIs can be developed to work with applications, operating systems, and other service related applications to provide a wide variety of customizations.

Example:

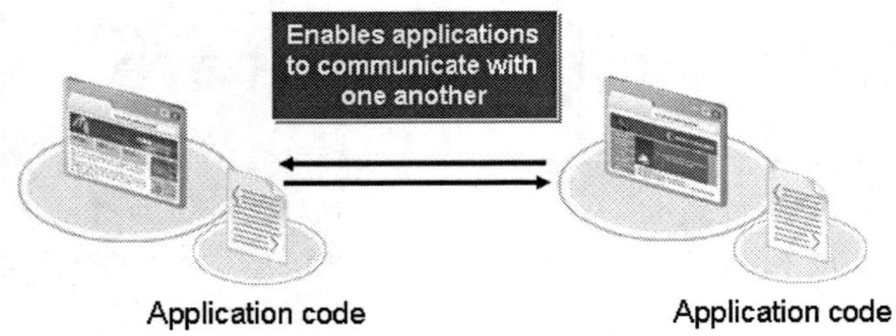

Figure 4-5: *An API.*

OS and Application Interoperability

Another consideration when installing applications within your network, is to verify that the application and operating system are compatible and meet the specifications of the application. Various operating systems, such as Unix, Linux, and Windows® systems have different requirements that must be evaluated prior to implementation.

Types of Servers

Within the healthcare computing environment, there may be a number of different servers used, each with a different purpose.

> It is important to remember that you are most likely concurrently running multiple servers on one machine.

Type	*Description*
Database server	A server that provides database services to other computers in a network. The database is usually connected in a client-server model.
Application server	A server that runs applications for client use. This type of server is also used by developers to store and share application components that can be used in web applications.
Mail server	A server that receives email requests from hosts on a network, and redirects them to the intended recipient. There are many different types of mail servers: • Simple Mail Transfer Protocol (SMTP) • Post Office Protocol 3 (POP3) • Internet Message Access Protocol (IMAP)
Web server	A server that displays web pages to clients. Web servers are assigned a domain name, and IP address. This information is used by clients to connect to a web page.
Proxy server	A server that isolates internal networks from the Internet by downloading and storing Internet files on behalf of internal clients.
DHCP server	A server that contains at least one DHCP scope. The scope contains a range of IP addresses and a subnet mask, and can contain other options, such as a default gateway address. When the scope is enabled, it automatically leases TCP/IP information to DHCP clients.

Type	Description
DNS server	A server that consists of databases that store domain name information and translate and resolve fully qualified domain name requests from clients.
File server	A server that is primarily used to share, store, and access files.
Time server	A server that provides the most accurate actual time to all clients in a computer network. The server synchronizes all devices.
FTP server	A server that uses the file transfer protocol (FTP) to exchange files over an Internet connection.
Fax server	A server or software program that enables users to send and receive fax messages through a network connection. The server is generally connected to a phone line and fax modem, and converts the messages and forwards them to the correct recipient.
Storage server	A server that stores files and programs. Types include *Network Attached Storage (NAS)* and *Storage Area Network (SAN).* NAS is a specialized file server designed and dedicated to support only data storage needs. There is no mouse, keyboard, or monitor present in the NAS server, which runs a streamlined operating system. The server can, however, contain a variety of storage devices such as large hard disk arrays or tape drives, or it can simply be a hard drive with an Ethernet port. A NAS server can be accessed over the network by clients and servers running different operating systems. SANs are special purpose high-speed networks dedicated to data storage. The SAN contains servers that share access to data storage devices such as disk arrays and tape drives. The servers and devices within the SAN interconnect using a high-speed networking technology such as Fiber Channel, Fiber Distributed Data Interface (FDDI), Asynchronous Transfer Mode (ATM), or high-speed Ethernet. Data can be stored and accessed quickly, and because the servers and storage devices all have redundant connections, data remains available during a server failure. The direct data traffic between servers and storage appliances on the SAN is separated from the traffic on the production network.

Interfaces

Server interfaces provide users with the ability to access and manage files, resources, services, and applications on a server. Functions will vary depending on the type of server installed.

ISPs

Definition:

An *Internet Service Provider (ISP)* is a company that provides Internet access to individuals and to businesses. Most ISPs charge a fee for this connection. Customers receive logon information, access to servers that provide name resolution and email services, dynamic or static IP configurations, and a method for connecting to the ISP. Once connected to the ISP, the customer can access the Internet.

A medical environment requires high levels of reliability and bandwidth guarantees, and choosing an ISP that can meet these demands is incredibly important.

Example:

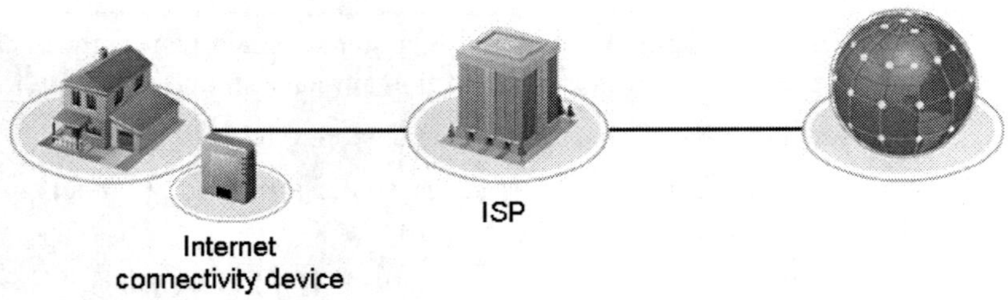

Figure 4-6: *An ISP.*

Cloud Computing

Definition:

Cloud computing is a method of computing that relies on the Internet to provide the resources, software, data, and services for a user, business, or organization. This method of computing relies on the Internet to provide computing capabilities that a single machine cannot. "The cloud" refers to anything available on the Internet. This could include business websites, consumer websites, storage services, IT-related services, file editing applications, and social networking websites. The main idea behind cloud computing is that you can access and manage your data and applications from any computer anywhere in the world while the storage method and location is hidden.

There is a high level of concern around implementing the cloud computing model in the medical environment, as there is the question of data security and availability due to the simple fact that all data and applications are being accessed through the Internet when using this model.

Example:

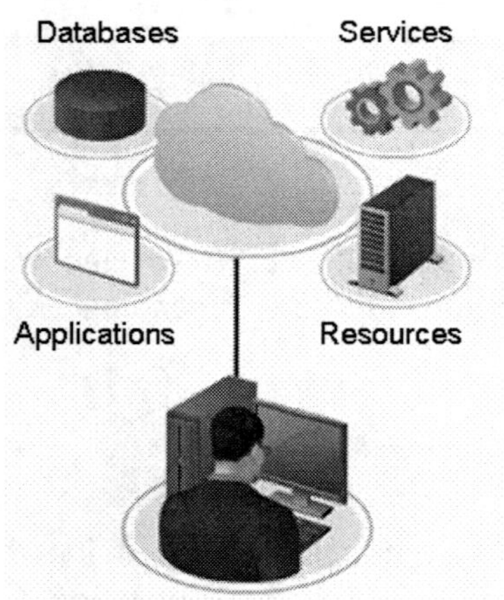

Figure 4-7: *A cloud computing architecture.*

Cloud Computing Service Types

Cloud computing provides three main services to users.

Service	Description
Software	*Software as a Service (SaaS)* refers to using the cloud to provide applications to users. This service eliminates the need for users to have the software installed on their computers and for organizations to purchase and maintain software versions.
Platform	*Platform as a Service (PaaS)* refers to using the cloud to provide virtual systems, such as operating systems, to customers.
Infrastructure	*Infrastructure as a Service (IaaS)* refers to using the cloud to provide access to any or all infrastructure needs a client may have. This can include data centers, servers, or any networking devices needed. IaaS can guarantee quality of service (QoS) for clients.

Virtualization

Definition:

Virtualization technology separates computing software from the hardware it runs on via an additional software layer. This enables a great deal of additional flexibility and increases hardware utilization by running multiple operating systems on a single computer, each thinking it is the only system present. In addition, virtualization allows hardware resources in an organization to be pooled and leveraged as part of a virtual infrastructure, increasing available processing and storage capacity. Virtualization has many uses in the modern IT environment:

- Running multiple operating systems on one computer, reducing hardware requirements.
- Separating software applications within a single operating system to prevent conflicts.
- Increasing the utilization of processing and storage resources throughout the organization by creating a "virtual infrastructure."
- And, making it simpler to provide server redundancy.

Example:

Figure 4-8: *Running multiple operating systems on one computer.*

Terminal Services

Terminal emulation services enable a client to connect remotely to a server. Terminals usually consist of just a keyboard and a monitor. Standard client computers that need to interact with host computers can run software called a *terminal emulator* so that they appear as dedicated terminals to the host. Terminal emulators are software that enables a standard client computer to appear to a host computer as a dedicated terminal. An example of a terminal service is Citrix.

Microsoft Windows Terminal Services

The technologies formerly known as Terminal Services were renamed Remote Desktop Services in Windows Server 2008 R2. Terminal Services is a client/server system that enables multiple clients to run applications or manage a server remotely. Terminal Services provides client access to all Windows-compatible applications by opening a user session on the Terminal Server. All application execution, data processing, and data storage is handled by the Terminal Server. Microsoft's terminal emulation software can be installed on almost any Windows operating system. Even handheld PCs running Windows® CE can connect to a Terminal Server and run applications. Web-based access is also available.

The low demands on the client have led a lot of companies to deploy Terminal Services as a way of extending the life of their outdated computers. It is possible for a Terminal Server to support hundreds of sessions. By spending money on a big server and using older clients, companies can sometimes save considerable upgrade money.

Citrix Clients

Because of Citrix's digital independence, almost anything can be a Citrix client, including desktop computers, net appliances, web browsers, or mobile devices. Net appliances are dedicated thin client workstations that have a keyboard, mouse, and video, but no hard drives or CD-ROM drives (they might or might not have floppy drives). The net appliance's operating system is embedded in a read-only memory (ROM) chip, it has lower central processing unit (CPU) power, and its entire job is to connect to a MetaFrame server. Even though it is a low-power device, it can run any application on the server.

Server Load and Utilization

Server utilization is managing the performance levels of server to ensure that critical operations are highly available to resources. The performance of a server is directly related to how it's being utilized within the infrastructure. *Server load* refers to the amount of work a server performs on a regular basis. High utilization and work load often results in poor performance, and low utilization and work load results in better performance. Server utilization is a key metric in long term planning and trending. Results will drive application migration and new server investments.

How to Manage Servers and Software

Managing servers and software can be challenging depending on how complex the IT environment is. Within an EMR or EHR environment, management tasks are vendor specific, and should be applied according to vendor recommendations and documentation. There are however, some high level guidelines you can apply when managing servers and software within the healthcare IT environment.

Guidelines

- Assign access control rights and privileges.
- Configure the security settings.
- Enable logging on the server to track activity.
- Set a baseline for server performance.
- Set up performance monitoring.

Example:

In the small physical therapy office you are supporting, there is a new server being installed to run an EMR system, that will eventually get networked with the affiliated hospital. Alex, the assigned technician, installs the server and gets it up and running on the network. Once he verifies that the server is connected, he assigns access control rights to the therapists and office staff according to the sensitivity guidelines. The next step is to make sure the server is secured from unauthorized access, and that logging and tracking settings are configured to identify any suspicious activity. Once he manages to secure the server, he can manage the performance monitoring configurations to make sure that the server is functioning as expected.

ACTIVITY 4-5

Verifying the Server Installation

This is a simulated activity that is available on the CD that shipped with this course. You can run this simulation on any Windows computer. The activity simulation can be launched either directly from the CD by clicking the **Interactives** link and navigating to the appropriate one, or from the installed data file location by opening the C:\HCIT\Simulations\Lesson 4\Verifying the Server Installation folder and double-clicking the executable (.exe) file.

Scenario:

You have replaced the various hardware components of a server and before you move on to installing the server software, you want to ensure that the hardware components are configured properly.

---

1. Verify the server installation.
   a. Browse to the C:\HCIT\Simulations\Lesson 4\Verifying the Server Installation folder.
   b. Double-click the Verifying the Server Installation executable file.
   c. In the **Open File - Security Warning** message box, click **Run.**
   d. Follow the on-screen steps for the simulation.
   e. Close the C:\HCIT\Simulations\Lesson 4\Verifying the Server Installation folder.

ACTIVITY 4-6

Configuring Roles and Features on the Server

This is a simulated activity that is available on the CD that shipped with this course. You can run this simulation on any Windows computer. The activity simulation can be launched either directly from the CD by clicking the **Interactives** link and navigating to the appropriate one, or from the installed data file location by opening the C:\HCIT\Simulations\Lesson 4\Configuring Roles and Features on the Server folder and double-clicking the executable (.exe) file.

Scenario:

You have installed an operating system and tested network connectivity on a new server. Now you want to create a domain, deptsrv.com, for the departmental server and clients, add users to the domain, and connect a client computer to the domain.

---

1. Configure roles and features on the server.

a. Browse to the C:\HCIT\Simulations\Lesson 4\Configuring Roles and Features on the Server folder.

b. Double-click the Configuring Roles and Features on the Server executable file.

c. In the **Open File - Security Warning** message box, click **Run.**

d. Follow the on-screen steps for the simulation.

e. Close the C:\HCIT\Simulations\Lesson 4\Configuring Roles and Features on the Server folder.

ACTIVITY 4-7

Viewing Event Logs

This is a simulated activity that is available on the CD that shipped with this course. You can run this simulation on any Windows computer. The activity simulation can be launched either directly from the CD by clicking the **Interactives** link and navigating to the appropriate one, or from the installed data file location by opening the C:\HCIT\Simulations\Lesson 4\Viewing Event Logs folder and double-clicking the executable (.exe) file.

Scenario:

In this activity, you will view the event logs of a server you manage for any events that might have been reported.

1. View event logs.

a. Browse to the C:\HCIT\Simulations\Lesson 4\Viewing Event Logs folder.

b. Double-click the Viewing Event Logs executable file.

c. In the **Open File - Security Warning** message box, click **Run.**

d. Follow the on-screen steps for the simulation.

e. Close the C:\HCIT\Simulations\Lesson 4\Viewing Event Logs folder.

ACTIVITY 4-8

Collecting Data for Baselining

This is a simulated activity that is available on the CD that shipped with this course. You can run this simulation on any Windows computer. The activity simulation can be launched either directly from the CD by clicking the **Interactives** link and navigating to the appropriate one, or from the installed data file location by opening the C:\HCIT\Simulations\Lesson 4\Collecting Data for Baselining folder and double-clicking the executable (.exe) file.

Scenario:

You are planning to upgrade your server, and your manager has asked you to collect the baseline data for the physical disk utilization and memory utilization on the departmental server before and after the upgrade. You decide to create a data collector set named baseline to collect the current performance data related to only these two parameters before performing the upgrade.

1. Collect data for baselining.

a. Browse to the C:\HCIT\Simulations\Lesson 4\Collecting Data for Baselining folder.

b. Double-click the Collecting Data for Baselining executable file.

c. In the **Open File - Security Warning** message box, click **Run.**

d. Follow the on-screen steps for the simulation.

e. Close the C:\HCIT\Simulations\Lesson 4\Collecting Data for Baselining folder.

TOPIC D

Hardware Support

In the previous topic, you identified the types of servers and how they are used within the EHR or EMR environment. But what about the hardware used within the system? In this topic, you will identify hardware components and how they are connected together to enable EMR or EHR systems to run.

There are a wide variety of hardware devices you may encounter while working in an IT environment. It is essential to your efficiency as a technician that you learn to identify and work with a wide variety of devices.

Physical Interfaces and Connection Types

Because of the wide variety of devices that may be used in a medical setting, you will probably encounter all types of ports and connections while supporting medical hardware.

Interface	***Description***
USB	A *Universal Serial Bus (USB)* connection is a personal computer connection that enables you to connect multiple peripherals to a single port with high performance and minimal device configuration. USB connections support two-way communications. All modern computer systems today have multiple USB ports and can, with the use of USB hubs, support up to 127 devices per port. USB cables may have different connectors at each end. The computer end of the cable ends in a Type A connector. The device end of the cable commonly ends in a Type B connector, or may also end in a Mini-A, Mini-B, Micro-AB, or Micro-B connector. The size of the connector varies depending on the device. USB connections transfer data serially, but at a much faster throughput than legacy serial connections.
Serial connections	A *serial connection* is a personal computer connection that transfers data one bit at a time over a single wire. Serial connections support two-way communications and are typically used for devices such as fax cards or external modems. Legacy serial ports have either 9-pin (DB-9) or 25-pin (DB-25) male connectors. A legacy serial cable ends with a female connector to plug in to the male connector on the system unit. On system units that have color-coded ports, the serial port is teal-colored.
Parallel connections	A *parallel connection* is a personal computer connection that transfers data eight or more bits at a time over eight or more wires. Any components connected by multiple data pathways may be considered to have a parallel connection, but the term is generally used to refer to a standard legacy parallel port that uses eight data wires, and is typically used to connect a printer to a system unit. Parallel connections in older personal computers support only one-way or unidirectional communications. Newer computers have parallel ports that support bidirectional communications. Standard parallel ports have 25-pin female connectors. A parallel cable has a 25-pin male connector to plug into the system unit and a 36-pin male Centronics connector at the other end to attach to the external device. On system units that have color-coded ports, the parallel port is burgundy or dark pink.

Interface	Description
FireWire	Also referred to as *IEEE 1394,* this is a personal computer connection that provides a high-speed interface for peripheral devices that are designed to use the IEEE 1394 standard. FireWire can support up to 63 devices on one FireWire port. FireWire 400 transmits at 400 Mbps and uses either a 6-pin bullet-shaped powered connector or a 4-pin square-shaped unpowered connector. FireWire 800 transmits at 800 Mbps and uses a 9-pin connector.
SCSI	*Small Computer System Interface (SCSI)* is an older connection standard, typically used for storage devices such as tape and hard drives, that remains in use due to its reliability and high speed. A SCSI adapter has a port for external devices and a connection for internal devices. SCSI devices themselves can have multiple ports, enabling you to connect up to seven devices in a chain to one SCSI adapter. Each device in the chain requires a unique ID, which you configure by using switches or jumpers. SCSI cables have 50-pin, 68-pin, or 80-pin connectors depending upon the type of SCSI in use.
PATA	A *Parallel Advanced Technology Attachment (PATA)* connection is a drive connection standard that provides a parallel data channel from the drive controller to the disk drives. Originally called *ATA,* Integrated Drive Electronics (IDE), Enhanced IDE (EIDE), or Ultra DMA (UDMA), PATA connections are used to connect internal hard drives, optical drives, and tape drives to the system board. On the system board, two sockets provide connections for up to two drives per socket. PATA cables are ribbon cables with 40 or 80 wires and 40-pin connectors.
SATA	A *Serial ATA (SATA)* connection is a drive connection standard that enhances PATA by providing a serial data channel between the drive controller and the disk drives. SATA transfer speeds are much higher than PATA for the same drive technologies. SATA's physical installation is also easier because the SATA power and data cables are much smaller, thinner, and more flexible than traditional PATA ribbon cables. SATA connectors have seven pins.
Bluetooth	*Bluetooth* is a wireless connection method that is used to communicate from one device to another in a small area, usually less than 30 feet. Bluetooth establishes a link using an radio frequency (RF)-based media and does not need line-of-sight to make connections. Bluetooth uses the 2.4 GHz spectrum to communicate a 1 Mbps connection between two devices for both a 232 Kbps voice channel and a 768 Kbps data channel. Bluetooth 2.0 will increase the overall speed to a data rate of 2.1 to 3 Mbps. Version 2.0 allows for communicating devices to be as far as 30 meters or 100 feet apart.

> IEEE 1394 is most often called FireWire, a name given to the standard by Apple Computer, Inc. Sony names the same standard i.Link™, which is often written iLink.

Imaging Devices

Imaging devices can be used in many different ways depending on the organizational structure and medical roles using the device. Installation and configuration guidelines vary depending on the device.

Imaging Device	*Installation and Configuration Considerations*
Barcode scanner	Typically, barcode scanners are wireless devices, but can also be wired. Barcode readers are used most often in a hospital setting to scan and identify patients using the unique barcode located on their ID wrist band. This system is used by clinicians when they administer medications or performing procedures. The wristband is used to positively identify the patient and automatically locate and open their electronic chart from the EMR/EHR system.
Document scanner	Document scanners are used to convert paper to electronic format and then associate the file with the proper patient.
Card/badge scanner	Card/badge scanners are used often to scan a patient's drivers license or insurance card to store within the EMR/EHR system.
Fax printer	Fax printers are used to fax prescriptions and patient data or to print out prescription or patient information from the EMR/EHR system. These printers are secured and in most environments used for printing prescriptions (or a locked tray), as the prescription paper is typically a pre-printed "form" that needs to be secured.
Camera	Cameras can be used to take pictures of patients, because some EMR/EHR systems allow for a patient picture to be tied to their electronic record. Also, for diagnostics in procedures, the camera is used to capture an image that will then be analyzed. So, pictures can show up as discrete "image data" in a patient's chart.
Signature pads	Signature pads are used for billing in most circumstances. When patients pay a co-payment with a credit card, the signature pad is used to capture the signature electronically. They are typically not used to capture a clinician signature, as "electronic signatures" are used instead.

Mobile Devices

A mobile device is a small handheld computing device. There are a number of devices that may be used within a medical environment by doctors, nurses and office staff.

Mobile Device Type	*Examples*
Smartphones	Examples include BlackBerries, Apple® iPhones®, and Android smartphones.
Portable media players	Examples include Apple® iPods®, Apple® iPod touch®, and other audio, video, and media players.
Tablet PCs	Also referred to as Wi-Fi enabled devices: Examples include Apple® iPads®, and Android-based and Windows-based tablets.

Portable Storage Devices

With the wide range of devices used within the healthcare field, portable storage capabilities can also vary.

Device	*Specifications*
Flash drives	Flash drives come in several form factors, including thumb drives and pen drives. Thumb drives can be small, from 50 to 70 mm long, 17 to 20 mm wide, and 10 to 12 mm tall. Data-storage capacities vary, from 128 MB up to 128 GB. Data-transfer rates also vary, from 700 KBps to 28 MBps for read operations, and from 350 KBps to 15 MBps for write operations.
SD cards	The original Secure Digital (SD) Memory Card is 32 mm long, 24 mm wide, and 2.1 mm tall. The miniSD Card measures 21.5 mm x 20 mm x 1.4 mm, and the microSD/TransFlash Card measures 15 mm x 11 mm x 1 mm. SD Memory Cards are currently available in several capacities, up to 2 TB. Data transfer rates range from 10 MBps to 20 MBps.
External hard drives	If you plan to install a USB external storage device, you will get the best possible performance from the device if you connect it to a port or hub that supports USB 2.0. Keep in mind that many hubs drop all ports down to the slower USB 1.1 speed if you connect any USB 1.1 devices. Try not to connect a slower speed device to the same hub in which you plan to connect a USB 2.0 storage device.
DVDs	DVDs typically hold 4.7 GB on one side of the disc; it is possible to write to both surfaces of the disc, in which case the disc can hold up to 9.4 GB. There are also dual-layer discs, which store additional data on each side, capable of holding up to 17 GB. DVD drives access data at speeds from 600 KBps to 1.3 MBps. Because of the huge storage capacity and fast data access, DVD discs are widely used to store full-length movies and other multimedia content. DVD drives use Universal Disk Format (UDF) as the file system. DVDs can be DVD-R (which can be written to once), or DVD-RW (which can be written to multiple times).
CDs	Compact discs store data on one side of the disc and most hold up to 700 MB of data, although older discs and drives may support only up to 650.4 MB of data. CDs are widely used to store music as well as data. To meet the audio CD standard, the CD drive on a computer must transfer data at a rate of at least 150 kilobytes per second (150 KBps).
Tapes	Data stored on tapes can be read in a tape drive only and must be read sequentially. Tapes are most commonly used to store backup copies of data.

Supporting Mobile Devices

When you are supporting mobile devices within a healthcare environment, there are many different devices that may need to be managed and secured for use.

Guidelines

To properly support mobile devices within the healthcare computing environment:

- Verify that all device air ducts are cleaned on a regular basis to prevent overheating.
- Follow proper care instructions from the manufacturer for device batteries.
- Verify that proper transport and handling procedures are followed to prevent loss or damage of devices.
- Verify that all mobile devices, such as laptops, mobile phones, and smartphones, must be properly stored and secured in a cabinet or safe when not in use.
- Ensure that security features and data encryption is configured on all portable media players used by clinical staff to protect any PHI data stored on the devices.
- Implement antivirus, anti-spyware, and anti-adware software to protect mobile devices against attacks.
- Ensure that strong password policies are used and enforced on all user end devices.
- Configure encryption settings on all mobile devices to meet specific HIPAA requirements.

Example:

Brian, an IT technician in a outpatient surgery center, has been asked to manage the smartphone implementation within the office. Each doctor in the practice will be issued a smartphone to use throughout the day to access email and the patient prescription database. The first thing Brian does is check the manufacturer's battery documentation to verify that the settings on the devices are acceptable. Brian then configures encryption on all the devices. Next, Brian verifies that sufficient antivirus software for mobile devices is installed on each phone. Then, Brian meets with the doctors in the office to review storage guidelines, handling procedures, and strong password guidelines.

WAP Basic Configuration Settings

There are a number of basic configuration settings used when installing or setting up a Wireless Access Point (WAP).

Setting	Countermeasures
Placement	To determine placement for the WAP, use the following questions to identify requirements: • Where are the nodes you wish to connect to the router located? • How long will the cable run between the WAP and the main network be? • Is there access to a power outlet? • Will the device be physically secure? • If necessary, is there access to a wired network drop? • Think about the various considerations for wireless networking including avoiding interference, signal range, and signal degradation. • Think about the sensitivity to imaging and radiology environments. Will the wireless router experience interference from imaging machines? To securely place the WAP: • Reduce your wireless LAN transmitter power. • Position the router or access point safely. The radio frequency range of each access point should not extend beyond the physical boundaries of the organization's facilities. • Consider the proximity of wireless devices to radiology environments.
Network	• Assign static IP addresses to devices. • Use Media Access Control (MAC) filtering for access control. • Use the Remote Authentication Dial-In User Service Plus (RADIUS+) network directory authentication where feasible. • Use a virtual private network (VPN). • Perform periodic rogue wireless access point scans. • Perform periodic security assessments.
SSID	• Don't broadcast your Service Set Identifier (SSID). • Change the default SSID naming broadcast.
Security	• Secure your wireless router or access point administration interface. • Change default administrator passwords (and user names). • Disable remote administration. • Secure/disable the reset switch/function. • Change the default Simple Network Management Protocol (SNMP) parameter, which monitors the state of the network. Default SNMP parameters may not provide enough security, and you may need to change the parameters to provide more security. • Change the default channel. • Regularly upgrade the Wi-Fi router firmware to ensure you have the latest security patches and critical fixes. • Apply MAC address filtering to verify the address assigned to each network card, and then permit or deny the device with that address from gaining access to your network. By configuring a WAP to filter MAC addresses, you can control which wireless clients may join your network.

Setting	Countermeasures
Encryption	• Enable Wi-Fi Protected Access (WPA2) encryption instead of Wired Equivalency Protocol (WEP). • Change the default encryption keys. • Avoid using pre-shared keys (PSK).
Guest network	• Ensure isolation from the network running the EMR. • Enable firewalls between the guest network and the network running the EMR system.

Installing a WAP

1. Begin by selecting and purchasing a WAP that will meet your needs.
2. Determine the correct placement for the WAP using the placement guidelines.
3. Using a laptop, or a workstation at a desk or workbench, configure the WAP prior to deployment:
    a. Connect a network cable to the WAP's uplink port.
    b. Power on the WAP.
    c. Connect to the WAP via the built-in web interface, or by using manufacturer supplied configuration software.
    d. Configure the desired settings:
        - Consult your network documentation for configuration parameters such as the WAP's SSID naming, DHCP settings, and security settings.
        - Consult the device manufacturer's documentation for information on how to configure and use the device's capabilities and settings.
    e. Save the settings once configured.
    f. Test the WAP's functionality by connecting a wireless client to it:
        - Ping or use traceroute to other computers and observe the results.
        - Use software tools to monitor the client's wireless signal strength and the WAP's behavior.
        - Connect to internal network shares.
        - Connect to the Internet.
4. Place the WAP in the chosen location.
5. Run the appropriate type of cabling from the main network to the WAP.

    Label the cable or drops on both ends so that there is no confusion as to where the cables go.
6. Power on the WAP.
7. Test the WAP's functionality in the live environment by repeating the tests from earlier.

8. Document your actions and their results, including any anomalies along the way.

Steps for Conducting a Site Survey

A *site survey* is an analysis technique that determines the coverage area of a wireless network, identifies any sources of interference, and establishes other characteristics of the coverage area. While an authorized site survey is a standard part of planning or maintaining a wireless network, unauthorized site surveys or a compromise of the site survey data can be a security risk. You use a site survey to help you install and secure a wireless LAN. Conducting a site survey requires you to complete the following steps:

1. Gather detailed information about the facility and its layout. If possible, obtain blueprints of the building. Be sure to document information such as the location of computers, power outlets, and structural components such as walls, doorways, floors and hallways. Also note the location of potential barriers to RF signals such as metal racks, partitions, file cabinets, radiology equipment and rooms, and firebreaks.
2. Use equipment to assess radio coverage. This step enables you to identify the optimal location for WAPs and antennas. Close all medical office and room doors during this step to be sure that the locations you select work well in this environment.
3. Analyze channel interference to determine the appropriate radio frequencies for your environment.
4. Install an access point at the preliminary locations you have identified. Then, measure data rates and signal strengths at various locations to verify that you have placed the access point appropriately.
5. Document your findings.

Router Installation and Configuration Settings

There are many different installation and configuration setting to be aware of when you install a router within a network.

Setting	Description
Password	The default password should be changed as soon as possible to prevent unauthorized access.
Internet connection	Internet connection configuration information can be assigned in the configuration page for the specific router.
SSID	For wireless routers, the SSID naming must be changed from the default name assigned by the manufacturer.
DHCP	DHCP should be turned off in most cases to prevent unauthorized users from obtaining an IP address from the router.
Firewall	When available, enable the firewall included with the router and verify that the configuration settings meet network requirements.

Firewall Installation and Configuration Considerations

When installing a firewall within a network infrastructure, there are a number of factors to consider:

- Place the firewall correctly within the network environment.
- Once the firewall is installed, test for security holes or other vulnerabilities.
- Verify that the firewall is set to block ICMP traffic.
- If applicable, configure stateful packet inspection settings.
- Disable remote administration options.
- Set up monitoring settings to be used to verify the firewall is functioning as expected.

ACTIVITY 4-9

Installing and Configuring Storage Devices

This is an animated demonstration that is available on the CD that shipped with this course. You can run this demonstration on any Windows computer. The animation can be launched either directly from the CD by clicking the **Interactives** link and navigating to the appropriate one, or from the installed data file location by opening the C:\HCIT\Simulations\Lesson 4\Installing and Configuring Storage Devices folder and double-clicking the executable (.exe) file.

Scenario:

You have been asked to upgrade all the workstation storage devices in the medical facility you support. You will install and configure a Parallel ATA drive and a SCSI drive.

1. View the installing and configuring storage devices demonstration.

a. Browse to the C:\HCIT\Simulations\Lesson 4\Installing and Configuring Storage Devices folder.

b. Double-click the Installing and Configuring Storage Devices executable file.

c. In the **Open File - Security Warning** message box, click **Run.**

d. View the animated demonstration and close the C:\HCIT\Simulations\Lesson 4\Installing and Configuring Storage Devices folder.

ACTIVITY 4-10

Discussing Hardware Support

Scenario:

In this activity, you will examine different hardware components and how they are installed and configured securely within a medical environment.

---

1. **What is the correct description for each type of imaging device?**

___	Barcode reader	a.	Used to scan a patient's driver licenses or insurance card.
___	Document scanner	b.	Used to fax prescriptions or to print out prescription information from the EMR/EHR system.
___	Card/badge scanner	c.	Used to capture a patient's signature.
___	Fax printer	d.	In diagnostics, used to capture an image that will then be analyzed.
___	Camera	e.	Used to convert paper to an electronic format.
___	Signature pads	f.	Used to scan and identify patients using information included on their ID wrist band.

---

2. **When placing a new router within an existing infrastructure, what should you consider before installing and configuring the device?**

---

3. **One of the doctors in the medical office that you are supporting asks you for a quick way to transfer patient notes taken on his smartphone to his laptop. He would like to be able to transfer data after each patient once he gets back to his office. What connection method would work well for these devices in this situation?**

   a) FireWire

   b) USB

   c) Bluetooth

   d) Serial

Lesson 4 Follow-up

In this lesson, you reviewed the basics of computer technology and how it is used within the healthcare environment. Now that you have reviewed the essential components that make up a computing environment, you can use that knowledge to fully support any technical issues that arise within the healthcare working environment.

1. **What technical components are you familiar with and how do you think you will use them in a medical environment?**

2. **What devices do you think are used the most within a healthcare setting?**

5 Providing Medical IT Support

Lesson Time: 3 hour(s), 30 minutes

Lesson Objectives:

In this lesson, you will provide IT support and solve IT problems in the medical workplace.

You will:

- Set up a user's computer at their work area.
- Troubleshoot basic IT issues.
- Troubleshoot medical IT problems.
- Identify how medical organizations select, implement, and deploy EMR systems.
- identify components of change control.

Introduction

In the previous lessons, you reviewed information about IT that you probably already knew, and gained new knowledge about the healthcare industry that you may need to have working knowledge of as you move into the healthcare field. Now it's time to put all those pieces together. In this lesson, you will identify tools and techniques for supporting IT and solving IT problems in the workplace, but more specifically, how those tools and techniques come into play when dealing with IT issues specific to the healthcare industry.

One of the most significant parts of an IT technician's job is solving IT problems. As you transition into the healthcare industry, you will need to know how to troubleshoot problems specific to the technology being used by healthcare professionals. Having the knowledge of how to support IT in a medical environment and to troubleshoot IT issues related to specific medical technology will make you a valuable asset to the healthcare industry.

TOPIC A

Set Up a Workstation

Solving IT problems as a professional in the healthcare industry requires the knowledge of basic IT troubleshooting and problem-solving skills, but specific to the kinds of devices, equipment, and scenarios you will encounter in the healthcare field. In this topic, you will perform the most common task any IT professional will likely have to perform: setting up a workstation.

Setting up a workstation is a basic yet vital part of IT support. Skipping a step, or forgetting a piece of equipment, can cost you time or result in a service call later, or even result in a privacy breach. Knowing all the components of a typical workstation set up will ensure that you are completing this task completely and efficiently.

Necessary Equipment

There are a number of pieces of equipment that are essential for setting up a workstation. Necessary equipment includes:

- A desk.
- A chair.
- A telephone.
- A system unit (such as a CPU or laptop).
- A display device (or monitor).
- And, input devices such as a mouse and keyboard.

Optional Equipment

There are a number of pieces of equipment that are not necessary for a workstation setup, but may be optional equipment required or requested by an employee. Optional equipment may include:

- A printer.
- A laptop docking station.
- External speakers.
- A DVD burner.
- An external hard drive.
- Portable storage devices.
- And, specific devices for a given medical setting, such as a card scanner for insurance documentation.

Software

In the medical environment, users will require both standard and specialized software, including:

- An operating system.
- Standard desktop applications such as web browsers, word processors, and email clients.
- And, specialized client software; for example, for accessing Electronic Medical Record (EMR) or Electronic Health Record (EHR) systems.

How to Set Up a Workstation

When setting up and configuring a workstation within a medical environment, you need to ensure that the station is available for use by the appropriate staff, without impeding other patient care activities that take place within the same location.

Guidelines

- Choose an appropriately accessible location within the work area.
- Place all equipment so that it can meet Health Insurance Portability and Accountability Act (HIPAA) privacy and security requirements.
- Ensure the installation location can meet the power needs of the new equipment.
- Ensure that the installation location meets communications needs, such as an available network drop.
- Set up and configure the standard and optional equipment according to the manufacturer's instructions.
- Use ghosting/imaging technology to simplify the software installation and to ensure a consistent set of hardware configuration specifications.

Example:

Adam receives a job ticket to set up a workstation in a new patient room. There is a desk in each patient room that will be a logical location for the workstation. It is near where patients will be seated, close to other medical devices that may be used during a patient visit, and already has ample power sources and a network drop that can be used for the workstation. Adam removes all the hardware for the workstation from boxes, places each device in the appropriate location, and connects all the equipment properly. He tests all the components to make sure they are functioning.

Adam uses ghosting software to install all of the necessary software and applications needed for the workstation, including the EMR system. This allows him to configure the workstation with the same applications and configurations as all other workstations in the office.

Adam makes sure to configure the workstation so that it requires a user to log in with a user name and password in order to access the system. He also configures the system to lock itself when the computer is not in use for more than one minute, ensuring that sensitive patient information is not accessible unless logged on with the appropriate credentials. Before leaving the room, Adam makes sure to lock the workstation.

OPTIONAL ACTIVITY 5-1

Setting Up a Basic PC Workstation

Scenario:

The hospital that you support as an IT technician has a new healthcare office opening on the third floor. You have been asked by your manager to set up the front desk computers. The machines have to be unpacked from the manufacturer boxes, set up, and essential components connected in preparation for the EHR or EMR environment setup.

---

1. Get all hardware and external components ready for setup.

   a. Remove each hardware component from the boxes and packaging.

   b. Get all the peripherals and connection wires out of the packaging.

   c. Move the system unit, LCD display, and peripherals to the desired location.

---

2. Connect and power up the peripherals and system unit.

   a. Connect the LCD cable to the system unit.

   b. Connect the LCD power cable to a power source.

   c. Connect the mouse to the system unit.

   d. Connect the keyboard to the system unit.

   e. Connect the system unit power cable to a power source.

   f. Connect the network cable to the system unit.

   g. Turn on the system unit and the LCD display and verify that the default operating system screen is displayed.

TOPIC B

Troubleshoot Basic IT Issues

In the previous topic, you performed a basic workstation setup, one of the most common and basic tasks of an IT professional's responsibilities. But your responsibilities don't end there; part of an IT professional's job role is to also provide day-to-day support for any issues that arise related to the IT equipment. In this topic, you will perform the day-to-day support tasks that an IT professional may be responsible for completing.

Day-to-day IT support keeps an organization running smoothly. This is particularly important in medicine, because common IT issues can waste valuable time and manpower that could be better used working with patients. Ensuring that you have the background knowledge of how to provide the essential day-to-day support for these common IT issues will make you a valuable addition to your healthcare organization, and allow the other staff members to do their jobs more easily.

Troubleshooting Network Issues

There are several common network issues you might be called upon to diagnose and resolve.

Network Issue	*Possible Problems and Solutions*
No network connectivity or connection lost	This could indicate a physical problem such as a loose cable or a defective network adapter. Check cables and connections and check for link lights on the network adapter. Reseat connections, replace cables, or reinstall/replace the adapter as necessary. On IP networks, check for a missing or incorrect IP address. If the address is manually configured, this could be a data entry error; reconfigure the connection. If automatically configured, the Dynamic Host Configuration Protocol (DHCP) server might be unavailable or unreachable. Make sure the DHCP server is up and that the client is physically connected to the network. On IP networks using DHCP, if a machine is statically assigned an IP address from the DHCP pool, this can cause duplicate IP addresses, resulting in a failure to communicate at either of the two machines with the same address. Locate statically assigned IP address and reconfigure appropriately.

Network Issue	Possible Problems and Solutions
Network communications are slow	The network might be experiencing high traffic and many collisions. Check the activity status indicator light for the collision frequency. This should be a temporary condition that will pass; if not, network engineers might need to upgrade the network bandwidth or data rate to increase throughput. A number of things could cause the network to run slow: • Improperly configured backup schedules. • Improper maintenance update schedules. • Internet Service Provider (ISP) issues. • Virtual private network (VPN) issues. • IP Domain Name System (DNS) failures. • Switch issues. • Improperly scheduled virus scans.
Local communications but no Internet connection	The proxy settings are incorrect. Check the proxy configuration of your network connection. There might be firewall settings causing issues with connectivity. Check the firewall settings.
Client can connect but cannot access resources	The user might have insufficient permissions, or the target network resource might be unavailable. Check to make sure the printer or server is running and connected to the network, and check to make sure the user has appropriate permissions.
Connections by IP address but not by name	The DNS configuration is incorrect or the DNS server is down. Or, the hosts file might be configured incorrectly. Check the IP configuration settings and verify that the DNS server is running. Check the hosts file to make sure it does not contain incorrect entries.
Intermittent signal quality issues	Electrical noise, or *electromagnetic interference (EMI)*, is a general term for unwanted signals on the network media that can interfere with network transmissions and cause transient problems. Interference or noise can come from natural sources, such as solar radiation or electrical storms, or from man-made sources, such as electronic interference from nearby motors or transformers. In hospital and healthcare settings, medical equipment (such as radiology equipment) is a major source of EMI. There is also lead shielding and steel cages that can impede wireless signals. In medical settings, it is best to use CAT6 twisted-pair or else fiber optic cable. Do not run data and power cables in the same conduits, and run network cables parallel to each other whenever possible. Keep network cables at least 20 inches away from fluorescent lights. Ground all equipment and electrical circuits according to the manufacturer's instructions and local building codes. When rewiring, it is also recommended to use subcontractors that specialize in computer cabling. In most cases, the IT technician will troubleshoot and the wiring specialists will fix the actual problem.

Troubleshooting Computer and Accessory Hardware Issues

There are a number of computer and accessory hardware issues that you might be called upon to diagnose and resolve.

Hardware	Possible Problems and Solutions
Monitor/display device	Possible problems include: • A dark screen, no image on screen, or an indicator light that is not lit. • A flickering, distorted, or erratic screen. • The monitor turns itself off. • A completely white display. • The monitor makes crackling or whining noises. Possible solutions for these issues include: • Always check the power source. Often the power is not turned on, the power cable is disconnected, or the power is on but the monitor is plugged into a power strip, surge protector, or Uninterruptible Power Supply (UPS) that is not turned on. • Check to see that the video graphics array (VGA) or high definition media interface (HDMI) cables are properly connected between devices. • Check the settings for the device, such as refresh rate, power settings, screen resolution, etc. • Check to see if the device is too close to other electronic or magnetic equipment that is causing interference. • Short of cleaning the exterior parts, noisy monitors should be replaced or repaired. • If the display device has been dropped or tipped, it may have sustained internal or external physical damage that cannot be corrected by any other troubleshooting technique. It is generally more economical and certainly safer to replace the device rather than attempting repair. Standby swap out units are common in this case.

Hardware	Possible Problems and Solutions
Keyboard	Possible problems include: • Sticking keys. • No input when keys are pressed. • Wrong characters when keys are pressed. • Multimedia buttons not working properly. • New keyboard will not plug into the same port as the old keyboard. Possible solutions for these issues include: • Foreign matter is stuck under the keys, and needs to be removed with compressed air. • The keyboard may be unplugged, plugged into the wrong port, connections are not seated properly, or the adapter is incorrect. • For wireless keyboards, check for connectivity issues, interference, and if batteries are needed. • The device driver needs updating or a file related to the button has been moved, renamed, or modified in some way. • Make sure your system and peripherals have compatible ports and connectors. • If keyboard failure is in a terminal emulation session, the keyboard mapping configuration file should be examined.
Mouse	Possible problems include: • Mouse pointer is jumping around on screen. • The mouse is not working at all. Possible solutions for these issues include: • The ball or rollers are dirty, or it is being rolled over an uneven or dirty surface. Clean the mouse; replace the mouse pad. • Use the Device Manager and Help utilities to check the status of the pointing device and to verify that the correct driver is installed. • Physically check the pointing device connection. • For wireless mice, check the batteries and replace if necessary. Verify that there is no obstruction between the transmitter and the receiver. Press the **Reset** or **Connect** buttons on each device to try to re-establish the connection. Verify that the receiver device is connected to the port. • Check the status of the root hub or USB host controller in Device Manager. Plug the mouse directly into a USB port on the computer; if this works, and the hub is working properly, the mouse is probably not getting enough power. Physically remove some of the devices on the same hub as the mouse to another port or hub or use a powered USB hub. • The device driver needs to be updated.

Hardware	Possible Problems and Solutions

Power supply	Possible power supply issues include:
	• The fan is not working.
	• The computer will not start or reboots after startup.
	• An odor is coming from the power supply.
	• A noise is coming from the power supply.
	Possible solutions for these issues include:
	• Dirt and dust may gather around the power supply, causing the fan bearings to wear and the fan to turn more slowly. Use compressed air to remove this debris from the system. In the healthcare environment, it is important to take precautions when performing any cleaning tasks. Considerations include:
	  ■ Due to sanitation issues, do not clean power supplies out in the medical environment.
	  ■ Proper and scheduled maintenance schedules should be in place to ensure no improper buildups within the computer.
	  ■ Mount the chassis off the floor and get units and cables securely out of the way to promote a cleaner environment.
	• If the fan becomes damaged due to dust, replace the power supply or have qualified personnel replace the fan.
	• Make sure that there is power to the outlet that the computer is plugged into.
	• Check that the connections from the power supply to the system board are secure and make sure the master switch to the power supply, at the rear of the system, is on before pressing the computer's power button.
	• Check power supply output voltages with a digital multimeter to verify that the necessary voltages are being provided to the board.
	• If there is an odor from the power supply, confirm that the odor is indeed coming from the power supply before contacting the manufacturer.
	• If a noise is not from the fan, but from another power supply component, replace the power supply or take it out and send it for service.

Cables	Possible problems include: • There is interference, packet loss, or temporary missing nodes on the workstation screen. • There is loss of network connection. Possible solutions for these issues include: • There is electromagnetic interference with the cables. Ensure that any source of EMI is at least 6 to 12 inches away from where cables will be located. • Check cable connections at the workstation, network adapter, router, and switch; ensure that cables are not looped or coiled, which can generate electrical interference; and inspect the cable for pinches or breaks and replace cable as needed. • Check that the cable is connected both to the source and the computer properly, and check that each end of the cable is not broken. Broken tabs are common and can cause a loose connection that can result in intermittent or complete loss of connectivity

Hardware	Possible Problems and Solutions
Printer	Possible problems include: • Jobs are in the print queue, but do not print. • The printer does not print the way the users expects it to. • A user cannot access a printer on the network. • The print output is garbled or showing ghosted images. • Print jobs do not appear in the print queue. Possible solutions for these issues include: • Check for physical problems with the printer (out of toner, ink, or paper). • Check to see that the user is aware of which printer their print job is being sent to. In an EMR system, printers are tied to specific tasks and workflows for security reasons. Certain print jobs will only print to specific printers configured within the EMR system. Make sure that the user is aware of which printer their print job will be sent to. • Check to see if the printer is paused in the operating system. • Check to see if the computer has an incompatible or incorrect printer driver installed. • Check to see if the print spooler service is stalled. • Check to see if the **Use Printer Offline** option has been activated. • Check the page setup options in the applications or the properties and settings of the printer. • Check printer connectivity to the network. You may need to reattach the printer to the network, check the status of the printer or print server and restart as necessary, verify or change the IP address on the printer to the correct address, or check the printer's power cycle. • Check whether you can install more memory, adjust the resolution in the printer settings, update or replace the driver, or replace the cable. • Check the network status of all devices, update user permissions, or move the spool folder or add disk space. • The last effort would be to contact the manufacturer or visit their website for troubleshooting information.

Proper Sanitation Procedures

It should be common practice to disinfect the components users touch on a regular basis. Improper disinfection procedures can gum up the mechanics of the device. Verify that proper procedures and supplies are present and used as directed.

Terminal Emulation Software

Terminal emulation software allows a computer to emulate a terminal to connect to legacy systems.

ACTIVITY 5-2

Troubleshooting Display Devices

This is an animated demonstration animation that is available on the CD that shipped with this course. You can run this demonstration on any Windows computer. The animation can be launched either directly from the CD by clicking the **Interactives** link and navigating to the appropriate one, or from the installed data file location by opening the C:\HCIT\Simulations\Lesson 5\Troubleshooting Display Devices folder and double-clicking the executable (.exe) file.

Scenario:

Several users have reported problems with their monitors. All the users need their systems to be fixed before they can continue with their work. You need to resolve the problems by using standard display device troubleshooting techniques.

---

1. View the troubleshooting display devices demonstration.

a. Browse to the C:\HCIT\Simulations\Lesson 5\Troubleshooting Display Devices folder.

b. Double-click the Troubleshooting Display Devices executable file.

c. In the **Open File - Security Warning** message box, click **Run.**

d. View the animated demonstration and close the C:\HCIT\Simulations\Lesson 5\Troubleshooting Display Devices folder.

ACTIVITY 5-3

Maintaining and Troubleshooting Input Devices

This is an animated demonstration animation that is available on the CD that shipped with this course. You can run this demonstration on any Windows computer. The animation can be launched either directly from the CD by clicking the **Interactives** link and navigating to the appropriate one, or from the installed data file location by opening the C:\HCIT\Simulations\Lesson 5\Maintaining and Troubleshooting Input Devices folder and double-clicking the executable (.exe) file.

Scenario:

Several users have reported problems with their keyboards and pointing devices. All the users need their systems to be fixed before they can continue with their work. You need to resolve the problems and get the users back to work.

1. View the maintaining and troubleshooting input devices demonstration.

a. Browse to the C:\HCIT\Simulations\Lesson 5\Maintaining and Troubleshooting Input Devices folder.

b. Double-click the Maintaining and Troubleshooting Input Devices executable file.

c. In the **Open File - Security Warning** message box, click **Run.**

d. View the animated demonstration and close the C:\HCIT\Simulations\Lesson 5\Maintaining and Troubleshooting Input Devices folder.

ACTIVITY 5-4

Troubleshooting Multimedia Devices

This is an animated demonstration animation that is available on the CD that shipped with this course. You can run this demonstration on any Windows computer. The animation can be launched either directly from the CD by clicking the **Interactives** link and navigating to the appropriate one, or from the installed data file location by opening the C:\HCIT\Simulations\Lesson 5\Troubleshooting Multimedia Devices folder and double-clicking the executable (.exe) file.

Scenario:

Several users have opened trouble tickets with the support center about problems with their speakers. You have been asked to resolve these problems.

---

1. View the troubleshooting multimedia devices demonstration.
   a. Browse to the C:\HCIT\Simulations\Lesson 5\Troubleshooting Multimedia Devices folder.
   b. Double-click the Troubleshooting Multimedia Devices executable file.
   c. In the **Open File - Security Warning** message box, click **Run.**
   d. View the animated demonstration and close the C:\HCIT\Simulations\Lesson 5\Troubleshooting Multimedia Devices folder.

Troubleshooting Mobile Devices

As a healthcare IT professional, you will be responsible for addressing issues with the laptop and tablet computers used in medical settings.

Portable Computer Issue	Description and Solutions
Display issues	Some common display device issues include: • Output to an external monitor, video device, or projector. Often this feature requires the user to toggle between display modes. Check the device documentation for more information on toggle modes for your specific device. • LCD not displaying. In some cases, the LCD cutoff switch remains stuck down even after the laptop lid is opened. You may need to connect the laptop to an external monitor to verify that the graphics card is still working properly. • Backlight functionality and pixelation have been changed. In some cases, the intensity of the backlight and the amount of pixelation can conserve power if configured correctly. Verify that the backlight and resolution settings are configured to suit the user's needs. Often, the laptop's display is optimized for certain dots per inch (DPI) and resolution settings. Changing these is not always recommended. • The screen goes dark and cannot be adjusted or the hues in the display are changing. This can be one of two issues: the screen has gone bad or the LCD inverter is bad. You may need to replace the screen or the inverter. Check the manufacturer's documentation to verify replacement options.
Short battery life	Device battery life can be maximized by configuring the power management features of your device. It is common to find most medical providers using tablets on a regular basis and need the devices available and working all the time. Configure sleep or standby modes for hard drives and displays, but leave the network interface controller cards active to stay connected to the network. Newer laptops and tablets are optimized for lower power consumption and are usually recommended. Many devices also offer extended life batteries. Replacing batteries is not uncommon and will need to be done periodically. Typically you will use high-capacity batteries, and some medical environments will provide battery-charging stations where spare batteries are constantly being kept charged and ready for use. It is common for medical facilities to utilize workstations on wheels (WOWs). These mobile rolling stations for laptops usually have a small UPS battery and can be plugged into AC supplies for recharging in examining rooms, nursing stations, and provider offices.
Laptop gets hot	Because laptops have very little space in between their internal components, you can have problems with laptops overheating, which leads to system lockups and even hardware failures. Strategies you can use to help reduce the heat within laptops include: • Use the power management features even when the laptop is connected to a power outlet, especially if you are using the laptop in a warm room. • Try to keep the bottom of the laptop ventilated. (For example, do not rest a laptop on a pillow in your lap.) • Medical facilities may offer cooling pads. • Be aware of the fan in the laptop. If you hear it running very fast on a regular basis, take steps to minimize heat in the laptop

Portable Computer Issue	Description and Solutions
Laptop power issues	Laptops have many possible power issues: • The laptop battery does not charge fully. Nickel-cadmium (Ni-Cad) batteries have battery memory—which means that they can lose most of their rechargeability if you repeatedly recharge them without draining the batteries first. The only solution to this problem is to use a conditioning charger, which is designed to first drain the Ni-Cd batteries before recharging them. Nickel-metal hydride (NiMH) batteries can be affected too. • The laptop not working properly when on battery power can be an indication that the battery contacts are dirty. You can clean them by using alcohol preps or even just a dry cloth. • If the laptop will not turn on when connected to AC power, the power cord or AC adapter might have failed, the outlet to which you are attempting to connect the laptop is bad, or the power supply in the laptop has failed. Try using a known good power cord and then an AC adapter to determine if either is the source of the problem. If this does not resolve the problem, verify that the power outlet is good by plugging in a known good electrical device and verifying whether you can turn it on. You might also test both AC and DC power by using a multimeter.
Pointing device issues	Causes of this problem include a corrupt driver, driver incompatibilities after an upgrade to a newer operating system, and a hardware failure. Steps to take to resolve this problem include reinstalling or upgrading the driver. If this does not resolve the problem, many portable devices allow users to connect an external mouse as a substitute for the touch pad or other integrated pointing devices. Laptops commonly have touch pads or pointing sticks. Touch pads can suffer from dirt and hand grease contamination that can make the touch pad behave erratically; make sure to clean with alcohol preps. Pointing stick heads can wear out and become slippery, making them very difficult to use; order replacements from the manufacturer or vendor. For touch screens on tablet PCs, the screens may need to be recalibrated to correct erratic input behavior.

Troubleshooting Smartphones

You may find that users will try to self-correct lockup problems with their smartphones by performing a factory reset or reinitialization. Unfortunately, in most cases this will not only not solve the problem, but will cause the user to lose all customized configuration settings and return to an out-of-the-box state. Try to discourage users from employing this technique.

ACTIVITY 5-5

Configuring Power Management for Mobile Computing

This is a simulated activity that is available on the CD that shipped with this course. You can run this simulation on any Windows computer. The activity simulation can be launched either directly from the CD by clicking the **Interactives** link and navigating to the appropriate one, or from the installed data file location by opening the C:\HCIT\Simulations\Lesson 5\Configuring Power Management for Mobile Computing folder and double-clicking the executable (.exe) file.

Scenario:

A user has indicated that the current power behavior on her portable system is not meeting her needs. You will create a new power plan for her laptop and also change the settings.

---

1. Configure power management settings.

   a. Browse to the C:\HCIT\Simulations\Lesson 5\Configuring Power Management for Mobile Computing folder.

   b. Double-click the Configuring Power Management for Mobile Computing executable file.

   c. In the **Open File - Security Warning** message box, click **Run.**

   d. Follow the on-screen steps for the simulation.

   e. Close the C:\HCIT\Simulations\Lesson 5\Configuring Power Management for Mobile Computing folder.

Troubleshooting Software Problems

There are a number of steps that can be taken when software crashes or error messages occur to try to find the cause and a potential fix to the problem. Any one or a combination of these may work to troubleshoot the software issue.

- Scan the system for possible viruses, spyware, or malware that may be causing the program to experience the problem.
- Close all other running programs and applications to free up random access memory (RAM). Close and immediately restart the program or application experiencing the problem. Close all programs, and restart the computer. Try launching the program or application again once the system has rebooted.
- Check to see if the firewall has for some reason been instructed to block the program experiencing the problem. Check the firewall settings for the user to see if the program is being blocked; if it has accidentally been blocked, change the settings to allow the program to run.
- Search online for instances of the same problem or if it is a known issue. Find out if there are any software patches/hotfixes/updates for the problem and install them.

- Undo any changes to the user's hardware or software to see if there are potential conflicts between newly installed parts or programs.
- Uninstall and reinstall the program experiencing the problem.
- If running a Windows-based system, defragment the hard drive.

Software Patches/Hotfixes/Updates

Software patches and updates are pieces of software created to fix problems with or provide updates to a program or application. This may include fixing known vulnerabilities or bugs, or improving functionality or performance. A *software hotfix* is a package of files used to address a specific problem, often specific to a particular customer's problem and not released to all customers at large. However, these terms can sometimes be used interchangeably. In most cases within a medical environment, software patches, hotfixes, and updates will be managed on an administrative level and typically administered through a patch management process.

ACTIVITY 5-6

Troubleshooting Basic IT Problems

Scenario:

As an IT professional, it is your job to diagnose and resolve the many common issues that medical staff might encounter on a daily basis. Today, you need to use your general computing knowledge and troubleshooting skills to solve a number of basic user problems.

---

1. **A doctor calls you, complaining that he cannot turn on his computer. It worked fine yesterday, but this morning he cannot get it to turn on. What is the first thing you should do?**

    a) Use compressed air to remove dirt and debris from the fan.

    b) Replace the monitor.

    c) Check all the power sources to the computer.

    d) Check the network connections to the machine.

---

2. **You receive a call from a practice manager who reports that she is unable to access any websites in Microsoft® Internet Explorer®. While talking with this user, you verify that none of the other users in the office can connect to websites in Internet Explorer. What might be the problem?**

    a) Her computer is configured with the wrong default gateway address.

    b) Her ISP's DNS server is down.

    c) Her computer is configured with the wrong subnet mask.

    d) Her ISP's default gateway server is down.

---

3. **You receive a call from an nurse practitioner who is having trouble with his laptop. He ran out of battery power during a meeting, and when he tried to turn it back on using the power cord, it still would not turn on. What are some of the possible causes of this issue?**

    a) The power outlet he was plugged into was not working.

    b) The power supply in the laptop has failed.

    c) The battery contacts are dirty.

    d) The power cord or AC adapter has failed.

---

4. **You receive a call from a physician's assistant who has been having ongoing issues with her keyboard. Sometimes it works fine; other times, when she presses certain keys, there is no input or the wrong characters are input. What is the most likely explanation for this issue?**

   a) The keyboard is plugged into the wrong port.

   b) There is interference between the keyboard and the computer.

   c) The device driver needs to be updated.

   d) There is foreign matter under the keys.

---

5. **You receive a call from a client who is experiencing an issue with one of her software applications. Every time she tries to launch the program, it will start to load but then a window pops up prompting her to go to an outside website and download antivirus software. She cannot close the window and access the program.**

   What is the most logical cause and solution to her issue?

   a) She is running an outdated version of the program and you need to install a software update.

   b) She is experiencing conflicts with another program that is open and you need to uninstall one of the programs.

   c) She accidentally blocked the program and you need to change the firewall settings to allow the program to run.

   d) She likely downloaded something with a virus or malware and you need to scan the system and remove it.

TOPIC C

Troubleshoot Medical IT Issues

In the previous topic, you described the day-to-day tasks you might perform as an IT professional in any industry. While core IT systems are important to a medical environment, the specialized medical systems, software, and tools are even more vital. In this topic, we will address specific techniques you can use to expedite medical IT troubleshooting.

As an IT professional, it is expected that you have the ability to perform day-to-day IT tasks like troubleshooting a variety of common hardware and software issues. However, as an IT professional hoping to work in the highly specialized healthcare industry, you will also need to have working knowledge of how to troubleshoot healthcare-specific IT issues. For example, you should know your EMR or EHR system inside and out to be ready to troubleshoot and support the clinical staff. This topic should give you a foundation for understanding how your skills will help resolve the specific IT problems that can occur within a medical setting.

Identifying Support Resources

The important thing to know for troubleshooting in a healthcare organization is knowing who within your organization may oversee specific programs or if you use outside support from the manufacturer of the device or program. Depending on the size of your organization, there may be onsite managers of an application or program. For smaller organizations, like a private practice, more than likely they will rely on support from the company that produces the device or program. Since within the organization there may be multiple systems in use at once—an EMR, a laboratory information system (LIS), medical billing software, and more—it is important for you to know who the appropriate person within or outside your organization would be to contact for troubleshooting issues for a specific medical device or application that is outside your area of knowledge.

Documentation for devices and applications and other support resources, such as online forums or support databases, are always a good place to start when trying to find information on troubleshooting specific issues.

Escalating Support Issues

If at any time in the troubleshooting process, you come across an issue that you cannot diagnose and resolve because of lack of access or knowledge, that issue should be escalated to the appropriate support staff, whether that be a site manager onsite at your organization, a manufacturer, or support staff for an application.

Integrating Medical Technology with Traditional IT Systems

With an EMR or EHR installation, the number of medical devices connected to the network can be substantial. Devices may include:

- Specialized printers, such as secured prescription printers, which may be accessible on the network from controlled workstations or authorized personnel.
- Speech recognition devices and software.
- And, specialized software to connect to external sources and to access medical diagnostic information.

Troubleshooting Medical Devices

There are a number of typical reasons that any medical device will not function properly. The following are the most common causes of an issue, which you should check first before escalating the problem to someone more knowledgeable about the specific device, such as the manufacturer.

Cause	*Description and Solution*
Power	Within a healthcare environment, power is very regulated. Dedicated power for computing equipment and medical equipment is usually designated to different power segments: ■ Institutional sized inline power redundancy systems. ■ Inline UPS. ■ Lines that switch to generators if/when power is lost. In hospital settings, it is crucial to keep key medical equipment such as ventilators powered due to the critical nature of the machine keeping patients alive. Check that all power sources are functioning properly and on a regular basis. A common problem is that the device is not working because the power source has been disrupted. Check the power source to ensure it is properly engaged and providing power to the device. Try disconnecting and reconnecting the power source.
Network	The device has lost connection with the network or was never properly set up with network access. Check the network status for the device and make sure that it was properly connected to the network.
Input/output	The device has lost connection with another device through an interface. Check that the interfaces are properly connected on both devices.
Configuration settings	The device does not have the proper configuration settings. Either the configuration settings were not properly set up initially, or a manual change to the configuration settings is causing a malfunction. Sometimes, even just moving a device to a different Universal Serial Bus (USB) port can cause misconfigurations to occur.

Troubleshooting HL7 Problems

Medical coders may experience issues with coding messages when trying to send information between the organization and the insurance company. There are a number of common causes for this issue, which you as the IT professional may be asked to troubleshoot.

Cause	Description and Solution

HL7 thread/nodes have been deactivated	Possible solutions if there are issues communicating with the HL7 node include:
	• Check the communication channel. Run ping and tracert to ensure a communication pathway is present.
	• Look at the configuration file:
	  ▪ To make sure that the thread is trying to contact the correct remote node.
	  ▪ For any credentials for logging into the remote node.
	  ▪ To ensure the correct ports are configured to the remote node.
	• Check to see if firewall policies have been changed or modified that might prevent communication.
	• Is the problem specific to your system? Communicate with the administrator of the remote node to verify that the node is operational and working with other systems.
	• Restart the node as a last resort.
	Possible solutions if the HL7 thread is no longer operating as normal include:
	• Check application event logs on the node.
	• Check the node's memory utilization to make sure the thread is not being shut down or is "not responding."
	• Stop/restart the named thread service.
	• Restart the node as a last resort.

Improperly formatted patient demographics	The demographic information for the patient may be incomplete or improperly formatted in the EMR, causing the coding message to fail. Have the appropriate staff member check that the patient demographic has been filled out completely and properly.
Communication link (fax, network, Internet) is not working or disconnected	The most likely cause of a failure is that the workstation is currently not communicating with the insurance company, clearinghouse, lab, Regional Health Information Organization (RHIO), etc., because either end is experiencing network or Internet downtime or interference. Check the connections between the two points, including access to the fax line, network, and Internet and verify that they are all working properly. Perform standard network troubleshooting, using ping, ipconfig, and tracert to detect the source of connectivity problems. Check with your ISP to determine if there are any issues on their end.
System upgrades	An upgrade on either end of the communication can affect HL7 segments. If you identify this as an issue, flag it for escalation to the software development team.

HL7 Threads and Nodes

An HL7 thread is the specific application, interface, or service running on a machine that provides the conversion or mapping of data between HL7-compliant EMR/EHR systems. An HL7 node is the server or machine that is running the software that is doing the conversion or mapping of HL7-complaint data.

RHIO

A *Regional Health Information Organization (RHIO)* is a health information organization comprised of key stakeholders in the healthcare industry within a specific geographical region who oversee the health information exchange of healthcare providers in the area to improve the overall health and care of the community. It is often used in non-hospital settings like private practices, which do not exchange lab orders or results or do not have their own clinical lab services.

Troubleshooting e-Prescriptions

The most common problem with e-prescriptions systems are errors or failures when trying to send the e-prescription. There are a number of common causes for this issue, which you as the IT professional may be asked to troubleshoot.

Issue	*Description and Solution*
Communication link (fax, network, Internet) is not working or disconnected	The most likely cause of a failure in sending a prescription is that the prescriber's device or workstation is currently not communicating with the pharmacy or the pharmacy is currently offline. Check the prescriber's connections that communicate to the e-prescription system, including access to the fax line, network, and Internet and verify that they are all working properly.
The selected pharmacy does not accept e-prescriptions	Not all pharmacies accept e-prescriptions, and will not be able to accept or fill a prescription sent electronically. The pharmacy will not be in the system. If a provider or patient wants to use such a pharmacy, the prescription will need to be issued and filled manually.
The person prescribing does not have the privileges assigned to them in the EMR	Only users with the necessary permissions will be able to prescribe medications using the e-prescription system. Make sure that the prescriber is logged in with their own user name and password. Verify that the person sending the prescription has been given the proper permissions in the system to send an e-prescription. If appropriate, provide that person with the proper permission if you have access to the system in that capacity, or escalate the issue to the responsible support staff.
Improperly formatted patient demographics	The demographic information for the patient may be incomplete or improperly formatted in the EMR, causing the e-prescription to fail. Have the prescriber check that the patient demographic information has been filled out completely and properly. If the patient demographic information is correct, and none of the other possible causes seem to be in play, escalate the issue to the appropriate support staff for the EMR or e-prescription service.

Issue	Description and Solution
Improperly formatted prescription	The prescription itself may be incomplete or improperly formatted in the system. Have the prescriber check that all the necessary fields have been filled in and the formatting requirements for an e-prescription have been met. If the all information has been properly filled in and formatting seems correct, and none of the other possible causes seem to be in play, escalate the issue to the appropriate support staff for the EMR or e-prescription service.
Deactivated medication	Medications that have been recalled or are no longer being prescribed can be deactivated in the system to prevent them from being accidentally prescribed. When a medication is deactivated in the system, it is not removed from the database nor from the records of patients who received it, so it may still appear in the database but cannot be prescribed. If a clinician tries to prescribe a deactivated medication, the system will return an informational message and the prescriber can select a different medication.
Controlled substance	As of the printing of this manual, controlled substances cannot be prescribed using an e-prescription system due to federal Drug Enforcement Administration (DEA) laws governing controlled substances. Many e-prescribers are working to meet newly established rules designed specifically with the advent of e-prescribing that will allow them to meet the two security credentials being required by the DEA to prescribe a controlled substance electronically. Clinicians should be aware that they will not be able to select this substance in the system to e-prescribe it.

Troubleshooting Billing Software Issues

There are a number of common problems with medical billing software that you may be asked to troubleshoot.

Problem	Description and Solution
Improperly formatted patient demographics	The demographic information for the patient may be incomplete or improperly formatted in the EMR, causing the billing process to fail. Have the appropriate staff member check that the patient demographic has been filled out completely and properly.

Problem	Description and Solution
Improperly formatted superbill	A *superbill* is an itemized form containing all the information needed to file a claim, including patient information and services rendered for a visit, that is compiled by the healthcare provider's medical biller and supplied to the insurance company or clearinghouse as the source for the claim. If the superbill is incorrectly formatted or is missing any piece of required data, it will not be transmitted properly, or may be rejected altogether. Have the medical biller check that all the information required has been added to the superbill and that active and accurate codes were added to the superbill.
Communication link (fax, network, Internet) is not working or disconnected	The most likely cause of a failure is that workstation is currently not communicating with the insurance company because either end is experiencing network or Internet downtime or interference. Check the connections between the two points, including access to the fax line, network, and Internet and verify that they are all working properly.
Network was not set up properly	Some software may need to access files that are stored on the network in order to run properly. It is possible that the program cannot access these files because the network connections on the user's system were not set up properly. Verify that the system is connected to the network and that all configuration settings are correct.
Input/output error	General device input/output (I/O) issues can impede the user from interacting properly with the system. Follow standard I/O troubleshooting.
Software configuration settings problem	Configurations settings for the software application could be preventing the program from working properly on the user's system. Even things as simple as screen resolution could be preventing the application from opening or working. Verify the configuration settings for the program from the manufacturer, and check that the end user's system is properly configured for the application to work. Verify that the user is logging in with the proper credentials to access the remote system.
Errors during installation causing software start-up issues	Errors during initial installation can cause problems down the line, the most common being that the application will not even start. It could be that the system is not compatible with the requirement, it does not have enough memory, or there were other programs running that should have been closed during installation (causing the registry to not be updated properly). Verify that the user's system meets the requirements for the software installation. Uninstall and reinstall the application with all other programs closed, including the firewall and virus scan software.

Superbill Information

Required information on a superbill includes:

- Provider information (full name and degree, service location and signature of provider; full name and degree, and the National Provider Identifier (NPI) code of the ordering/referring/attending physician).
- Patient information (full name, date of birth, insurance provider and ID, date of onset, and date of last visit).
- Visit information (date of visit, Current Procedural Terminology [CPT] procedure codes for services rendered, National Drug Code Identifications [NDC IDs] for any drugs prescribed, International Statistical Classification of Diseases and Related Health Problems, 10th revision [ICD-10] diagnosis codes for diagnosis, modifiers, time, units, quantity of drugs, and authorization information, if necessary).
- Additional information (with notes or comments, if needed).

Troubleshooting Lab Orders and Results

There are a number of issues concerning lab orders and results that you may be asked to troubleshoot.

Problem	*Description and Solution*
Status of an order does not change from "open" to "sent"	Despite the order being sent, the system is not verifying that the order was actually sent. It may or may not be accompanied by an error message in the system. One possible cause for this issue may be that the EMR or lab interface is not running or needs to be restarted. Contact the appropriate manager for the interface to see if they are experiencing issues or to have them restart the interface. Try to resend the order from the requesting end to see if this has solved the issue.
Lab results not received	Lab results have not been received or the system shows them "in progress" for an inordinate amount of time and much longer than it should have taken for the lab to be performed and results sent back. First, contact the lab to make sure that the test has been performed. If the test has been performed, the lab should retrigger the results to be sent to the requesting facility. Improperly formatted patient demographics can cause the lab results to be stuck in a queue without being assigned to the patient. Check to see if the results have not been linked to the proper patient file.
Error messages appear when trying to submit an order	When the submitting facility tries to send an order, an error message such as "patient not found," "no active patient selected," or "no diagnosis codes selected" appears. Not all of the necessary information or fields have been populated. Have the person entering the information for the lab order double check that all of the information has been properly added, especially to the field related to the error message (was a patient currently selected when trying to select a test?)

Problem	Description and Solution
Error messages when trying to view results	When trying to view the result reports in a browser-based EMR client, an error message appears. In a browser-based EMR client, results typically open in a new window, and it is possible that the user's pop-up blocker is preventing the report from opening. Turn off the pop-up blocker or change the settings to allow for the report to open, and try opening the results report again.
Cannot print to lab printer or label printer	The user may not be selecting the lab printer when they send the print request. Ensure that the printer is installed, the drivers are properly installed, and that the user is selecting the lab printer when trying to print labels and not using another printer by default. If the user is selecting the lab printer and the labels are still not printing, it could be that the printer settings are not set up properly in the lab system software. Check the printer settings from within the application to make sure the settings are correct.

How to Troubleshoot Medical IT Issues

Troubleshooting IT problems in general is an important task in any organization; however, within the healthcare industry, there is the added intensity of need for a solution when you are dealing with personal and sensitive information regarding the health and well-being of countless people.

Guidelines

When troubleshooting medical IT problems, consider the following guidelines:

- Follow a tried and true process for all troubleshooting tasks: gather information and identify the symptoms; review the data and establish a possible cause; identify and test a solution.
- Locate the affected modules or fields.
- Determine the file or data types.
- Once you have identified the problem, begin to ascertain the scope of the issue. Find out first and foremost how many users are experiencing the issue to determine the severity of the problem.
- Regardless of the scope of the problem, however, treat all problems regarding medical IT equipment as equally important to solve.
- If the scope of the problem seems large, raise red flags now and make the solution a priority, to avoid an "all-hands-on-deck" response when the problem becomes a crisis.
- Make sure to keep all stakeholders apprised of progress as frequently as possible, but do not let status reports become the focus of the work.
- When determining possible causes, remember: often the first and simplest reason is the correct one.
- There is not always just one root cause. Make sure that you are finding the source of the entire problem, and not just one symptom of the problem. One error message might only just be the most recent error message in a string of error messages that points to a much larger problem with a more intensive solution.
- Many systems and subsystems have audit trails and error logs that can be reviewed to help you diagnose the issue.

- Make sure to test your solution and give it adequate time to prove the true solution. Best practice is to give your solution 24 hours on full load to ensure that the solution is working.
- Be aware that the problem my require the activation of manual backup procedures and workflows.
- If necessary, follow escalation procedures to the proper support tier for the problem, including vendor or local application support as needed.

Example:

Mike receives a help desk call from a client, Sarah, who cannot access the EMR system for the practice. This is incredibly important as it is the middle of the work day, and more patients will be coming in shortly and the office staff need to be able to access patient data.

Mike first asks for as much information from Sarah as possible to help diagnose the issue. She can access the office network and Internet, but cannot access the practice management system. The same is true of all other computers attempting to access the system. It is clear that the problem is an overall outage for the entire practice. Knowing this, Mike needs to get the practice up and running with the system as soon as possible.

Knowing that the entire office does not have access, and that the practice has a hosted server, Mike thinks that the problem is likely with the practice management system's server. He places a call to the network admin for the practice management system, who tells him that they are experiencing unexpected server downtime. He assures Mike that no data will be lost during the downtime, and that the server should be up and running again in the next half an hour. Mike relays this message back to Sarah, letting her know that they should expect to regain access to the server within the hour. He will continue to check for connectivity, and will notify her again when the issue has been resolved.

After the system server is back online, Mike verifies with Sarah that they can once again access the system at the practice's office. Over the next 24 hours, Mike continues to check that the system server and the office equipment still have connectivity, to make sure that the problem has really been resolved.

DISCOVERY ACTIVITY 5-7

Troubleshooting IT Issues in the Medical Environment

Scenario:

Use the knowledge of troubleshooting medical IT issues that you gained in this topic to answer the following questions.

---

1. **Which of the following are common causes of issues in many medical software systems? (Select all that apply.)**

   a) The superbill or prescription is not properly formatted.

   b) Patient demographics are formatted incorrectly or missing necessary information.

   c) Necessary nodes needed for proper communication have been deactivated.

   d) The communication link between systems is not working or is disconnected.

---

2. **You receive a call from a physician's assistant (PA), Sherri, who is having problems with the e-prescription service. Today is her first day working for the practice, and she is having difficulty sending any prescriptions. After talking with Sherri for a minute, you know that her colleagues are not having the same issues. One colleague even checked her work for some of the possible formatting errors, and she couldn't find anything that might be causing the problem.**

   Based on this information, what is the most likely cause of the problem?

   a) The pharmacy Sherri selected to receive the prescription does not accept e-prescriptions.

   b) The e-prescription was not filled out completely or was formatted improperly.

   c) Sherri has not been assigned the necessary privileges in the system to be able to send e-prescriptions.

   d) Sherri was trying to send a prescription for a controlled substance.

---

3. **Though you were able to troubleshoot Sherri's problem, you do not have the authorization to provide the solution.**

   What should you do?

   a) Have another employee send the e-prescriptions for Sherri.

   b) Contact the manufacturer and make sure they are aware of the problem with the system.

   c) Contact the system administrator for the system, who can provide Sherry the privileges she needs.

   d) Have another employee send the e-prescription for Sherri while you contact the system administrator to provide Sherri with the necessary privileges.

---

4. **What should you do if the issue you have been called to troubleshoot is outside of the realm of your knowledge or skills?**

TOPIC D

Implementation of an EMR/EHR System

Up to this point, you have identified all the components that make up an EMR or EHR implementation including IT and the roles and responsibilities assigned to use the system. How do combine all of that into deploying an EMR system? In this topic, you will implement an EMR or EHR system.

The implementation of EMR systems is a tremendous opportunity for IT providers to penetrate the healthcare market. Your advanced knowledge of the implementation process and associated hurdles will give you a significant advantage over those who have net been exposed to an EMR or EHR implementation. This topic will be an excellent starting point if you are ever involved with an EMR or EHR system implementation

EMR/EHR Implementation Goals

General goals for any type of EMR or EHR implementation include:

- Improve overall patient care.
- Streamline process workflows for clinical and administrative tasks.
- Support medical professionals in day-to-day operations.
- Promote consistency of patient records.
- Improve prescription management processes.
- Enhance patient care by providing quick access to comprehensive health records.
- And, meet criteria for meaningful use and the associated funding incentives.

The EMR Project Lifecycle

There are a number of general phases in the EMR implementation project lifecycle.

Phase	Description
Planning	In this phase there are a number of factors that must be considered: • Identify the project stakeholder. • Form a project team or committee. • Define the main goals and objectives for the project • Determine the scope of the EMR implementation. This may include an IT assessment to identify existing network infrastructure components and to identify all potential IT needs. • Identify specific practice needs and requirements for EMR systems. • Research potential EMR hosting options versus an in-house implementation. • Determine the cost for each component, each application, contract services, system downtime, etc. • Identify the necessary resources for completing the implementation. • Identify major workflows that are used traditionally, that will change once the system has been implemented. • Research grant and funding options and plan for the grant application process.
Selection	In this phase an EMR system is selected and purchased by the practice. Purchase agreements and service contracts are established. Other EHR system requirements are defined based on the hardware needs analysis done during the planning phase.
Implementation	In this phase, an EMR implementation plan, and/or checklist is created to communicate general implementation information such as: • Approved timelines for implementation tasks agreed upon by the client and vendor. • Targeted sites for hardware installation. • If necessary, security controls needed to secure EMR servers and systems. • Installation and configuration details for hardware and EHR system software. • Requirements for preparing the environment for implementation, such as installing HVAC in a designated server room. • Site identification for all EMR installations. • Implementation readiness guidelines for each site targeted in the plan. • Needs for training of key personnel.
Configuration	This phase includes specific configurations of the EMR system to align with workflows and processes for a specific medical office or facility. Configurations will be specific to each healthcare environment and be based on the services provided at each site.
Training	Create an EMR training plan for all affected clinicians and staff: • Identify workflow changes that will require re-training of existing staff. • Decide on training methods. • Assess staff to determine the level of training needed. • For large-scale implementations, create and distribute resources to support staff members and users of the system, such as an online wiki, reference cards, job aids, and an EMR help desk support system or team.

Phase	***Description***
Post implementation	A post implementation review is conducted to determine that the system has been implemented properly to meet the goals and objectives that were identified in the planning phase. Future updates and system changes may also be identified at this phase. A change control process should be put in place to manage system changes appropriately.

EMR Implementation Project Team Members

Because of the implementation of an EMR/EHR system requires time, patience, and commitment, the team must be chosen carefully. Members should be people who will support and embrace change, and can represent their job functions respectively. The team should include key roles that will can contribute to the system design, implementation, and training.

Project Management Principles

Solid project management principles help the EMR and EHR implementation staff manage the phases of an EMR rollout project such as initiating, planning, executing, monitoring, controlling, and closing. The project manager will:

- Define the needs and specifications for the project, and obtain a commitment to move forward from stakeholders.
- Plan and develop a strategy for how to accomplish the work in the project.
- Verify that tasks and processes are completed within the scope of the project.
- Verify that required progress was made in the project, or in the different project phases, and is moving toward completion.
- Report progress made to the appropriate individuals.
- Regularly document issues, progress, and tasks completed.
- Use good communication practices.
- Use appropriate project management software tools.

EMR Hosting Options

There are two main EMR or EHR hosting options available for system implementation.

Option	Description
Application service provider (ASP)	A system that is hosted remotely in the cloud. This option involves purchasing an EMR/EHR managed service from a vendor. The infrastructure used to provide the ASP service is already HIPAA compliant. Advantages include: • Technical issues are managed by the service provider. • It is cheaper to implement that the client-server environment, because the number of machines is minimal. • It provides easy remote server access and computing capabilities. Disadvantages include: • Over time the cost may increase and could eventually be just as expensive as the client-server option. • Customization options may be minimal. • Maybe processing speeds are slower because the Internet is used to access records. • Accountability issues with vendors can lead to data loss.
Client-server	In a client-server environment, the hardware and application is onsite within the medical facility. The server is usually managed by the practice IT department. Advantages include: • Quick application response times. • Internet access is available. • Data can be managed by medical personnel. Disadvantages include: • Initial implementation cost can be substantial. • A significant increase in hardware and implementation support. • In-house control of data can lead to issues with unauthorized access and possible theft of hardware.

EMR/EHR Clients

There are three general client types used to provide access to EMR or EHR systems:

- A browser-based client is used when the EMR or EHR system is ASP hosted.
- An application-based client is used when the EMR or EHR application is installed on workstations.
- A terminal, or remote-access client connects to either a server or the Internet to access EMR or EHR applications.

Structured Data

Definition:

Structured data is data that fits into a well-defined data model. Structured data is identified by a data model, and then classified into a type and stored accordingly. EHR or EMR system data is best stored and managed if it is structured. This enables a more standardized approach to managing medical records, and promotes consistency between multiple medical providers.

Example: HL7 Structured Data

HL7 is an example of structured data in an EMR or EHR system. HL7 uses messages, segments, data types, numeric fields, fixed lengths for codes, and so forth to structure data that can be communicated and understood amongst different systems. The structure is inherent within the system.

Environment Size Considerations

It is extremely important to take into consideration the size of your organization and what affect it will have on your IT support team when implementing an EMR or EHR system, and it is important to consider this at all phases of the process: as you determine which solution is the best for your specific organization, as you implement and roll out the solution, and how you will maintain and support the system once it is in place. Different solutions may be better for smaller organizations, like a private practice, while others are better suited for a large organization like a hospital. Beyond that, it is also important to determine, given the size of the environment and the scope of the solution, if there is enough staff, especially in IT, to support the implementation of the system.

Funding

EMR and EHR implementations are costly and should be planned carefully. Government has started offering incentives for physicians who implement an EMR by a certain date and can demonstrate "meaningful use" of an EMR system. Once practices have qualified for the government incentives, then they could potentially receive anywhere from $2,000 to $18,000 in Medicare and Medicaid reimbursements per eligible provider per year.

The Software Vendor Selection Process

When selecting a software vendor to provide your EMR and EHR services, there are many factors to consider.

Phase	Description
Needs	Basic needs for any medical environment must be met by the software application. This includes: • Billing. • Prescription management. • Scheduling functionality. • Lab ordering and management services. • Data collection requirements. • Data types supported. • Data conversion services. • Storage space limitations. Any software that is certified by the Certification Commission for Health Information Technology (CCHIT), will meet most of the basic needs of a EMR application. If the needs are more specific and do not fall into the basic needs category, then further needs assessment planning must be done. Most practices will require a request for proposal (RFP) to carefully document and identify all software requirements for their practice.
Requirements	Provide all potential vendors with your requirements to verify that the software capabilities meet your needs. This may include: • Vendor installation requirements and limitations. • Product limitations and benefits. • Medical environment infrastructure requirements. • Practice needs vs. wants.
Hosting	You must decide which hosting option suits your needs and meets the identified requirements. Hosting options include either a cloud-based ASP implementation, or a client-server in-house implementation.
Vendor evaluation	In most cases, a consultant will be helping you with the process of evaluating and identifying the right software vendor to meet your specific needs. This phase includes: • Evaluation of the all options provided by the software vendor. • Demonstrations of software from all potential vendors. • Usability testing with medical infrastructure. • Reference checking and visits to sites where the vendor's product is already installed.
Negotiation	The negotiation process can be tedious and long. This phase involves: • Creating a payment schedule. • Establishing customer support requirements. • Researching training options for users. • Creating the service-level agreement (SLA). • Agreement on the implementation timeline and phases.

Server Storage Space and Limitations

When installing an EMR/EHR environment, you must consider the specific needs of a medical facility's application and storage needs. There are a number of factors that should be negotiated between the vendor and the medical facility:

- Type of data stored on servers.
- The amount of legacy data being transferred into the EMR/EHR system.

There are also a number of factors to ensure that the system requirements will meet the future needs of the practice:

- The number of physicians in the organization.
- The number of locations supported by the EMR/EHR environment.
- The number of patients managed by the practice.

CCHIT

The *Certification Commission for Health Information Technology (CCHIT)* is a not-for-profit organization that promotes the adoption of healthcare IT systems, as well as certifies health record technology. For more information visit **www.cchit.org/**

RFPs

A *request for proposal (RFP)* is an invitation for vendors to submit a plan and bid for the delivery of a product or service. Invitations to respond to an RFP are generally offered to as many vendors as is possible so as to best determine the most cost-effective solution. RFPs typically contain:

- Product versus system requirements.
- Vendor references.
- The vendor's financial stability.
- Availability of documentation.
- Vendor support services.
- Availability of source code.
- Number of years' experience offering the service or product.
- Number of current clients using the service/product.
- Specifications for user acceptance testing.

EMR/EHR Hardware Considerations

The hardware chosen to provide the EMR or EHR software is one of the most important decisions made in the implementation process. There are a number of requirements and factors that should be considered:

- Determine the required and recommended hardware specifications for both the EMR and EHR servers hosting the application and the client computers before purchasing any hardware.
- Verify that the vendor hardware requirements are met. This may include a hardware validation from the vendor.
- Secure all hardware components and systems properly per HIPAA regulations.
- Replace slow or outdated devices that may not be able to handle running the EMR or EHR application.

- Wireless offers more portability with devices, but can be more expensive to maintain due to limited battery life and potential for damage due to the handling of devices.
- Wired implementations end up being less expensive and are easier to maintain, due to easy system component replacement.
- Environment size, number of locations, and configuration may affect the choice of hardware components.
- Backup guidelines and procedures will need to be determined and established.
- System downtime procedures, both scheduled and unscheduled, will need to be determined and established.

Secondary Software Dependencies

EMR and EHR systems may store many different types of files such as scanned documents, graphical data, and maybe even some voice data. Secondary software programs may be needed to view these files. When applications are installed on user workstations for viewing and possibly amending any EMR related files, then the installations must meet the EMR and EHR vendor specifications. Before installing any secondary applications, be sure to verify all vendor specifications and recommendations.

Additionally, you must understand how data is used within secondary software programs, such as where data will be accessed from, how it will be accessed and what software is needed. For example, ultrasound machines usually have a software interface for the technician to capture, diagnose, and record information. This program is usually device dependent, so another program may be needed for a specialist to view and submit diagnosis information.

Interoperability with Legacy Systems

Legacy systems and hardware must be evaluated before the EMR implementation. Careful planning and testing must be done at the beginning to work through all issues before the installation occurs, to limit post-installation downtime. Some legacy systems and resources will remain in place even after the EMR or EHR system is in place, and the transition from traditional medical record processes to an EMR or EHR system may result in many different interoperability issues. For example, many offices use vendor-specific applications, such as billing and scheduling, that may not be compatible with a newer system. The hardware used within a medical facility should be of commercial quality and able to run EMR applications and services, and may require newer hardware to be purchased to meet these requirements. In the end, it may be more cost-effective for some organizations to purchase newer hardware with a current operating system versus spending money to upgrade older systems.

Implementation Strategies

An EMR or EHR implementation is a huge undertaking and can take several months to a year or more. The entire project should be tracked so any parallel activities, processes, requirements, personnel, milestones, and target dates are tracked and documented all in one place and can be systematically reviewed and adjusted as the project moves forward. Some implementations may be done in stages or phases, depending on the size of the medical facility or facilities.

The Implementation Process

Once you have selected your EMR or EHR vendor, the implementation process can be started. The process consists of four general phases.

Phase	Description
Prepare and install environment	In this phase the location for hardware should be assessed and prepped for delivery. Placement of servers, workstations, network devices and other components should be carefully planned and configured properly. Installation steps include: • Secure servers. • Assign strong passwords to workstations. • Install and configure network security devices.
Data conversion	This phase of the EMR implementation involves converting demographic data and clinical data, if available, safely to the EMR system. There are a number of steps in data conversion: • The data must be extracted from the legacy system. • Data must be analyzed to verify that it can be imported into the new system. • Data is filtered to identify errors or coding issues. • Data is imported into the EMR by the EMR vendor.
Workflows	Standardize workflows and processes within the system. Existing processes and workflows should be updated and altered to align directly with the EMR system.
Training	Training of key personnel is a crucial phase of the EMR implementation. In this phase, there are a number of methods used to deliver the training to new users: • Train the trainer. In this scenario, the vendor trains a select few and then those individuals are responsible for training the rest of the users. This method can be effective in large practices, where it can get expensive to send everyone to a training class or facility. • Web-based training may be offered by some EMR vendors, and can be a cost effective way to train a large number of users quickly. • Classroom-based training may be required when a more hands on instructor led approach is needed. This option can be effective when training specific job functions. • Onsite training may be held when this is more convenient for clinicians and staff.

Timing and Scheduling of Rollout Events

Every EMR implementation must have a plan to roll out the EMR within the targeted environment. Many factors come into play when determining how the EMR system will be distributed among various healthcare environments. The rollout schedule must be based on how the medical staff will use the EMR, and how they will be using the system while supporting patients. Some environments may require a staggered rollout schedule, with the primary office being first. This provides the EMR support staff with the opportunity to fix issues and test the environment before implementing at the satellite medical facility locations.

Vacation and Patient Load Restrictions

The IT professional may be responsible for communicating parameters around the timing and rollout of the EMR/EHR system. During implementation there is a timeframe where all practice staff should be present in the office (e.g. no approved vacations) and it is strongly suggested that there be a reduction in patient load. Be prepared to have this discussion with medical staff when planning implementation of the system.

ACTIVITY 5-8

Implementing an EMR/EHR System

Scenario:

In this activity, you will identify implementation steps for EMR and EHR systems.

1. **Your medical practice is in the process of selecting a vendor for the EMR implementation planned for early next year. You have been asked to take part in the demonstrations given by the top three choices. What phase of the process does this occur in?**

2. **How does the size of a medical environment effect the EMR implementation process?**

3. **A small private practice is looking to move their traditional patient record system to an EMR. They do not want to purchase additional computer equipment other than the three workstations they use at the front desk. The office manager also does not want to have to hire an administrator to manage the system onsite. What implementation option would best suit the needs of the small office?**

   a) A client-server implementation

   b) An ASP implementation

4. **What are the three general types of EMR/EHR clients?**

5. **What phase of the EMR project lifecycle is described?**

___	Planning	a. Environment readiness is determined.
___	Selection	b. The scope of the EMR installation is determined.
___	Implementation	c. Purchase agreements are created.
___	Configuration	d. Goals and objectives are verified against the EMR plan.
___	Post implementation	e. EMR resources are distributed to users of the system.
___	Training	f. Processes are aligned with the EMR system.

TOPIC E

Change Control

In the last topic, you worked through the stages of an EMR or EHR system implementation. After implementation, an important ongoing task is managing change within the system. In this topic, you will identify components of change control and how to manage this process within a healthcare environment.

Uncontrolled change can cause many problems within an IT infrastructure, both immediate and long-term. By implementing and following appropriate change control processes and policies, IT departments will save time and money when issues arise and changes to existing systems must be made.

Why Control Change?

Within the IT world, change is inevitable; it happens every day. Technology will continue to evolve as computing becomes more portable and efficient. Because of this, the healthcare environment must adapt to technological changes that affect workflows. Change must be controlled and managed by a governance board, whose responsibilities include governing and organizing the manner in which changes will be requested, approved or rejected, implemented, reviewed, controlled, and coordinated. The goal is to make sure that changes to any system or environment are managed with the least amount of disruption to cost, time, and quality.

The Governance Board

The governance board is made up of individuals from different departments who play a crucial role in deciding what changes will take place and how they will be implemented.

Change Control Environments

There are generally four different environments in which change control is applied.

- Development environments, to limit changes based on necessity.
- Quality assurance and testing environments, to manage critical changes.
- User testing environments, to manage changes that arise from users.
- And, production/live environments, to manage improvement changes to systems.

Change Control Considerations

There are specific things to consider when implementing change within the healthcare IT environment:

- Plan for the potential reaction to change.
- Establish appropriate scheduling of change procedures and processes.
- Establish a system patching and updates installation schedule.
- Establish a systematic method to implement customization within a system.
- Expect that needs must be met by all departments.
- Recognize that in some cases, when change occurs there is a loss.
- Manage expectations from all users and departments.
- And, manage and plan for negative effects resulting from changes made.

ACTIVITY 5-9

Examining Change Control

Scenario:

In this activity, you will examine the different elements of change control.

---

1. **True or False? When considering how a system-wide EMR/EHR update will affect users, you should plan for all types of responses, including any negative reactions to the updates.**

   __ True

   __ False

---

2. **What are the four environments where change must be controlled?**

---

3. **Why is controlling change of great importance in the healthcare environment?**

Lesson 5 Follow-up

As an IT professional working in the healthcare industry, many of the day-to-day activities you will be performing require knowledge of industry-specific terms, hardware, software, and systems. In this lesson, you identified tools and techniques for solving IT problems in the workplace, and how those tools and techniques can be used to solve IT issues specific to the healthcare industry.

1. **How is troubleshooting IT issues for the medical environment different from other IT troubleshooting jobs you may have experience with?**

2. **As an IT professional in the healthcare industry, you may not always have the knowledge or skills to troubleshoot every problem brought to you. How can you handle this possible dilemma?**

6 Security

Lesson Time: 2 hour(s), 30 minutes

Lesson Objectives:

In this lesson, you will integrate security best practices into your daily healthcare IT workflow.

You will:

- Apply physical and logical security measures to mitigate against common threats.
- Implement best practice security techniques for wireless networks, passwords, and PHI.
- Manage remote access.
- Implement best practices for wireless security.
- Implement backup and disaster recovery plans for your organization.

Introduction

In the previous lessons, you've learned about healthcare fundamentals, IT in the medical workplace, and IT technology basics in the medical workplace. A very important requirement to all of that is how to keep your data and devices secure. This lesson will identify components of security in the IT medical workplace.

Increased use of IT in the medical environment carries a commensurate increased risk of security and privacy violations. Staff that may be used to old methods could unintentionally expose patient data, or unscrupulous individuals could attempt to gain access to data. With a strong understanding of the potential risks, and how to mitigate against them, you can demonstrate the value of IT security to uninformed individuals and organizations.

TOPIC A

Manage Physical and Logical Security

There are many risks that can threaten your organization, starting with the physical and logical components of your network and your organization's overall physical locations. In this topic, you will identify the types of risks that are directed against the physical and logical resources in your organization and learn how to manage their security.

The basis of all IT security is controlling access to both physical assets and information. This topic will provide you with an understanding of theses vital aspects so that you may better secure assets you are responsible for.

Physical vs. Logical Security

Definition:

Physical security refers to the implementation and practice of various control mechanisms that are intended to restrict physical access to facilities. In addition, physical security involves increasing or assuring the reliability of certain critical infrastructure elements such as electrical power, data networks, and fire suppression systems. Physical security may be challenged by a wide variety of events or situations, including:

- Facilities intrusions.
- Electrical grid failures.
- Fire.
- Personnel illnesses.
- Or, data network interruptions.

Logical security refers to software protection for systems in an organization. Standards are in place to ensure that only those with authorization have the ability to access information on a network or workstation. It involves particular authentication elements such as user IDs, tokens, and passwords.

Example: Security in a Hospital Server Room

Mariah is a network administrator for a large hospital. She needs to check the performance of one of their servers. The servers are in a protected area of the hospital, and only authorized users can gain access. Mariah has the code to unlock the door, allowing her physical access to the server room. Once she is in the room, she will then need provide her logical security credentials to authenticate herself on the server using her unique user name and password.

The CIA Triad

Information security seeks to address three specific principles: confidentiality, integrity, and availability. This is called the *CIA triad*. The three principles work together to support the goals of HIPAA. If one of the principles is compromised, the security of the organization is threatened.

Principle	Description
Confidentiality	This is the fundamental principle of keeping information and communications private and protecting them from unauthorized access. Confidential information includes trade secrets, personnel records, health records, tax records, and military secrets.
Integrity	This is the property of keeping organization information accurate, free of errors, and without unauthorized modifications. For example, in the 1980s movie *War Games,* actor Matthew Broderick was seen modifying his grades early in the movie. This means that the integrity of his grade information was compromised by unauthorized modification.
Availability	This is the fundamental principle of ensuring that systems operate continuously and that authorized persons can access the data that they need. Information available on a computer system is useless unless the users can get to it. Consider what would happen if the Federal Aviation Administration's air traffic control system failed. Radar images would be captured but not distributed to those who need the information.

Common Security Risks

There are many types of security risks that you should be aware of.

Risk	Details
Social engineering	A *social engineering attack* is a type of attack that uses deception and trickery to convince unsuspecting users to provide sensitive data or to violate security guidelines. Social engineering is often a precursor to another type of attack. Because these attacks depend on human factors rather than on technology, their symptoms can be vague and hard to identify. Social engineering attacks can come in a variety of methods: in person, through email, or over the phone.
Physical security	Physical security threats and vulnerabilities can come from many different areas. They can be internal, external, natural, or man made.
Hardware	A *hardware attack* is an attack that targets a computer's physical components and peripherals, including its hard disk, motherboard, keyboard, network cabling, or smart card reader. One goal of a hardware attack is the destruction of the hardware itself or acquisition of sensitive information through theft or other means. A second goal of a hardware attack is to make important data or devices unavailable through theft or vandalism. This second goal is meant to disrupt a company's business or cause embarrassment due to data loss.
Environmental	Environmental threats pose system security risks and can be addressed with specific mitigation These threats include fire, hurricanes and tornadoes, floods, extreme temperatures, and extreme humidity.

Risk	Details
Software	Attacks against software resources including operating systems, applications, protocols, and files. The goal of a software attack is to disrupt or disable the software running on the target system, or to somehow exploit the target system to gain access to the target system, to other systems, or to a network. Many software attacks are designed to surreptitiously gain control of a computer so that the attacker can use that computer in the future, often for profit or further malicious activity.
Network	Attacks that are targeted at the physical or wireless networks within an organization. This can also include social network attacks that are targeted towards social networking sites such as Facebook, Twitter, and MySpace. The goal of a network attack is to retrieve sensitive data, or attempt access to systems and services within the network.
Phishing	This is a common type of email-based social engineering attack. In a phishing attack, the attacker sends an email that seems to come from a respected bank or other financial institution. The email claims that the recipient needs to provide an account number, Social Security number, or other private information to the sender in order to "verify an account." Ironically, the phishing attack often claims that the "account verification" is necessary for security reasons. Individuals should never provide personal financial information to someone who requests it, whether through email or over the phone. Legitimate financial institutions never solicit this information from their clients. A similar form of phishing called *pharming* can be done by redirecting a request for a website, typically an e-commerce site, to a similar-looking, but fake, website.

Physical Access Controls

Definition:

Physical security controls are security measures that restrict, detect, and monitor access to specific physical areas or assets. They can control access to a building, to equipment, or to specific areas, such as server rooms, finance or legal areas, data centers, network cable runs, or any other area that has hardware or information that is considered to have important value and sensitivity. Determining where to use physical access controls requires a risk/benefit analysis and must include the consideration of any regulations or other compliance requirements for the specific types of data that are being safeguarded.

Example: Controlling Facility Access

The main entrance in a hospital has a visitor center with a receptionist to log and monitor visitors as they come and go. There is also a security guard on duty in the main lobby.

Physical Security Threats and Vulnerabilities

Physical security threats and vulnerabilities can come from many different areas.

Physical Security Threat and Vulnerability	Description
Internal	It is important to always consider what is happening inside a medical facility, especially when physical security is concerned. For example, disgruntled individuals may be a source of physical sabotage of important security-related resources.
External	It is impossible for any facility to fully control external security threats. For example, an external power failure is usually beyond a IT specialist's control because most medical facilities and practices use a local power company as their source of electrical power. However, risks posed by external power failures may be mitigated by implementing devices such as an *Uninterruptible Power Supply (UPS)* or a generator.
Natural	Although natural threats are easy to overlook, they can pose a significant threat to the physical security of a medical facility. Buildings, rooms, or areas within the facility that contain important computing assets should be protected against likely weather-related problems including tornados, hurricanes, snow storms, and floods.
Man-made	Whether intentional or accidental, people can cause a number of physical threats. For example, a backhoe operator may accidentally dig up fiber optic cables and disable external network access. On the other hand, a disgruntled individual may choose to exact revenge by deliberately cutting fiber optic cables. Man-made threats can be internal or external.

Types of Physical Access Controls

There are a number of physical access controls available to ensure the protection of an organization's physical environment.

<table>
<tr><th>Physical Security Control</th><th>Description</th></tr>
<tr><td>Locks</td><td>There are a number of different locks that can be used to restrict unauthorized access to information resources:
● Bolting door locks are a traditional lock-and-key method that requires a non-duplicate policy for keys to access a door.
● Combination door locks, or cipher locks, use a keypad or dial system with a code or numeric combination to access a door.
● Electronic door locks use an access ID card with an electronic chip or token that is read by the electronic sensor attached to a door.
● Biometric door locks are commonly used in highly secure environments. This method uses an individual's unique body features to scan and identify the access permissions for a particular door.
● Hardware locks can be attached to a laptop, hard drive, or file cabinet to secure it from being opened or turned on.</td></tr>
<tr><td>Logging and visitor access</td><td>Logging should be used at all entrances that are open to the general public. This method requires all visitors to sign in and out when entering and leaving the building. Logging requirements will vary depending on the organization, but should include the following:
● Name and company being represented.
● Date, time of entry, and time of departure.
● Reason for visiting.
● Contact within the organization.
When possible, one single entry point should be used for all incoming visitors. This decreases the risk of unauthorized individuals gaining access to the building.</td></tr>
<tr><td>Identification systems</td><td>Badges, such as swipe cards or security cards, provide identity information about the bearer, which is then checked against an appropriate access list for that location. The cards can be used along with a proximity reader to verify identification and grant access. A badge can also include a picture or some other identification code for a second authentication factor. Badges should be required for all employees and should be visible at all times.</td></tr>
<tr><td>Surveillance</td><td>Video or still-image surveillance can be put in place to deter or help in the prosecution of unwanted access. These systems can be placed inside and outside the building. All video recording should be saved and stored in a secure environment.</td></tr>
<tr><td>Security guards</td><td>Human security guards, armed or unarmed, can be placed in front of and around a location to protect it. They can monitor critical checkpoints and verify identification, allow or disallow access, and log physical entry occurrences. They also provide a visual deterrent and can apply their own knowledge and intuition to potential security breaches.</td></tr>
<tr><td>Bonded personnel</td><td>Contracted services personnel, such as cleaning services, should be bonded to protect an organization from financial exposures.</td></tr>
</table>

Physical Security Control	Description
Mantrap doors	A mantrap door system, also referred to as a deadman door, is a system with a door at each end of a secure chamber. An individual enters a secure area through an outer door. The outer door must be closed before an inner door can open. An individual's identity is sometimes verified before they enter the secure area through the first door, and other times while they are confined to the secure area between the two doors. This system also requires that one person enter at a time. This system typically requires two separate authentication processes, with the second one being done while the authenticated person is isolated inside a reinforced enclosure.
Physical barriers	The location of highly secure resources, such as a server room, should not have windows or be visible from the outside of a building. This creates a more secure barrier from the outside. Common medical areas to physically secure include: • Offices usually contain Personal Health Information (PHI) materials and other computer equipment that can be used to access the Electronic Medical Record (EMR) or Electronic Health Record (EHR) system. • Servers must be kept out of public areas in a medical environment and should be kept in a secured room. • Data closets should be kept secured with a lock, or other physical security method to prevent unauthorized access to PHI data and materials. • *Intermediate Distribution Frame (IDF)* systems store networking hardware and provide networking services to local area networks within a medical environment. These systems are usually located in designated IDF rooms, or closets. • A *Main Distribution Frame (MDF)* is a hardware rack that holds networking equipment to provide connections from public lines coming into the physical building, generally from the Internet Service Provider (ISP), to all the IDFs located throughout the medical facility. • Backup storage areas or systems. These locations should be secured using door locks or other physical security controls.
Alarms	Alarms activated by an unauthorized access attempt require a quick response. Locally stationed security guards or police may respond to alarms. These responding individuals may trigger access control devices in the facility to automatically lock.

Biometrics

Biometrics are authentication schemes based on individuals' physical characteristics. This can involve a fingerprint scanner, a retinal scanner, a hand geometry scanner, or voice-recognition and facial-recognition software. As biometric authentication becomes less expensive to implement, it is becoming more widely adopted.

Biometric Authentication Tokens

Biometric user data can be scanned and encoded once and then stored on a chip on some form of portable electronic security token such as a smart card or a digital *keyfob*. To authenticate, the user presents the token instead of submitting to another biometric scan. Because the token could be lost or stolen, it is best to combine this type of authentication with a password or PIN, or at least to include a user photograph on the card for visual confirmation of the user's identity.

Physical Security Considerations

Hardware placement and the hardware environment are important to consider when implementing your physical security systems.

Physical Security	*Considerations*
IT hardware location	The location of IT hardware must be considered when determining how to implement physical security controls. Servers, network hardware components, printers, scanners, and copiers all need to be secured physically from unauthorized access. Considerations include: • What floor is the hardware located on; is that floor secured from unauthorized access? • Are all the servers located in a single server room with a secured door? • Are the office scanner, copiers, and printers in a secured location that the general public cannot gain access to? • Are network hardware components, such as Wireless Access Points (WAPs), secured throughout the facility?
Environmental controls	There are certain environmental controls that can be implemented to help control a facility's physical environment: • An HVAC system controls the environment inside a building, such as humidity and temperature control. • Security lighting should be installed in all medical facilities to provide necessary lighting in the event of an emergency or disaster. • Hot and cold aisles may be used to control temperatures in data centers and server rooms. • EMI shielding is used to prevent electromagnetic transfers from cables and devices by creating a conductive material protective barrier. • Generators or UPSs should be installed to protect computer systems, as well as provide electricity to the medical facility during a power outage or disaster. • The main control panel for an organization's alarm system should be protected and secured from any type of exposure. The panel must be in a separate location and protected from unauthorized access, and be accessible by the fire department, encased in a waterproof and climate-controlled box, powered by a dedicated circuit, and programmed to function by zone within an organization. • Various fire detection systems are used to identify the threat of a fire • *Fire suppression* systems extinguish fires using special gases in areas with a large number of computers or servers.

Physical Security	*Considerations*
Personnel	The general safety and concern for personnel working within a medical facility must be considered when implementing physical security controls within the environment. In the event of an environmental disaster, security precautions must be documented and distributed to all personnel working within the medical facility, so safety procedures are followed by all staff.

Fire Suppression Systems

Fires in computer facilities are especially dangerous. The damage done to computing systems is extremely expensive, and the chemicals used in the machines may emit toxic substances during fires. In some cases, small fires may be extinguished using hand-held fire extinguishers. These systems must be placed in the appropriate locations within a facility and should be inspected regularly. When it is not practical to fight these fires with small extinguishers or to douse fires with water, then special gases should be used to extinguish fires in areas with a large number of computers or servers.

Frequently, local jurisdictions mandate water-based fire extinguishing systems, even though gaseous systems often provide more appropriate protection for computer equipment. To satisfy each requirement, organizations are outfitted with both. Here is what occurs: if the gas system does not suppress the fire, the sprinkler system will then activate, but is otherwise maintained as the official back-up extinguisher. The best practice is to contact your local fire authorities when designing a fire suppression system.

Logical Access Controls

Definition:

Logical access controls are protection mechanisms used to identify, authenticate, and authorize access to computers and their corresponding systems. Their elements administer access control for computer systems, programs, processes, and information. They can vary from being embedded directly in an operating system, to specific applications that are designed to manage access. Logical access controls can also be policies and procedures to manage the protection mechanisms in place.

Example:

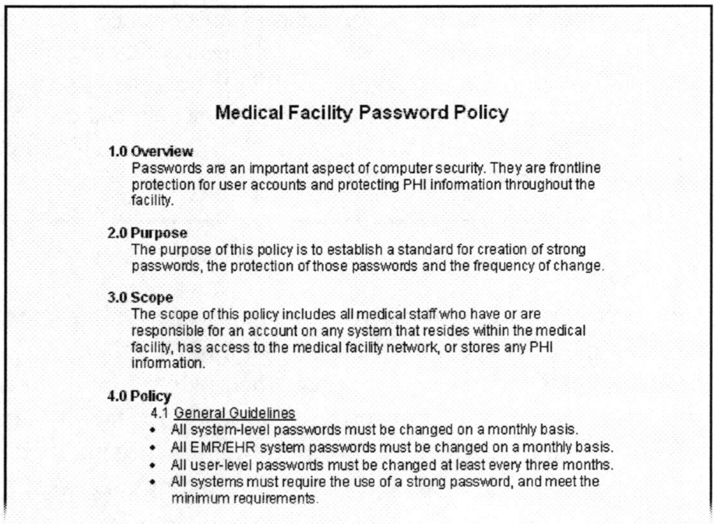

Medical Facility Password Policy

1.0 Overview
Passwords are an important aspect of computer security. They are frontline protection for user accounts and protecting PHI information throughout the facility.

2.0 Purpose
The purpose of this policy is to establish a standard for creation of strong passwords, the protection of those passwords and the frequency of change.

3.0 Scope
The scope of this policy includes all medical staff who have or are responsible for an account on any system that resides within the medical facility, has access to the medical facility network, or stores any PHI information.

4.0 Policy
4.1 General Guidelines
- All system-level passwords must be changed on a monthly basis.
- All EMR/EHR system passwords must be changed on a monthly basis.
- All user-level passwords must be changed at least every three months.
- All systems must require the use of a strong password, and meet the minimum requirements.

Figure 6-1: *A password policy is a logical access control.*

Security Users and Groups

Definition:

Rights and permissions can be assigned to individual user accounts. However, this is an inefficient security practice, because so many permission assignments must be duplicated for users with similar roles and because individual users' roles and needs can change frequently. It is more efficient to create groups of users with common needs, and assign the rights and permissions to the user groups. As individual users' needs change, the users can be placed in groups with the appropriate security configuration.

Example:

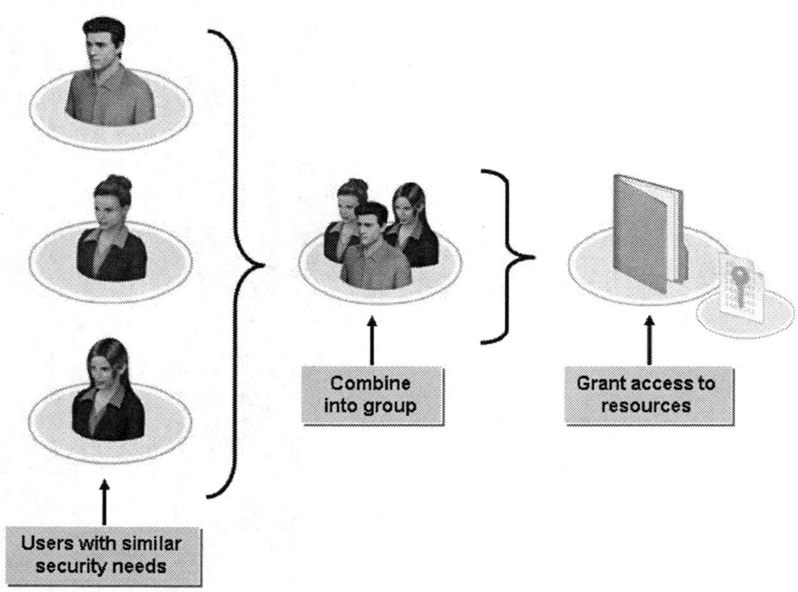

Figure 6-2: *Security users and groups.*

Permissions

A *permission* is a security setting that determines the level of access a user or group account has to a particular resource. In many IT systems, there are four general levels of permissions that can be assigned to different user roles based on their access needs.

- Read, to view information only.
- Write, to create information.
- Modify, to change contents and attributes of information.
- And, full access, to create, change, and delete items.

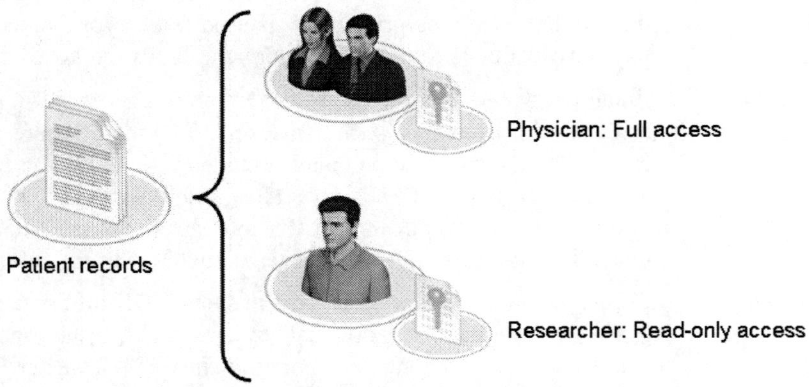

Figure 6-3: *Permission levels.*

Most EMR and EHR systems maintain role-based profiles that determine the overall user functionality within the system. For example, a medical doctor role will be able to place an order, while a technician role cannot.

Encryption

Encryption is a process in which information is transcribed into an unreadable form by anyone who does not have the encryption code. There are several types of encryption that can be utilized to protect information.

Encryption Type	***Details***
Manual encryption	Computer programs that will encrypt pieces of information. This is done manually by the user by choosing the files that need to be encrypted and then choosing the encryption type from the designated security system. This is beneficial for personal computing because users can encrypt personal files in the best suitable way.
Transparent encryption	A type of computer software encryption that can be downloaded to a computer to automatically encrypt everything. It is the most secure type of encryption because it won't leave out anything that may have been forgotten during a manual encryption.

Encryption Type	Details
Symmetric encryption	A two-way encryption scheme in which encryption and decryption are both performed by the same key. The key can be configured in software or coded in hardware. The key must be securely transmitted between the two parties prior to encrypted communications. Symmetric encryption is relatively fast, but is vulnerable if the key is lost or compromised. Some of the common names for symmetric encryption are secret-key, shared-key, and private-key encryption.
Asymmetric encryption	This is a secure and easy way to encrypt information that you will be receiving. There are two encryption keys used: a public one and a private one. The public key is given to whomever you want or you can post it for the public to see. The private key is used to decrypt the code, and is generally only available to the one person who holds the key.
Email encryption	Email encryption commonly uses asymmetrical encryption methods. Emails can't be read by others, such as hackers. Two methods are used to encrypt email. The first is when an email provider is the only one to decide who gets the private key. This is generally given only to the email address user. The second method allows the user to control who gets the encryption key, thus allowing others to read encrypted emails with the private key.
Communication encryption	Communication encryption is used to secure PHI information that may be shared with authorized individuals by email, fax, instant message chat applications, smartphone, collaboration sites, File Transfer Protocol (FTP) sites, over the phone, or by using Voice over IP (VoIP) software. All these communication methods should have encryption configured for data that is transmitted, shared, and accessed.
Storage encryption	Storage encryption is used to encrypt and decrypt data on storage devices. In many cases, there will be PHI data stored on a number of different devices within a medical environment. To ensure that the PHI data is secure, encryption is used. Storage devices used within the medical environment that should utilize encryption include: • Flash drives • Desktop computers • Laptops • Secure Digital (SD) cards • External drives • Servers • Network-Attached Storage (NAS) • Storage Area Networks (SANs)

Encryption Algorithms

Some algorithms are used for symmetric encryption.

Symmetric Algorithm	Description
Data Encryption Standard (DES)	A block-cipher symmetric encryption algorithm that encrypts data in 64-bit blocks using a 56-bit key with 8 bits used for parity. The short key length makes DES a relatively weak algorithm.

Symmetric Algorithm	Description
Triple DES (3DES)	A symmetric encryption algorithm that encrypts data by processing each block of data three times using a different key each time. It first encrypts plaintext into ciphertext using one key, it then encrypts that ciphertext with another key, and it last encrypts the second ciphertext with yet another key.
Advanced Encryption Standard (AES) algorithm	A symmetric 128-, 192-, or 256-bit block cipher developed by Belgian cryptographers Joan Daemen and Vincent Rijmen and adopted by the U.S. government as its encryption standard to replace DES. The AES algorithm is called Rijndael (pronounced "Rhine-dale") after its creators. Rijndael was one of five algorithms considered for adoption in the AES contest conducted by the National Institute of Standards and Technology (NIST) of the United States.

Encryption Protocols and Utilities

There are a number of encryption protocols and utilities used to secure data.

Protocol	Description
SSL	*Secure Sockets Layer (SSL)* is a security protocol that combines digital certificates for authentication with public key data encryption. SSL is a server-driven process; any web client that supports SSL, including all current web browsers, can connect securely to an SSL-enabled server.
HTTPS	*Hypertext Transfer Protocol Secure (HTTPS)* is a secure version of HTTP that supports web commerce by providing a secure connection between a web browser and a server. HTTPS uses SSL to encrypt data. Virtually all web browsers and servers today support HTTPS. An SSL-enabled web address begins with the protocol identifier *https://*
SSH	*Secure Shell (SSH)* is a protocol used for secure remote login and secure transfer of data. SSH consists of a server and a client. Most SSH clients also implement login terminal-emulation software to open secure terminal sessions on remote servers. To ensure security, the entire SSH session, including authentication, is encrypted using a variety of encryption methods. SSH is the preferred protocol to File Transfer Protocol (FTP) and is used primarily on Linux and Unix systems to access shell accounts. Microsoft® Windows® does not offer native support for SSH, but it can be implemented by using a third-party tool.
PGP	*Pretty Good Privacy (PGP)* is a publicly available email security and authentication utility that uses a variation of public key cryptography to encrypt emails: the sender encrypts the contents of the email message and then encrypts the key that was used to encrypt the contents. The encrypted key is sent with the email, and the receiver decrypts the key and then uses the key to decrypt the contents. PGP also uses public key cryptography to digitally sign emails to authenticate the sender and the contents.

Uses for Encryption

Encryption is used to promote many security goals and techniques. Encryption enables confidentiality by protecting data from unauthorized access. It supports integrity because it is difficult to decipher encrypted data without the secret decrypting cipher. It supports non-repudiation, because only parties that know about the confidential encryption scheme can encrypt or decrypt data. In addition, some form of encryption is employed in most authentication mechanisms to protect passwords. Encryption is used in many access control mechanisms as well. It is commonly used within EMR and EHR systems to secure communications between server storage systems to workstations, to email, and to external storage devices.

ACTIVITY 6-1

Using File Encryption

This is a simulated activity that is available on the CD that shipped with this course. You can run this simulation on any Windows computer. The activity simulation can be launched either directly from the CD by clicking the **Interactives** link and navigating to the appropriate one, or from the installed data file location by opening the C:\HCIT\Simulations\Lesson 6\Using File Encryption folder and double-clicking the executable (.exe) file.

Scenario:

You are the support person in a small, family-owned business that uses a workgroup-based Windows 7 Ultimate network. One of your sales representatives is gathering confidential information about a prospective client, and wants to protect the information in the event that his laptop is ever lost or stolen when he is on the road.

1. Use file encryption.
   a. Browse to the C:\HCIT\Simulations\Lesson 6\Using File Encryption folder.
   b. Double-click the Using File Encryption executable file.
   c. In the **Open File - Security Warning** message box, click **Run.**
   d. Follow the on-screen steps for the simulation.
   e. Close the C:\HCIT\Simulations\Lesson 6\Using File Encryption folder.

Removable Media Considerations

Removable media can be very useful, but due to their small size, can be easily lost, thus causing the potential for a serious security threat to your organization. To minimize the risk of exposing PHI on these devices you should follow several steps.

Steps to Follow	***Details***
Security policy	Initiate a security policy for your employees to set expectations and management of such devices. Make sure your employees read and sign the policy.
Education	By educating your employees about the importance of security and data protection, you are informing them about the implications that exist. Don't just impose controls without explaining them otherwise users may ignore them.

Steps to Follow	***Details***
Encryption	There are solutions available to protect data on removable media device types. These encryption solutions can be managed by the IT department. They automatically encrypt data loaded onto devices and access is granted only to users who have the password. Products are fast and transparent, thus not disrupting real-time work.
Control	Implement control solutions for removable devices that will allow you control over what devices can or cannot be connected and what executable files can and cannot be run.
Audit and measure	By running regular audits, you can find out who is using removable media and if they are following policies and procedures set in place.

Types of Malicious Software

There are several major types of malicious software.

Malicious Software Type	***Description***
Viruses	A *virus* is a piece of code that spreads from one computer to another by attaching itself to other files. The code in a virus corrupts and erases files on a user's computer, or performs other destructive or annoying tasks, when the file to which it was attached is opened or executed. Viruses and other types of malicious code are frequently introduced via email attachments. The term "virus" is often used as an umbrella term to refer to many types of malicious software.
Worms	A *worm* is a piece of code that spreads from one computer to another on its own, not by attaching itself to another file. Like a virus, a worm can corrupt or erase files on your hard drive or perform other destructive or annoying operations.
Trojans	A *Trojan*, or *Trojan horse*, is malicious code that masquerades as a harmless file. When a user executes the Trojan, thinking it is a legitimate application, it can perform damaging or annoying operations. Or, it can continue to masquerade as a legitimate program, while in the background it captures input from the user and transmits the data to an attacker.
Logic bombs	A *logic bomb* is a piece of code that sits dormant on a user's computer until it is triggered by a specific event, such as a specific date. Once the code is triggered, the logic bomb "detonates," erasing and corrupting data on the user's computer or performing other destructive or annoying operations.

Malicious Software Type	Description
Malware	There are generally three types of malware: • *Spyware* is unwanted software that runs in the background to monitor system activities and send collected personal user data to a third party. • *Adware* is unwanted software loaded onto a system for the purposes of presenting commercial advertisements to the user. The adware can run in the background and collect data about the user in order to present customized advertisements. The adware can also function as spyware. The user is often unaware that the adware has penetrated the system. The adware itself can create annoyances or adverse system conditions, or the adware can be a vector for introducing other types of malicious software. • *Grayware* is a general classification for any unwanted software that produces harmful or annoying effects. A joke program that makes the computer screen image vibrate or a drive door open or shut would be a form of grayware.
Spam	In the electronic world, *spam* is generally taken to mean unsolicited commercial email. Spamming creates nuisance conditions by filling user mailboxes with unwanted messages, and impedes email system performance by filling up email servers' storage areas and generating excessive network traffic. Although not technically software, spam travels via email software, which is why it is often considered to be a type of malicious software.
Hoaxes	A *hoax* is any message containing incorrect or misleading information that is disseminated to multiple users through unofficial channels. Hoaxes do not have to be electronic, although electronic distribution systems facilitate their propagation. Although not technically software, some hoaxes travel via email software, which is why they are often considered to be a type of malicious software. Hoaxes can be relatively benign, such as an email letter soliciting "get well" cards for a fictitious ill child. In this case, the main threat is from users who widely disseminate the hoax email, clogging communications systems and annoying other recipients. However, hoaxes often improperly alert users to the existence of unsubstantiated virus threats. Rather than validating the information, users often react by following instructions in the hoax that might cause system damage or introduce further malicious software.

Types of Network Attacks

There are a number of network-based attacks that can cause damage to your network.

Attack	Description
Port scanning	A type of network attack where a potential attacker scans the computers and devices that are connected to the Internet or other networks to see which TCP and UDP ports are listening and which services on the system are active. Port scans can be easily automated, so almost any system on the Internet will be scanned almost constantly. Some monitoring software can detect port scans, or they might happen without your knowledge.

Attack	Description
Eavesdropping	Also, referred to as *sniffing*, uses special monitoring software to gain access to private network communications, either to steal the content of the communication itself or to obtain user names and passwords for future software attacks. Attackers can eavesdrop on both wired and wireless network communications. On a wired network, the attacker must have physical access to the network or tap in to the network cable. On a wireless network, an attacker needs a device capable of receiving signals from the wireless network. Eavesdropping is very hard to detect, unless you spot an unknown computer leasing an IP address from a DHCP server.
Replay	A network attack where an attacker captures network traffic and stores it for retransmitting at a later time to gain unauthorized access to a specific host or a network. This attack is particularly successful when an attacker captures packets that contain user names, passwords, or other authentication data. In most cases, replay attacks are never discovered.
Man-in-the-middle	A form of eavesdropping where the attacker makes an independent connection between two victims (two clients or a client and a server) and relays information between the two victims as if they are directly talking to each other over a closed connection, when in reality the attacker is controlling the information that travels between the two victims. During the process, the attacker can view or steal information to use it fraudulently.
Denial of service (DoS)	A type of network attack in which an attacker attempts to disrupt or disable systems that provide network services by various means, including: • Flooding a network link with data to consume all available bandwidth. • Sending data designed to exploit known flaws in an application. • Sending multiple service requests to consume a system's resources. • Flooding a user's email inbox with spam messages, causing the genuine messages to get bounced back to the sender. A Distributed Denial of Service (DDoS) attack is a type of DoS attack that uses multiple computers on disparate networks to launch the attack from many simultaneous sources. The attacker introduces unauthorized software that turns the computer into a *zombie* or *drone* that directs the computers to launch the attack.
Session hijacking	Involves exploiting a computer in session to obtain unauthorized access to an organization's network or services. It involves stealing an active session cookie that is used to authenticate a user to a remote server and using that to control the session thereafter. The main intent in session hijacking attacks is to execute denial of service to either the client's system or the server system, or in some cases, both systems.
Peer-to-peer (P2P)	Launched by malware propagating through *P2P* networks. P2P networks typically have a shared command and control architecture, making it harder to detect an attacker. A P2P attack can be used to launch huge DoS attacks. Within a P2P network, personal computers with high-speed connections can be compromised by malware such as viruses and Trojans. An attacker can then control all these compromised computers to launch a DDoS attack.

Attack	Description
ARP poisoning	Address Resolution Protocol (ARP) is the mechanism by which individual hardware Media Access Control (MAC) addresses are matched to an IP address on a network. ARP poisoning occurs when an attacker with access to the target network redirects an IP address to the MAC address of a computer that is not the intended recipient. At this point, the attacker could choose to capture and alter network traffic before forwarding it to the correct destination, or create a DoS condition by pointing the selected IP address at a non-existent MAC address.
Transitive access	The access given to certain members in an organization to use data on a system without the need for authenticating themselves. The information regarding the list of members that have transitive access is usually saved in a log or host file. If an attacker can access and modify the file, then that will give transitive access to all data and programs to the attacker. Therefore, a *transitive access attack* is an attack that takes advantage of the transitive access given in order to steal or destroy data on a system.

How to Manage Physical and Logical Security

Managing physical and logical security is the basis of all IT security.

Guidelines

Some steps you might take to manage physical and logical security include:

- Lock the server room. Ensure that there are locks on the doors and that the doors are locked at all times.
- Set up surveillance to your server room so that you can keep track of who comes and goes and when.
- Store backups elsewhere. Keep a set of backups offsite and make sure they are secure at the offsite location.
- Make sure that users log off and lock all servers and workstations when they are not in use.
- Maintain a list of employees and their access control rights. Update the list every time there is a change in your organization.
- Manage group and user accounts to ensure they only have rights to access the information they need.
- Do not allow the use of non-approved external devices.
- Have a removable media policy in place and ensure that users have been trained on and understand the policy. Properly secure any removable media when not in use.
- Initiate a security policy to your employees to set expectations and management of such devices. Make sure your employees read and sign the policy.
- Educate your employees about the importance of security and data protection.

Example:

A healthcare company that uses a security policy to determine how employees can access the Internet and other network resources is employing an important logical security practice.

ACTIVITY 6-2
Managing Physical and Logical Security

Scenario:

In this activity, you will discuss the ways in which you can manage physical and logical security.

---

1. **Any employee gets to work and realizes that he forgot his laptop in the car. Upon exiting the building, he props the door open with a rock so he won't have to use his swipe card to get back in. Does this pose a security threat to the company?**

   a) Yes. Leaving an otherwise locked door open allows anyone to enter the building and access systems and data.

   b) No. He is just running to his car and will be fast enough to ensure that no one else will have a chance to enter the building.

---

2. **Why is it better to create groups instead of managing individual user accounts?**

---

3. **Match the type of security threat with its correct definition.**

___	Social engineering	a.	An attack that targets a computer's physical components and peripherals.
___	Physical security	b.	An attack that uses deception and trickery to convince unsuspecting users to provide sensitive data or to violate security guidelines.
___	Hardware attacks	c.	These can be internal, external, natural or man made.
___	Environmental threats	d.	Threats include fire, hurricanes and tornadoes, floods, extreme temperatures and extreme humidity.

---

4. **Which of the following are ways you can protect your environment from social engineering attacks? (Select all that apply.)**

   a) Do not give out passwords over the phone or in email.

   b) Users should immediately answer phone callers who make unusual requests.

   c) Organizations should implement security policies but don't need to train users to follow them.

   d) Users should report possible attacks.

   e) Users should employ common sense. If anything sounds forced, too good to be true, or otherwise unusual, it is best to err on the side of caution.

TOPIC B

Implement Security Best Practices and Threat Mitigation Techniques

In the last topic, you identified some basic concepts of physical and logical security. Now you can start thinking of how to apply them to mitigate threats against your organization. In this topic, you will implement various security best practices.

How does it all work together to ensure your network is secure on a day-to-day basis? Leveraging common best practices and mitigation techniques can discourage casual hackers and increase your organizations resiliency against more determined foes. This topic will apply all the security measures to day-to-day scenarios to ensure your network is secure.

Threat Prevention Methods

An organization may take steps to eliminate threats through mitigation. By eliminating the threat, no risk is present. With no risk, avoidance is implemented. There are several methods to follow.

Method	*Details*
Security policies	A *security policy* is a formalized statement that defines how security will be implemented within a particular organization. It describes the means the organization will take to protect the confidentiality, availability, and integrity of sensitive data and resources, including the network infrastructure, physical and electronic data, applications, and the physical environment. It often consists of multiple individual policies. All implemented security measures should conform with the stated policy.
User training	Medical facility security plans can only succeed when all members of an organization understand the necessary security practices and comply with them. IT professionals are often the ones responsible for educating employees and encouraging their compliance with security policies. There are three important components that work together in order to ensure proper employee security training: • Awareness. Users must understand the importance of information security and security policies, and have an awareness of the potential threats to security. • Communication. The lines of communication between medical staff and the IT team must remain open. • Education. Medical staff should be trained and educated in security procedures, practices, and expectations from the moment they walk through the door.

Method	Details
Change management	*Change management* is a systematic way of approving and executing change in order to assure maximum security, stability, and availability of information technology services. When an organization changes its hardware, software, infrastructure, or documentation, it risks the introduction of unanticipated consequences. Therefore, it is important for an organization to be able to properly assess risk; to quantify the cost of training, support, maintenance, or implementation; and to properly weigh benefits against the complexity of a proposed change. By maintaining a documented change management procedure, an organization can protect itself from potential adverse effects of hasty change.
Software updates	Software manufacturers regularly issue different types of system updates that can include security-related changes to the software. These can include patches, hotfixes, and roll up and service packs.
Antivirus software	*Antivirus software* is a category of protective software that scans computers and sometimes networks for known viruses, Trojans, worms, and other malicious programs. Some antivirus programs attempt to scan for unknown harmful software. It is advisable to install antivirus software on all computers, and keep it updated according to your organization's patch management policy. In addition to detection, most antivirus software is capable of logging scan and detection information. These logs should be monitored to make sure that scans are taking place and ensure that infections are reported properly. There is also specialized antispyware software you can install to protect against spyware threats.
Internet email virus protection	Because almost all computer systems today are connected to the Internet, Internet email is a source of serious virus threats. Companies can implement Internet email virus protection by: • Screening the Internet gateway computers for viruses. • Employing good desktop antivirus software. • Scanning incoming email between the Internet and the email server. • Scanning email again at the desktop. • If a virus attack is detected, disabling all Internet connections and isolating affected systems.
Anti-spam solutions	Spam detection has become an important task for end users. There are many different ways end users can protect themselves against spammers. Detection can include an anti-spam filtering program that will detect specific words that are commonly used in spam messages. Other detection methods are used to block Internet Protocol (IP) addresses of known spammers or to pose an email address that is not in use or is too old to collect spam.
Anti-malware solutions	Consists of protective software that scans individual computers and entire enterprise networks for known viruses, Trojans, worms, and other malicious programs. Some programs attempt to scan for unknown harmful software. It is advisable to install anti-malware software on all computers to restrict user access control capabilities for downloading and installing applications.

Method	Details
MAC filtering	MAC address filtering provides a simple method of securing a wireless network. By configuring a Wireless Access Point (WAP) to filter MAC addresses, you can control which wireless clients may join your network. Typically, an administrator configures a list of client MAC addresses that are allowed to access the network. Those pre-approved clients are granted access if the MAC address is "known" by the access point. A note of caution, though: it is not difficult for someone with a little skill and know-how to change a MAC address, falsely gain authorization using another computer, and gain access to your network. While MAC filtering is usually implemented on wireless networks, it can also be used on wired networks.
NAC	*Network Access Control (NAC)* is a general term for the collected protocols, policies, and hardware that govern access on device network interconnections. NAC provides an additional security layer that scans systems for conformance and allows or quarantines updates to meet policy standards. Security professionals will deploy a NAC policy according to an organization's needs based on three main elements: authentication method, endpoint vulnerability assessment, and network security enforcement. Once the NAC policy is determined, professionals must determine where NAC will be deployed within their network structure.
IDS	An *intrusion detection system (IDS)* is a detection control system that scans, audits, and monitors the security infrastructure for signs of attacks in progress. IDS software can also analyze data and alert security administrators to potential infrastructure problems. An IDS can comprise a variety of hardware sensors, intrusion detection software, and IDS management software. Each implementation is unique, and depends on an organization's security needs and the components chosen.

Protecting Against Social Engineering

To protect against social engineering attacks, such as shoulder surfing, programmers should employ simple programming techniques that circumvent echoing passwords or prevent masking password entries with characters such as asterisks (*). You can help eliminate the risk of phishing by educating users, and by educating yourself about how criminals use advanced network analysis tools and techniques to bypass the protections that are in place.

Social Engineering Attack Scenarios

These are a few typical social engineering attack scenarios:

- An attacker creates an executable program file (for example, a file with a .vbs or .exe file extension) that prompts a network user for his user name and password. The attacker then emails the executable file to the user with the story that the user must double-click the file and log on to the network again to clear up some logon problems the organization has been experiencing that morning.
- An attacker contacts the help desk pretending to be a remote sales representative who needs assistance setting up his dial-in access. Through a series of phone calls, the attacker obtains the phone number for remote access and the phone number for accessing the organization's private phone and voice-mail system.

- An attacker sends an executable file disguised as an online greeting card or as a patch for an operating system or a specific application. The unsuspecting user launches the executable, which might install email spamming software or a key-logging program, or turn the computer into a remote "zombie" for the hacker.

Social Engineering Targets

Social engineering typically takes advantage of users who are not technically knowledgeable, but it can also be directed against technical support staff if the attacker pretends to be a user who needs help.

Social Engineering Awareness

The most effective way to prevent damage from social engineering attacks is to educate users. Users must be able to recognize and respond to these attacks properly.

- Users should not automatically believe everything they see, hear, or read, particularly on the Internet.
- Organizations should implement security policies and train users to follow them.
- Users should report possible attacks.
- Users should not give out passwords over the phone or in email.
- Users should not comply with phone or email requests for personal or company information or access to company resources.
- Users should transfer phone callers who make unusual requests to a system operator.
- And, above all, users must employ common sense. If anything sounds forced, too good to be true, or otherwise unusual, it is best to err on the side of caution.

Strong Passwords

Definition:

A *strong password* is a password that meets the complexity requirements that are set by a system administrator and documented in a security policy or password policy. Strong passwords increase the security of systems that use password-based authentication by protecting against password guessing and brute force password attacks.

Password complexity requirements should meet the security needs of an individual organization, and can specify:

- The minimum length of the password.
- Required characters, such as a combination of letters, numbers, and symbols.
- And, forbidden character strings, such as the user account name or dictionary words.

Example:

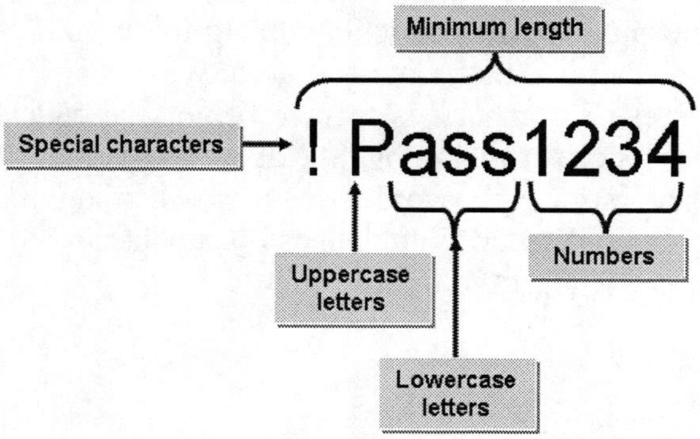

Figure 6-4: *A strong password.*

Communicating Passwords

It's important that you communicate passwords in a secure fashion so they don't fall into the wrong hands. Password best practices should be followed:

- Never include the password in or on same document as the user name or other identifying information pertaining to the user account.
- Verify that once the user knows the password that they have destroyed the document that password has been written on.
- Never share your password with anyone.
- Never write down a password, or put it in an email, give it over the phone, or through an instant message conversation.
- And, password reuse should be restricted within a medical environment when accessing multiple systems.

How to Implement Security Best Practices and Threat Mitigation Techniques

By following security best practices and knowing what techniques to use to mitigate threats, you can ensure that your network and data will be secure.

Guidelines

These are some guidelines to follow for security best practices and threat mitigation techniques:

- Make sure that systems are in secure areas and only authorized users can access them.
- Log off systems when they aren't being used.
- Set a time-out feature for your systems so that they will lock if a user forgets to log off or lock it.
- Ensure you have a strong password policy in effect.
- Ensure that access control has been applied to protect against malware.
- Educate your users on basic security practices.
- Periodically scan your systems for vulnerabilities and unauthorized user attempts.

Example:

Lee is an IT support technician for a large hospital and has been asked by her supervisor to verify that the guidelines of the hospital security policy are being followed. She starts at the front entrance to the hospital, since that is a busy area and usually has many visitors coming and going. She verifies that the greeter's computer is secured behind the counter, and cannot be seen by anyone standing at the desk, or walking by. She also verifies that the time-out feature is set on the machine, and that a strong password is required when logging on. Before she goes to the next area, she posts a general security guidelines document next to the computer for the greeter to reference if she needs to in the future.

ACTIVITY 6-3

Verifying Password Policies

> This is a simulated activity that is available on the CD that shipped with this course. You can run this simulation on any Windows computer. The activity simulation can be launched either directly from the CD by clicking the **Interactives** link and navigating to the appropriate one, or from the installed data file location by opening the C:\HCIT\Simulations\Lesson 6\Verifying Password Policies folder and double-clicking the executable (.exe) file.

Scenario:

To support the security needs on your network, you want to enforce the use of strong passwords. You decide to verify that the default password settings in Windows Server® 2008 require complex passwords.

---

1. Verify the password policies.
   a. Browse to the C:\HCIT\Simulations\Lesson 6\Verifying Password Policies folder.
   b. Double-click the Verifying Password Policies executable file.
   c. In the **Open File - Security Warning** message box, click **Run.**
   d. Follow the on-screen steps for the simulation.
   e. Close the C:\HCIT\Simulations\Lesson 6\Verifying Password Policies folder.

TOPIC C

Manage Remote Access

You've learned the types of risks that can be directed against the physical and logical resources in your organization and how to secure them. You now need to consider security in connection to any employees who may work remotely, whether it be from time to time or full time. This topic will cover remote access technologies and how to support them.

Remote access is a common way for workers and third parties to use IT systems. If you are not familiar with the technologies and systems, you will be unable to effectively support these systems when needed.

Remote Access

Definition:

Remote access is the ability to connect to network systems and services from an offsite or remote location using a remote access method. Remote access enables authorized users to access and use systems and services through a secure Internet connection.

Example:

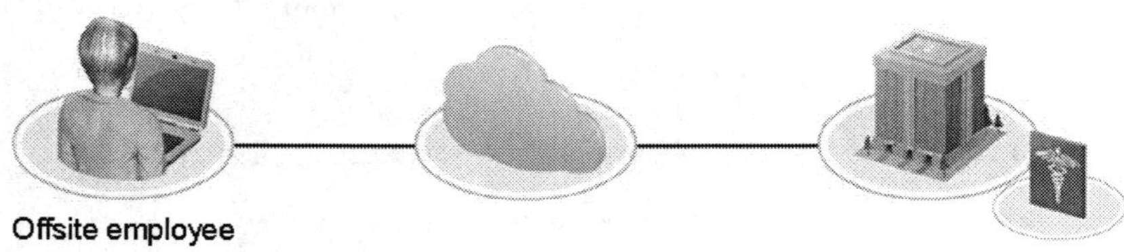

Figure 6-5: *A remote access connection.*

Remote Access Protocols

There are a number of common protocols used to provide remote access to networks.

Protocol	***Description***
Point-to-Point Protocol (PPP)	This is an Internet standard for sending IP datagram packets over serial point-to-point links. Its most common use is for dial-up Internet access. It can be used in synchronous and asynchronous connections. Point-to-Point Protocol over Ethernet (PPPoE) and Point-to-Point Protocol over ATM (PPPoA) are more recent PPP implementations used by many Digital Subscriber Line (DSL) broadband Internet connections. PPP can dynamically configure and test remote network connections, and is often used by clients to connect to networks and the Internet. It also provides encryption for passwords, paving the way for secure authentication of remote users.

Protocol	Description
Point-to-Point Tunneling Protocol (PPTP)	A Microsoft® VPN Layer 2 protocol that increases the security of PPP by providing tunneling and data encryption for PPP packets. It uses the same authentication types as PPP, and is the most widely supported VPN method among older Windows® clients. PPTP encapsulates any type of network protocol and transports it over IP networks.
Layer Two Tunneling Protocol (L2TP)	An Internet-standard protocol combination of PPTP and Layer 2 Forwarding (L2F) that enables the tunneling of PPP sessions across a variety of network protocols, such as IP, frame relay, or Asynchronous Transfer Mode (ATM). L2TP was specifically designed to provide tunneling and security interoperability for client-to-gateway and gateway-to-gateway connections. L2TP does not provide any encryption on its own and L2TP tunnels appear as IP packets, so L2TP employs IP Security (IPSec) Transport Mode for authentication, integrity, and confidentiality.
Secure Socket Tunneling Protocol (SSTP)	This protocol uses the Hypertext Transfer Protocol over Secure Sockets Layer (HTTP over SSL) protocol and encapsulates an IP packet with a PPP header and then with an SSTP header. The IP packet, PPP header, and SSTP header are encrypted by the SSL session. An IP header containing the destination addresses is then added to the packet. It is supported in all current Windows operating systems.

> L2TP has wide vendor support because it addresses the IPSec shortcomings of client-to-gateway and gateway-to-gateway connections.

VPNs

Definition:

A *virtual private network (VPN)* is a private network that is configured by tunneling through a public network, such as the Internet. VPNs provide secure connections between endpoints, such as routers, clients, or servers, by using tunneling to encapsulate and encrypt data. Special *VPN protocols* are required to provide the VPN tunneling, security, and data encryption services.

Example:

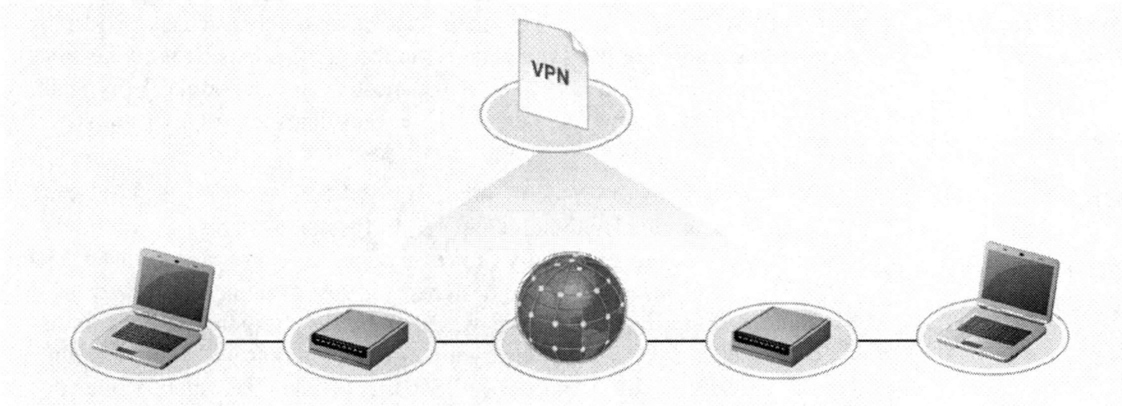

Figure 6-6: *A VPN.*

Advantages and Disadvantages of Remote Access

There are advantages and disadvantages of remote access.

Advantage/ Disadvantage	***Details***
Advantages	• Can be very secure when requests for connections are verified, confirmed, and granted at both ends. • Allows your employees to work from remote locations, thus increasing productivity. • Can help to reduce an organization's cost by cutting down on overhead.
Disadvantages	• Since there are employees working from remote locations and using a variety of personal devices, it can become challenging to offer simple and secure remote access. • If your operating system has vulnerabilities that are not patched, you could experience security risks such as malware and hackers. • Can increase network traffic due to multiple remote connections.

How to Manage Remote Access

Remote access enables authorized users to access and use systems and services through a secure Internet connection. You must ensure that access is secure to protect your organization's data.

Guidelines

Some guidelines to follow to ensure your remote access connections are secure include:

- Initiate a remote access policy. Train users on the policy and make sure they understand it.
- Keep your antivirus software up to date.
- Apply the latest security patches.
- Ensure there is a firewall enabled.
- Only give remote access to people who really need it.
- Set up connections to time out when they aren't used.
- Ensure that proper security controls are in place for a Remote Desktop Client (RDC), VPN, and any remote control application installations.
- Log remote access attempts so you can see who is trying to access your network.

Example:

AFR Health System is a large regional healthcare company with a central office and several branches in various locations across the region. They have employees who work from home from time to time. These employees have to follow the written remote access policy. The policy dictates that they can only connect to the VPN using a company-issued device such as a laptop. In addition, if their connection is inactive after 10 minutes, they will be automatically disconnect and will have to log back in.

RADIUS

Remote Authentication Dial-In User Service (RADIUS) is an Internet standard protocol that provides centralized remote access authentication, authorization, and auditing services. When a network contains several remote access servers, you can configure one of the servers to be a RADIUS server, and all of the other servers as RADIUS clients. The RADIUS clients will pass all authentication requests to the RADIUS server for verification. User configuration, remote access policies, and usage logging can be centralized on the RADIUS server.

ACTIVITY 6-4

Implementing RADIUS for Remote Access

This is a simulated activity that is available on the CD that shipped with this course. You can run this simulation on any Windows computer. The activity simulation can be launched either directly from the CD by clicking the **Interactives** link and navigating to the appropriate one, or from the installed data file location by opening the C:\HCIT\Simulations\Lesson 6\Implementing RADIUS for Remote Access folder and double-clicking the executable (.exe) file.

Scenario:

You are an IT technician for a mid-size medical facility with a growing number of remote connectivity needs. You plan to implement Remote Authentication Dial-In User Service (RADIUS) for remote authentication, and you want to use it in tandem with wireless authentication for an added layer of security on a wireless network that is mainly accessed by traveling employees. You want to test RADIUS in a lab environment before deploying it in production. On a test Routing and Remote Access Server (RRAS) system, you will install a RADIUS server and reconfigure an RRAS server to use RADIUS authentication.

---

1. Implement RADIUS for remote access.
   a. Browse to the C:\HCIT\Simulations\Lesson 6\Implementing RADIUS for Remote Access folder.
   b. Double-click the Implementing RADIUS for Remote Access executable file.
   c. In the **Open File - Security Warning** message box, click **Run.**
   d. Follow the on-screen steps for the simulation.
   e. Close the C:\HCIT\Simulations\Lesson 6\Implementing RADIUS for Remote Access folder.

ACTIVITY 6-5

Securing a Remote Access Server

This is a simulated activity that is available on the CD that shipped with this course. You can run this simulation on any Windows computer. The activity simulation can be launched either directly from the CD by clicking the **Interactives** link and navigating to the appropriate one, or from the installed data file location by opening the C:\HCIT\Simulations\Lesson 6\Securing a Remote Access Server folder and double-clicking the executable (.exe) file.

Setup:

The Microsoft® Windows Server® 2008 R2 Server computer has a physical local area network (LAN) adapter and also a virtual Microsoft Loopback Adapter to simulate the presence of an external connection object. The Microsoft Loopback Adapter has been configured with default IP settings. The RRAS is configured to use Dynamic Host Configuration Protocol (DHCP) to distribute IP addresses to remote access clients.

Scenario:

An important task as a medical facility's IT technician is to make sure your remote access servers are secure. In the past, there have been problems with attackers accessing services and data that they were not supposed to have access to through VPN connections. You will now provide VPN services through new Windows Server 2008 R2 RRAS servers, which you will secure before connecting them to the network. The IT department will install the new VPN RRAS server in the demilitarized zone (DMZ). The DMZ has already been secured. Also, the Active Directory team has already created a remote access security policy to determine who will have VPN access to RRAS servers in your domain.

You need to configure the VPN server with system-wide security settings that include:

- Permitting only L2TP clients with IPSec encryption to connect.
- Blocking PPTP packets from external networks.

---

1. Secure the Remote Access Server.
   a. Browse to the C:\HCIT\Simulations\Lesson 6\Securing a Remote Access Server folder.
   b. Double-click the Securing a Remote Access Server executable file.
   c. In the **Open File - Security Warning** message box, click **Run.**
   d. Follow the on-screen steps for the simulation.
   e. Close the C:\HCIT\Simulations\Lesson 6\Securing a Remote Access Server folder.

ACTIVITY 6-6

Setting Up Remote Access Authentication

This is a simulated activity that is available on the CD that shipped with this course. You can run this simulation on any Windows computer. The activity simulation can be launched either directly from the CD by clicking the **Interactives** link and navigating to the appropriate one, or from the installed data file location by opening the C:\HCIT\Simulations\Lesson 6\Setting Up Remote Access Authentication folder and double-clicking the executable (.exe) file.

Scenario:

As part of your remote access implementation, the senior network administrator in your organization favors implementing Network Policy Server (NPS) so that the administrators can obtain detailed authentication information and use a single remote access policy for all RRAS servers. She also recommends configuring the policy to automatically disconnect users if their connections are idle for 15 minutes.

---

1. Set up remote access authentication.

a. Browse to the C:\HCIT\Simulations\Lesson 6\Setting Up Remote Access Authentication folder.

b. Double-click the Setting Up Remote Access Authentication executable file.

c. In the **Open File - Security Warning** message box, click **Run.**

d. Follow the on-screen steps for the simulation.

e. Close the C:\HCIT\Simulations\Lesson 6\Setting Up Remote Access Authentication folder.

TOPIC D
Manage Wireless Security

Wireless network access is extremely common, whether it be used in the work environment, in homes, or in retail locations such as coffee shops. Securing your data over a wireless connection is just as vital as securing it in any other form. This topic will cover how to manage wireless access security so your data stays protected.

Wireless technologies enable a more mobile and productive workforce. In any wireless data environment, there are increased concerns regarding security, and this is particularly prominent in a medical setting. Familiarity with wireless security ensures you are properly securing your data over your wireless network.

Wireless Security

Definition:

Wireless security is any method of securing your wireless LAN network to prevent unauthorized network access and network data theft. You need to ensure that authorized users can connect to the network without any hindrances. Wireless networks are more vulnerable to attacks than any other network system. For one thing, most wireless devices such as laptops, mobile phones, smartphones, and tablets search and connect automatically to the access point offering the best signal, which can be coming from an attacker. Wireless transmissions can also be scanned or sniffed out of the air, with no need to access physical network media. Such attacks can be avoided by using relevant security protocols.

Example:

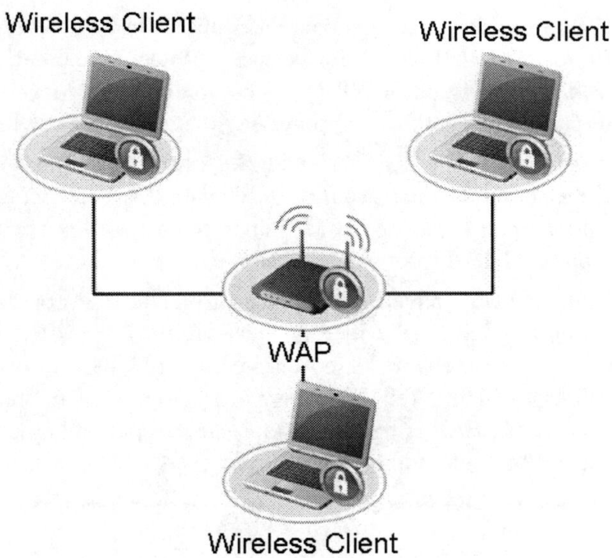

Figure 6-7: *A wireless security design.*

Wireless Security Protocols

There are several major wireless security protocols.

Security Protocol	Description
Wired Equivalent Privacy (WEP)	Provides 64-bit, 128-bit, and 256-bit encryption using the Rivest Cipher 4 (RC4) algorithm for wireless communication that uses the 802.11a and 802.11b protocols. While WEP might sound like a good solution at first, it ironically is not as secure as it should be. The problem stems from the way WEP produces the keys that are used to encrypt data. Because of a flaw in the method, attackers could easily generate their own keys using a wireless network capture tool, such as Kismet, to capture and analyze as little as 10 MB of data transferred through the air.
Wireless Transport Layer Security (WTLS)	The security layer of the Wireless Application Protocol that uses public key cryptography for mutual authentication and data encryption. In most cases, WTLS is meant to provide secure WAP communications, but if it is improperly configured or implemented, it can expose wireless devices to attacks that include email forgery and sniffing data that has been sent in plaintext.
802.1x	An IEEE standard used to provide a port-based authentication mechanism for wireless communications using the 802.11a and 802.11b protocols. 802.1x uses the Extensible Authentication Protocol (EAP) to provide user authentication against a directory service.
Wi-Fi Protected Access (WPA/WPA2)	The security protocol introduced to address some of the shortcomings in WEP. WPA was introduced during the development of the 802.11i IEEE standard, and WPA2 implemented all the mandatory components of the standard. It provides for dynamic reassignment of keys to prevent the key-attack vulnerabilities of WEP. • WPA provides improved data encryption through the *Temporal Key Integrity Protocol (TKIP),* which is a security protocol created by the IEEE 802.11i task group to replace WEP. It is combined with the existing WEP encryption to provide a 128-bit encryption key that fixes the key length issues of WEP. • In addition to TKIP, WPA2 adds Advanced Encryption Standard (AES) cipher-based *Counter Mode with Cipher Block Chaining Message Authentication Code Protocol (CCMP)* encryption for even greater security and to replace TKIP. It provides a 128-bit encryption key. • Both standards have been extended to include several types of user authentication through EAP, which is considered poor in WEP. WEP regulates access to a wireless network based on a computer's hardware-specific MAC address, which is relatively easy to figure out, steal, and use (that is, sniff and spoof). EAP is built on a more secure public key encryption system to ensure that only authorized network users can access the network.

Security Protocol	Description
EAP	A framework that allows clients and servers to authenticate with each other using one of a variety of plug-ins. Because EAP does not specify which authentication method should be used, it enables the choice of a wide range of current authentication methods, and allows for the implementation of future authentication methods. EAP is often utilized in wireless networks and can also be used in wired implementations. Two common EAP implementations include: • *Protected Extensible Authentication Protocol (PEAP),* which is an open standard developed by a coalition made up of Cisco Systems, Microsoft, and RSA Security. • *Lightweight Extensible Authentication Protocol (LEAP),* which is Cisco Systems' proprietary EAP implementation.

Wireless Threats and Vulnerabilities

Wireless networks have an increasing number of specific vulnerabilities.

Wireless Threat and Vulnerability	Description
Rogue access point	This is an unauthorized wireless access point on a corporate or private network. Rogue access points can cause considerable damage to an organization's data. They are not detected easily, and can allow private network access to many unauthorized users with the proper devices. A rogue access point can allow man-in-the-middle attacks and access to private information. Organizations should protect themselves from this type of attack by implementing techniques to constantly monitor the system, such as installing an IDS.
Evil twins	These are rogue access points on a network that appear to be legitimate. Although they can be installed both in corporate or private networks, typically they are found in public Wi-Fi hotspots where users do not connect transparently and automatically as they do in a corporate network, but rather select available networks from a list. Evil twins can be more dangerous than other rogue access points because the user thinks that the wireless signal is genuine, making it difficult to differentiate from a valid access point with the same name.
Interference	In wireless networking, this is the phenomenon by which radio waves interfere with the 802.11 wireless signals. It usually occurs at home because of various electronic devices, such as microwaves, operating in a bandwidth close to that of the wireless network. When this occurs, it causes the 802.11 signals to wait before transmitting and the wait can be indefinite at times.

Wireless Threat and Vulnerability	Description
Bluejacking	This is a method used by attackers to send out unwanted *Bluetooth* signals from mobile phones, smartphones, tablets, and laptops to other Bluetooth-enabled devices. Because Bluetooth has a 30-foot transmission limit, this is a very close-range attack. With the advanced technology available today, attackers can send out unsolicited messages along with images and video. These types of signals can lead to many different types of threats. They can lead to device malfunctions, or even propagate viruses, including Trojan horses. Users should reject anonymous contacts, and should configure their mobile devices to non-discoverable mode.
Bluesnarfing	This is a method in which attackers gain access to unauthorized information on a wireless device using a Bluetooth connection within the 30-foot Bluetooth transmission limit. Unlike bluejacking, access to wireless devices such as mobile phones, smartphones, tablets, and laptops by bluesnarfing can lead to the exploitation of private information including email messages, contact information, calendar entries, images, videos, and any data stored on the device.
War driving	War driving is the act of searching for instances of wireless networks using wireless tracking devices such as mobile phones, smartphones, tablets, or laptops. It locates wireless access points while traveling, which can be exploited to obtain unauthorized Internet access and potentially steal data. This process can be automated using a GPS device and war driving software.
War chalking	War chalking is the act of using symbols to mark off a sidewalk or wall to indicate that there is an open wireless network which may be offering Internet access.
IV attack	In this attack, the attacker is able to predict or control the *initialization vector (IV)* of an encryption process. This gives the attacker access to view the encrypted data that is supposed to be hidden from everyone else except the authentic user or network.
Packet sniffing	This can be used as an attack on wireless networks where an attacker captures data and registers data flows, which allow the attacker to analyze the data contained in a packet. In its benign form, it also helps organizations monitor their own networks against attackers.

Wireless Security Best Practices

There are several best practices to follow to ensure your wireless network is secure.

Practice	Information
Configuration	• Secure your wireless router or access point administration interface. • Change default administrator passwords (and user names). • Disable remote administration. • Secure/disable the reset switch/function. • Change the default Simple Network Management Protocol (SNMP) parameter. • Change the default channel. • Regularly upgrade the Wi-Fi router firmware to ensure you have the latest security patches and critical fixes. • Apply MAC address filtering. By configuring a WAP to filter MAC addresses, you can control which wireless clients may join your network.
SSID	• Don't broadcast your Service Set Identifier (SSID). • Change the default SSID naming broadcast.
Encryption	• Enable WPA2 encryption instead of WEP. • Change the default encryption keys. • Avoid using pre-shared keys (PSK).
Network	• Assign static IP addresses to devices. • Use MAC filtering for access control. • Use the Remote Authentication Dial-In User Service Plus (RADIUS+) network directory authentication where feasible. • Use a VPN. • Perform periodic rogue WAP scans. • Perform periodic security assessments.
Antennae placement and power level configuration	• Reduce your wireless LAN transmitter power. • Position the router or access point safely. The radio frequency range of each access point should not extend beyond the physical boundaries of the organization's facilities. • Adjust the power level controls on routers and access points as needed to help minimize power consumption within the wireless network. It can be difficult to manage the power of wireless to reduce the power used, while providing the right level of power to operate the network.
Guest network settings	• Do not auto-connect to open Wi-Fi networks. • Enable firewalls on each computer and the router.
HIPAA concerns	The matter of security has always been a concern with wireless standards. With the inception of Health Insurance Portability and Accountability Act (HIPAA), wireless security becomes even more crucial. Your wireless environment should meet or exceed the standards set by the HIPAA Advisory Committee and the Wi-Fi Alliance.

How to Manage Wireless Security

When you secure wireless traffic, you must prevent unauthorized network access and the theft of network data while ensuring that authorized users can connect to the network.

Guidelines

Some steps you might take to manage wireless security include:

- Keep sensitive data private. Do not include any data on a wireless device, such as a smartphone, that you are not willing to lose if the device is lost or stolen.
- Install antivirus software if it is available for your wireless devices.
- Update the software on wireless devices and routers to provide additional functionality as well as to close security holes in wireless devices such as:
  - To prevent bluejacking and bluesnarfing attacks, disable the discovery setting on Bluetooth connections.
  - Set Bluetooth connections to hidden.
- Implement a security protocol.
- Implement appropriate authentication and access control, such as MAC address filtering or user authentication, against a directory service to prevent authentication attacks such as war driving.
- To protect against a rogue access point and other wireless attacks, implement an IDS on the wireless network for monitoring network activity.
- Implement your hardware and software manufacturers' security recommendations.
- Test the functionality of systems after hardening them to make sure that required services and resources are accessible to legitimate users.
- Document your changes.

Example:

AFR Health System has many healthcare professionals who use wireless laptops to work in different locations within the main office or in branch offices. They also use mobile devices to check email and web-based patient information from any location. All wireless devices have antivirus software installed, and all software patches are kept up to date.

Wireless routers are also patched with the latest firmware updates. AFR Health System employs the 802.11i security protocol for data encryption. All authentication is performed through EAP against the Active Directory accounts database.

ACTIVITY 6-7

Securing Wireless Traffic

This is a simulated activity that is available on the CD that shipped with this course. You can run this simulation on any Windows computer. The activity simulation can be launched either directly from the CD by clicking the **Interactives** link and navigating to the appropriate one, or from the installed data file location by opening the C:\HCIT\Simulations\Lesson 6\Securing Wireless Traffic folder and double-clicking the executable (.exe) file.

Setup:

This is a simulated activity using a Cisco Linksys Wireless-G broadband router, model WRT54G2.

Scenario:

You have been assigned the task of tightening security for your medical facility. Many of the clinicians are mobile users, and it is your responsibility to set up Windows laptop and desktop computers with wireless cards so that users can communicate with each other without having to run any cables. The practice manager is concerned that attackers may steal patient information by accessing the router. You have successfully tested Internet access through the router on a desktop computer. Now, you need to configure the router's security features.

---

1. Configure the wireless security on your wireless router.
    a. Browse to the C:\HCIT\Simulations\Lesson 6\Securing Wireless Traffic folder.
    b. Double-click the Securing Wireless Traffic executable file.
    c. In the **Open File - Security Warning** message box, click **Run.**
    d. Follow the on-screen steps for the simulation.
    e. Close the C:\HCIT\Simulations\Lesson 6\Securing Wireless Traffic folder.

TOPIC E

Perform Backups and Disaster Recovery

Now that you've learned how to secure your network, hardware, and people, you need to make sure you have systems in place to recover if there is ever a disaster such as an accident or system failure. This topic addresses planning for disaster and how to recover from one.

Accidents and hardware failures do occur. This topic will prepare you to deal with these incidents by presenting best practices for backup and recovering from an incident.

DRP

Definition:

A *disaster recovery plan (DRP)* is a policy that defines how people and resources will be protected in a disaster, and how the organization will recover from the disaster. In any disaster situation, the safety of personnel is the first concern, regardless of the implications for physical and information security. The DRP can include a list of individuals responsible for recovery, an inventory of hardware and software, and a series of steps to take to respond to the disaster and rebuild affected systems.

Example:

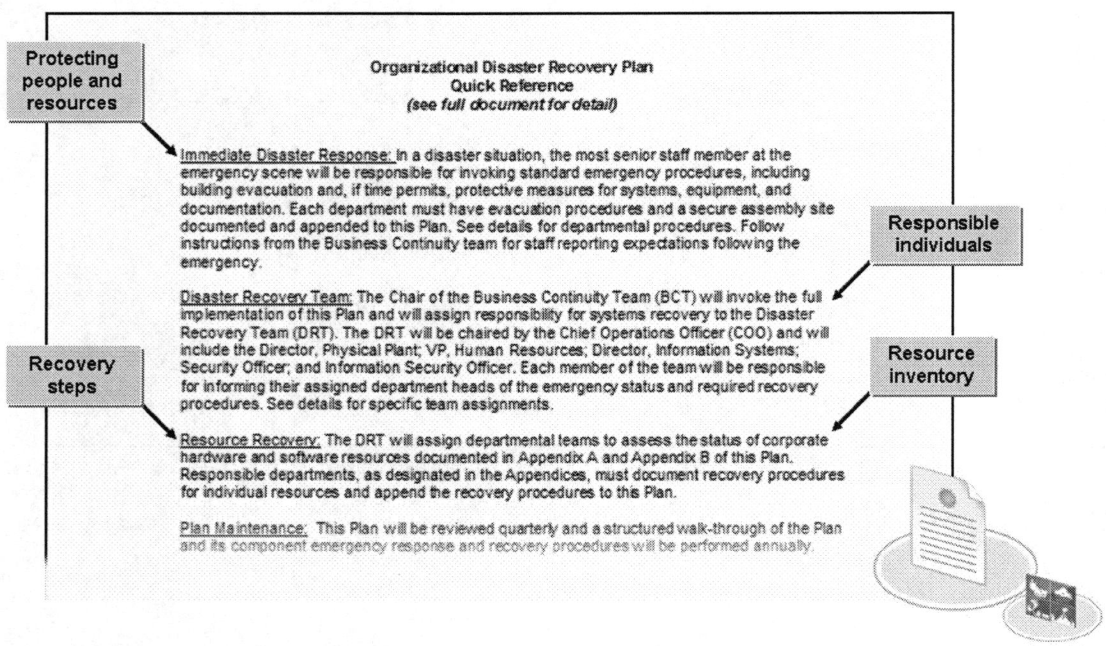

Figure 6-8: *A DRP.*

Backup Uses

Backups are a key component to any disaster recovery plan. There are two specific purposes for using a backup. The main purpose is to perform a recovery if data has been lost, whether the loss was caused by a corruption or accidental deletion. A second purpose for a backup is to restore data from an earlier state.

Backups for Disaster Recovery

Backups should be a main component of your DRP but should not be the only component. Restoring data from backup may not reconstitute a full computer system.

Backup Types

There are several backup types available to protect your data.

Backup Type	***Description***
Full backup	All selected files, regardless of the state of the archived bit, are backed up. The *archive flag*, also referred to as the archive bit, is a file property that essentially indicates whether the file has been modified since it was last backed up. A full backup then clears the archive flag.
Daily backup	All selected files that have been changed on a daily basis. The daily backup does not clear the archive flag.
Differential backup	All selected files that have changed since the last full backup are backed up. A differential backup does not clear the archive bit. When differential backups are used, you must restore the last full backup plus the most recent differential backup.
Incremental backup	All selected files that have changed since the last full or differential backup are backed up. It clears the archive bit. An incremental backup typically takes less time to perform than a differential backup because it includes less data. When incremental backups are used, you must restore the last full backup plus all subsequent incremental backups.

Backup Storage

The data that you back up must need to be stored on appropriate media.

Storage Type	***Information***
Tape drive	A *tape drive* is a personal computer storage device that stores data magnetically on a tape that is enclosed in a removable tape cartridge. Data on the tape must be read sequentially. The size of external tape drives varies, but internal drives have a 5.25-inch form factor. Tape drives are most commonly used to store backup copies of data.

Storage Type	Information
Hard disk	A *hard disk drive (HDD)* is a personal computer storage device that uses fixed media, which means that the disk is built into the drive and the drive remains in the computer unless you are performing an upgrade or a repair. Hard drives connect directly to the system board via at least one cable for data and one for power. The hard disk itself consists of several metal or hard plastic platters with a magnetic surface coating. Data is stored magnetically and can be accessed directly. Most hard drives are internal, but some are external.
Optical storage	An *optical disk* is a personal computer storage device such as a CD or DVD that stores data optically, rather than magnetically. The removable plastic disks have a reflective coating and require an optical drive to be read. In optical storage, data is written by either pressing or burning with a laser to create pits (recessed areas) or lands (raised areas) in the reflective surface of the disc. A laser in the optical drive then reads the data off the disc. Optical drives can be internal or external, and they generally have a 5.25-inch form factor.
Solid state storage	*Solid state storage* is a personal computer storage device that stores data in special types of memory instead of on disks or tape. Common types of solid state storage include the USB devices commonly known as jump drives or thumb drives, flash memory cards, and secure digital (SD) memory cards. Solid state storage uses non-volatile memory to emulate mechanical storage devices, but solid state storage is much faster and more reliable than mechanical storage because there are no moving parts.
Cloud-based backups	You can subscribe to a vendor-supplied cloud-based backup service that takes continual snapshots of the changed data. The snapshots stream to the cloud to create redundant online backups.

Backup Storage Options

The magnetic tapes or other physical media used to create data backups must be stored securely, but must remain accessible in case the data is needed. Many organizations employ both onsite and offsite backup storage. The onsite storage location is for the most recent set of backups, so that they can be accessed quickly if a data restoration is needed during normal operations. The offsite location is a secure, disaster-resistant storage facility where the organization keeps either a duplicate or an older backup set to protect it against any damage caused by disaster conditions at the primary site.

Another option is to use a secure bonded courier service to extract backup data, media, and disks from your medical facility and transport it to the designated backup location for storage.

Secure Backup Transfer Methods

When backing up files and patient records stored within an EMR or EHR system, there are a number of methods that can be used to ensure that this process is completed securely:

- The use of SSL encryption during data transfer.
- The use of encryption during authentication.
- The use of strong passwords to access files once they are backed up.

How to Plan for Disaster Recovery

To plan for disaster recovery, you must properly assess your organization's current state of readiness, and you must know when and how to improve any limitations of the current strategy.

Guidelines

To plan for disaster recovery, keep the following guidelines in mind:

- If your organization has not tested the BCP recently, do so. Conduct several offline scenarios that only utilize backup resources.
- If you are creating or improving the BCP and/or DRP, research any available templates that might help guide you. Websites such as **www.disasterrecoveryforum.com** or **www.disasterrecoveryworld.com** are good places to begin.
- Ensure that there are redundancy measures in place for servers, power supplies, and your ISP.
- Verify that the company has access to spare hardware and peripherals for emergency use, and that the devices are secure enough to conduct business with.
- Review any service-level agreements (SLAs) that are in place so that you have an idea of what constitutes acceptable downtime.
- Create a line of communication that does not make use of company resources, so it does not break should the company lose power after hours. Do the same in the event that the city or regional power is down.
- Identify and document all single points of failure, as well as any up-to-date redundancy measures.
- Make sure that the company's redundant storage is secure.
- Be sure that your DRP includes provisions for regular tests of the plan. You might want to schedule a "fire drill," where one day, all managers are moved to an offsite location, unannounced. This helps to simulate a disaster or emergency, which does not always provide ample warning.
- Employees must receive training to understand the importance of the DRP.

Example:

You work for a very large healthcare organization that supports a number of different hospitals and practices. Every 12 to 18 months, the IT department you work with revisits the preparedness of the organization to withstand a disaster. They begin with an analytical look at both the BCP and the DRP as they currently exist, and then they modify them as necessary; this only comes after a careful assessment of the organization's recent security history, as well as an assessment of the landscape of security in the general healthcare business.

While it is not always financially feasible for the organization to have an unannounced offsite fire drill, the IT department does regularly test the viability of all hospital locations backup servers for the intranet, the secure servers that contain patient billing and financial information, and those servers that actually host the EMR. After conducting these tests, the IT department members determine how many backup resources they need to maintain uptime, how many spare peripherals they need to save in case of an emergency, and how many options they have should their ISP lose service for an extended period of time.

The IT department also revisits the emergency contact information for all those employees identified in the BCP and DRP who will have a hand in disaster recovery and those that need to report to the hospital or practice locations. Those employees are then tested on how quickly they can get the backup networks operational, and how quickly they can use spare hardware and peripherals to function as secure, temporary network devices. Consistent and systematic planning saves time and money in the long run should something unforeseeable happen to a healthcare organization's network resources.

How to Perform Backups

Procedure Reference: Perform Backups

To perform backups and plan for disaster recovery:

1. Open the Backup and Restore utility on your system.
2. Set your backup settings:
   - Determine where to back up files are stored and what storage media will be used.
   - Determine what files will be backed up.
   - Select the drives and folders you want to back up.
   - If necessary, configure the backup schedule settings, and determine how often you want to back up system files.
   - Perform a backup inventory as needed to verify that the backup data is secure and valid.

Supported Backup Locations

If you want to back up your files on a particular partition, you cannot choose the same partition as the backup location. You need to choose a different partition, a local storage device, or a network location. By default, the partition where you have installed Windows 7 will always be included in the backup. You can neither remove it from the backup nor choose it as the backup location.

For example, suppose that you have three disks, C, D, and E, and you have Windows 7 installed on the C drive. If you want to back up the files stored on the D drive, you must choose the E drive as the backup location. Since Windows 7 is installed on your C drive, you cannot choose that disk as your backup location. Also, you cannot choose the D drive as your backup location since you want to back up the files on that disk.

ACTIVITY 6-8

Creating a Backup Copy of Files and Folders

This is a demonstration animation that is available on the CD that shipped with this course. You can run this animation on any Windows computer. The animation can be launched either directly from the CD by clicking the **Interactives** link and navigating to the appropriate one, or from the installed data file location by opening the C:\HCIT\Simulations\Lesson 6\Creating a Backup Copy of Files and Folders folder and double-clicking the executable (.exe) file.

Scenario:

You have stored project-related documents on your computer. You update the reports and documents after every status meeting. You need to save a copy of these documents every week to prevent the files from being corrupted or accidentally deleted. After your initial backup, you have created new files and also modified some of the existing files. So, you want to make a backup of these files immediately. You also want to ensure that you back up only the modified files and not all the files.

---

1. Create a backup copy of files and folders.

a. Browse to the C:\HCIT\Simulations\Lesson 6 folder.

b. Double-click the Creating a Backup Copy of Files and Folders executable file.

c. In the **Open File - Security Warning** message box, click **Run.**

d. Follow the on-screen steps for the simulation.

e. Close the C:\HCIT\Simulations\Lesson 6 folder.

ACTIVITY 6-9

Creating a DRP

Scenario:

You are a security professional at Ristell Health Center, a small but rapidly growing health clinic. With a growing roster of employees, a larger network infrastructure, and more remote network access by traveling employees, the company has decided that it has outgrown its original security policies. You have been asked to create the company's first DRP.

---

1. **Which are common components that should be in a medical facility's DRP? (Select all that apply)**

   a) A list of employees' personal items.

   b) Contact information for key individuals.

   c) An inventory of important hardware and software.

   d) Plans to reconstruct the network.

---

2. **Assume that Ristell Health Center is located in a climate and location identical to the company you work for now. What are some unique geographical or weather-related conditions you might need to account for, but that might not be a consideration for other companies?**

---

3. **Assume that a high-level manager has expressed some dissatisfaction with the notion of a "fire drill" to test the clinic's preparedness for a disaster; it seems he is leery of so much paid time being used in an unproductive way, and he wonders if you cannot just write a detailed plan instead. What are some things you can mention to help persuade him that such an unannounced drill is necessary?**

---

4. **Once you have the DRP and other components in place, what do you do to make sure it works smoothly?**

Lesson 6 Follow-up

In this lesson you learned how to integrate security best practices into your daily healthcare IT workflow. You now have a strong understanding of potential risks and how to mitigate them. With this knowledge in hand, you can successfully secure your IT environment and demonstrate the value of IT security to others within your department and organization.

1. **Which of the basic security concepts in this lesson were familiar to you, and which were new?**

2. **Consider your current security measures that are in place. Are there any areas that are at risk? What can you do to improve upon them?**

Follow-up

In this course, you identified essential healthcare and IT concepts and terminology and took various steps to integrate the two realms of practice within the healthcare IT technician job role. With this general background understanding of the healthcare IT environment as well as your own IT support skills, you should be well-positioned to pursue both certification and potential employment within the healthcare IT industry.

What's Next?

After completing this course and taking time for additional review of courseware materials, you may choose to pursue the CompTIA® Healthcare IT certificate examination, as well as job opportunities in the healthcare field. Depending on the healthcare environment in which you work, you may need to pursue specialized training from a software or hardware vendor. You may also want to pursue training to prepare for CompTIA certifications you may not currently hold, such as CompTIA A+, Network+, Security+, or Server+.

A Mapping Course Content to the CompTIA® Healthcare IT Technician (Exam HIT-001) Objectives

The following tables can assist you in your preparation for the CompTIA® Healthcare IT Technician exam by mapping the content of the course to the exam objectives.

Exam Objective	***CompTIA Healthcare IT Technician (Exam HIT-001) Lesson and Topic Reference***
Domain 1.0 Regulatory Requirements	
1.1 Identify standard agencies, laws, and regulations.	
• HHS	Lesson 1, Topics A and C
• ONC	Lesson 1, Topic C
• CMS	Lesson 1, Topic C
• HIPAA	Lesson 1, Topics A and D
• Medicare	Lesson 1, Topic C
• Medicaid	Lesson 1, Topic C
• ARRA	Lesson 1, Topic C
• HITECH	Lesson 1, Topic C
• Meaningful use	Lesson 1, Topic C
• Eligible provider	Lesson 1, Topic C
• NIST	Lesson 1, Topic C

Exam Objective	***CompTIA Healthcare IT Technician Lesson and Topic Reference***
1.2 Explain and classify HIPAA controls and compliance issues.	
• PHI	Lesson 1, Topic A

Exam Objective	CompTIA Healthcare IT Technician Lesson and Topic Reference
1.2 Explain and classify HIPAA controls and compliance issues.	
• Covered Entity	Lesson 1, Topics A and C
• Security	Lesson 1, Topics C and D
• HIPAA Security	Lesson 1, Topic D
■ Violations	Lesson 1, Topic D
■ Fines	Lesson 1, Topic D
■ Requirements	Lesson 1, Topic D
• Release of information	Lesson 1, Topic D Lesson 2, Topic C
• Access permissions	Lesson 1, Topic D

Exam Objective	CompTIA Healthcare IT Technician Lesson and Topic Reference
1.3 Summarize regulatory rules of record retention, disposal, and archiving.	
• Documentation requirements	Lesson 3, Topic C
■ Time of storage	Lesson 3, Topic C
• Types of records	Lesson 1, Topic A
■ Public records	Lesson 1, Topic A
■ Private records	Lesson 1, Topic A
■ Legal health records	Lesson 1, Topic A
• Methods of record disposal	Lesson 3, Topic C

Exam Objective	CompTIA Healthcare IT Technician Lesson and Topic Reference
1.4 Explain and interpret legal best practices, requirements, and documentation.	
• Waivers of liability	Lesson 3, Topic C
• Business Associate Agreements (BAA)	Lesson 3, Topic C
• Third-party vendor review and agreements (SLA, MOU)	Lesson 3, Topic C

Exam Objective	CompTIA Healthcare IT Technician Lesson and Topic Reference
Domain 2.0 Organizational Behavior	
2.1 Use best practices for handling PHI in the workplace.	
● PC placement	Lesson 3, Topic C
● Privacy screens	Lesson 3, Topic C
● Printer placement	Lesson 3, Topic C
● Screensavers	Lesson 3, Topic C
● Time lockout	Lesson 3, Topic C

Exam Objective	CompTIA Healthcare IT Technician Lesson and Topic Reference
2.2 Identify EHR/EMR access roles and responsibilities.	
● Medical roles	Lesson 3, Topic A
■ MD	Lesson 3, Topic A
■ RN	Lesson 3, Topic A
■ PA	Lesson 3, Topic A
■ DA	Lesson 3, Topic A
■ PCT	Lesson 3, Topic A
■ MA	Lesson 3, Topic A
■ NUC	Lesson 3, Topic A
■ UA	Lesson 3, Topic A
■ LPN	Lesson 3, Topic A
■ PM	Lesson 3, Topic A
■ Office Mgr.	Lesson 3, Topic A
■ Staff	Lesson 3, Topic A
● Technical roles	Lesson 3, Topic A
■ Security administrator	Lesson 3, Topic A
■ Network administrator	Lesson 3, Topic A
■ System administrator	Lesson 3, Topic A
■ Desktop support	Lesson 3, Topic A
■ Database administrator	Lesson 3, Topic A
● Business Associate Access and Contractor Access	Lesson 3, Topic A

Exam Objective	CompTIA Healthcare IT Technician Lesson and Topic Reference
2.2 Identify EHR/EMR access roles and responsibilities.	
● Access limitations based on role and exceptions	Lesson 3, Topic A Lesson 6, Topic A
■ Emergency access (break the glass)	Lesson 3, Topic A
● Access based on sensitive patient data	Lesson 3, Topic A
■ Sensitivity labels and clearance	Lesson 3, Topic A

Exam Objective	CompTIA Healthcare IT Technician Lesson and Topic Reference
2.3 Apply proper communication methods in the workplace.	
● Email	Lesson 3, Topic B
● IM vs. secure chat	Lesson 3, Topic B
● EMR system	Lesson 3, Topic B
● Fax	Lesson 3, Topic B
● Secure FTP	Lesson 3, Topic B
● Phone	Lesson 3, Topic B
● VoIP	Lesson 3, Topic B

Exam Objective	CompTIA Healthcare IT Technician Lesson and Topic Reference
2.4 Identify organizational structures and different methods of operation.	
● Organizational Structures	Lesson 2, Topic A
■ Hospital	Lesson 2, Topic A
■ Private practice	Lesson 2, Topic A
■ Nursing homes	Lesson 2, Topic A
■ Assisted living facilities	Lesson 2, Topic A
■ Home healthcare	Lesson 2, Topic A
■ Hospice	Lesson 2, Topic A
■ Surgical centers	Lesson 2, Topic A
● Methods	Lesson 2, Topic A
■ Differences in scope of work	Lesson 2, Topic A
■ Availability of resources	Lesson 2, Topic A
■ Formality of procedures	Lesson 2, Topic A

Exam Objective	CompTIA Healthcare IT Technician Lesson and Topic Reference
2.5 Given a scenario, execute daily activities while following a code of conduct.	
• Communicate in a professional fashion	Lesson 3, Topic B
• Adapt procedural behavior according to different situations and environments	Lesson 3, Topic B
• Imaging room	Lesson 3, Topic B
■ Procedural room	Lesson 3, Topic B
■ Recovery room	Lesson 3, Topic B
■ Examination room	Lesson 3, Topic B
■ Float room	Lesson 3, Topic B
■ Emergency room	Lesson 3, Topic B
• Adapt social behavior based on sensitivity of the environment	Lesson 3, Topic B
• Use proper sanitation steps - follow medical precautionary guidelines	Lesson 3, Topic E
• Conform to requirements set forth by project manager	Lesson 3, Topic B

Exam Objective	CompTIA Healthcare IT Technician Lesson and Topic Reference
Domain 3.0 IT Operations	
3.1 Identify commonly used IT terms and technologies.	
• Protocol terms	Lesson 4, Topic B
■ TCP/IP	Lesson 4, Topic B
■ DNS	Lesson 4, Topic B
■ DHCP	Lesson 4, Topic B
■ FTP	Lesson 4, Topic B
■ Wireless (802.11x)	Lesson 4, Topic B
■ RDP	Lesson 4, Topic B
• Devices	Lesson 4, Topic B
■ Switch	Lesson 4, Topic B
■ Domain controller	Lesson 4, Topic B
■ Printer server	Lesson 4, Topic B

Exam Objective	CompTIA Healthcare IT Technician Lesson and Topic Reference
Domain 3.0 IT Operations	
3.1 Identify commonly used IT terms and technologies.	
• Industry terms	Lesson 4, Topics B and C Lesson 5, Topic D
■ ASP	Lesson 5, Topic D
■ ISP	Lesson 4, Topic C
■ Client-server model	Lesson 5, Topic D
■ Mainframe	Lesson 4, Topic B
■ Cloud Computing	Lesson 4, Topic C
■ Virtualization	Lesson 4, Topic C
■ Terminal services	Lesson 4, Topic C
■ APIs	Lesson 4, Topic C
■ Fiber	Lesson 4, Topic B
• Languages	Lesson 4, Topic C
■ XML	Lesson 4, Topic C
■ SQL	Lesson 4, Topic C
■ HTML	Lesson 4, Topic C
■ Flash	Lesson 4, Topic C
■ PHP	Lesson 4, Topic C
■ ASP	Lesson 4, Topic C

Exam Objective	CompTIA Healthcare IT Technician Lesson and Topic Reference
3.2 Demonstrate the ability to set up a basic PC workstation within an EHR/ EMR environment.	
• Basic installation, configuration and maintenance procedures	Lesson 5, Topic A
• Basics of operating systems, mouse, keyboard, monitor and applications	Lesson 4, Topic A

Exam Objective	CompTIA Healthcare IT Technician Lesson and Topic Reference
3.3 Given a scenario, troubleshoot and solve common PC problems.	
• Malfunctioning hardware	Lesson 5, Topic B

Exam Objective	CompTIA Healthcare IT Technician Lesson and Topic Reference
3.3 Given a scenario, troubleshoot and solve common PC problems.	
■ Mouse	Lesson 5, Topic B
■ Printer	Lesson 5, Topic B
■ Power	Lesson 5, Topic B
■ Monitor	Lesson 5, Topic B
■ Cables	Lesson 5, Topic B
● Software patches/hotfixes/updates	Lesson 5, Topic B
● Documentation	Lesson 3, Topic C Lesson 4, Topic A Lesson 6, Topic B

Exam Objective	CompTIA Healthcare IT Technician Lesson and Topic Reference
3.4 Install and configure hardware drivers and devices.	
● Imaging devices	Lesson 4, Topic D
■ Barcode scanner	Lesson 4, Topic D
■ Document scanner	Lesson 4, Topic D
■ Card/badge scanner	Lesson 4, Topic D
■ Fax printer	Lesson 4, Topic D
■ Camera	Lesson 4, Topic D
■ Signature pads	Lesson 4, Topic D
● Physical interfaces	Lesson 4, Topic D
■ USB	Lesson 4, Topic D
■ IEEE 1394	Lesson 4, Topic D
■ SCSI	Lesson 4, Topic D
■ Serial	Lesson 4, Topic D
■ Bluetooth	Lesson 4, Topic D
● Mobile storage devices	Lesson 4, Topic D
■ Flash drives	Lesson 4, Topic D
■ External hard drives	Lesson 4, Topic D
■ DVDs	Lesson 4, Topic D
■ CDs	Lesson 4, Topic D
■ Tapes	Lesson 4, Topic D

Exam Objective	CompTIA Healthcare IT Technician Lesson and Topic Reference
3.4 Install and configure hardware drivers and devices.	
■ SD cards	Lesson 4, Topic D
• Mobile devices	Lesson 4, Topic D
■ Tablet PCs	Lesson 4, Topic D
■ Smart phones	Lesson 4, Topic D
■ Portable media players	Lesson 4, Topic D

Exam Objective	CompTIA Healthcare IT Technician Lesson and Topic Reference
3.5 Compare and contrast basic client networks and tools.	
• DHCP vs. static IP	Lesson 4, Topic B
• Adhoc vs. infrastructure	Lesson 4, Topic B
• Command line prompts	Lesson 4, Topic B
■ ping	Lesson 4, Topic B
■ ipconfig	Lesson 4, Topic B
■ tracert	Lesson 4, Topic B

Exam Objective	CompTIA Healthcare IT Technician Lesson and Topic Reference
3.6 Set up basic network devices and apply basic configuration settings.	
• Wireless access point	Lesson 4, Topics B and D Lesson 6, Topic D
■ Security settings	Lesson 4, Topic D Lesson 6, Topic D
■ SSID	Lesson 4, Topic D
■ Guest network	Lesson 4, Topic D
■ Access point placement	Lesson 4, Topic D
• Router	Lesson 3, Topic D Lesson 4, Topic B
■ DHCP	Lesson 3, Topic D
■ Port forwarding	Lesson 4, Topic B
• Internet modem	Lesson 4, Topic B

Exam Objective	CompTIA Healthcare IT Technician Lesson and Topic Reference
3.7 Given a scenario, troubleshoot and solve common network problems.	
• Cabling	Lesson 4, Topic B Lesson 5, Topic B
• Power	Lesson 5, Topic B Lesson 5, Topic C
• IP settings	Lesson 5, Topic B
• ISP	Lesson 5, Topic B
• Interference	Lesson 4, Topic B Lesson 5, Topic B
• Signal issues	Lesson 5, Topic B

Exam Objective	CompTIA Healthcare IT Technician Lesson and Topic Reference
3.8 Explain the features of different backup configurations and the associated maintenance practices.	
• Daily	Lesson 6, Topic E
• Differential	Lesson 6, Topic E
• Incremental	Lesson 6, Topic E
• Archive flags	Lesson 6, Topic E

Exam Objective	CompTIA Healthcare IT Technician Lesson and Topic Reference
3.9 Classify different server types, environments, features, and limitations.	
• Database server	Lesson 4, Topic C
• Application server	Lesson 4, Topic C
• Interfaces	Lesson 1, Topic C
• Physical connections	Lesson 4, Topic D
• Server load and utilization	Lesson 4, Topic C
• Application services	Lesson 4, Topic C
• OS and application interoperability	Lesson 4, Topic C
• Storage space limitations based on application usage and electronic record storage	Lesson 5, Topic D

Exam Objective	CompTIA Healthcare IT Technician Lesson and Topic Reference
3.10 Compare and contrast EHR/EMR technologies and how each is implemented.	
• ASP/Cloud vs. client-server (locally-hosted)	Lesson 5, Topic D
• Browser vs. installed application vs. terminal/ remote access	Lesson 5, Topic D
• Hardware requirements	Lesson 5, Topic D

Exam Objective	CompTIA Healthcare IT Technician Lesson and Topic Reference
Domain 4.0 Medical Business Operations	
4.1 Identify commonly used medical terms and devices.	
• Interfaces	Lesson 2, Topic C Lesson 2, Topic D
■ HL7	Lesson 2, Topic D
■ e-Prescribing	Lesson 2, Topic D
■ CCD	Lesson 2, Topic D
■ CCR	Lesson 2, Topic D
■ ICD–10	Lesson 2, Topic C
■ CPT	Lesson 2, Topic C
■ SNOMED CT	Lesson 2, Topic C
■ NDC ID	Lesson 2, Topic C
■ PACS	Lesson 2, Topic D
■ E/M codes	Lesson 2, Topic C
• Devices	Lesson 2, Topic B
■ Portable x-ray machine	Lesson 2, Topic B
■ MRI	Lesson 2, Topic B
■ Vitals cuff	Lesson 2, Topic B
■ EKG	Lesson 2, Topic B
■ EEG	Lesson 2, Topic B
■ Ultrasound	Lesson 2, Topic B
■ PET	Lesson 2, Topic B
■ CT	Lesson 2, Topic B
■ Vascular/nuclear stress test	Lesson 2, Topic B

Exam Objective	CompTIA Healthcare IT Technician Lesson and Topic Reference
Domain 4.0 Medical Business Operations	
4.1 Identify commonly used medical terms and devices.	
■ Glucose monitor	Lesson 2, Topic B
● Clinical software and modules	Lesson 2, Topic B
■ Patient tracking	Lesson 2, Topic B
■ Scheduling	Lesson 2, Topic B
■ Order entry	Lesson 2, Topic B
■ Practice management	Lesson 2, Topic B
■ Billing/coding	Lesson 2, Topic B
■ Tracking/auditing	Lesson 2, Topic B
● Basic clinical terms	Lesson 2, Topic B
■ Imaging	Lesson 2, Topic B
■ PCP	Lesson 2, Topic B
■ Stat	Lesson 2, Topic B
■ Acuity	Lesson 2, Topic B
■ Code blue/rapid response	Lesson 2, Topic B
■ Trauma levels	Lesson 2, Topic B
■ Controlled substance (levels)	Lesson 2, Topic B
■ EHR/EMR	Lesson 2, Topics A and B
● Common medical departments	Lesson 2, Topic A
■ Inpatient	Lesson 2, Topic A
OB/GYN	Lesson 2, Topic A
ONC	Lesson 2, Topic A
PEDS	Lesson 2, Topic A
FBC/L&D/Stork/NICU	Lesson 2, Topic A
ICU/CCU	Lesson 2, Topic A
TCU/PCU	Lesson 2, Topic A
MED/SURG	Lesson 2, Topic A
Behavior health	Lesson 2, Topic A
PACU	Lesson 2, Topic A
OR/UR	Lesson 2, Topic A
ER	Lesson 2, Topic A
■ Outpatient	Lesson 2, Topic A

Exam Objective	CompTIA Healthcare IT Technician Lesson and Topic Reference
Domain 4.0 Medical Business Operations	
4.1 Identify commonly used medical terms and devices.	
OB/GYN	Lesson 2, Topic A
ONC	Lesson 2, Topic A
PEDS	Lesson 2, Topic A
Plastic surgery	Lesson 2, Topic A
ENT	Lesson 2, Topic A
Respiratory	Lesson 2, Topic A
Physical therapy	Lesson 2, Topic A
Cardiovascular	Lesson 2, Topic A
Occupational therapy	Lesson 2, Topic A
Ambulatory/day surgery	Lesson 2, Topic A
Radiology	Lesson 2, Topic A
Laboratory	Lesson 2, Topic A
Ophthalmology	Lesson 2, Topic A
Dermatology	Lesson 2, Topic A
Nuclear	Lesson 2, Topic A

Exam Objective	CompTIA Healthcare IT Technician Lesson and Topic Reference
4.2 Explain aspects of a typical clinical environment.	
● Basic workflow	Lesson 2, Topic A
■ Registration	Lesson 2, Topic A
■ Consultation	Lesson 2, Topic A
■ Examination	Lesson 2, Topic A
● Clinical processes	Lesson 2, Topics A and B
■ Computerized physician order entry	Lesson 2, Topics A and B
■ Transcription	Lesson 2, Topic A
■ Dictation	Lesson 2, Topic A
■ Referrals/consults	Lesson 2, Topic A
■ Digital signatures	Lesson 2, Topic A

Exam Objective	CompTIA Healthcare IT Technician Lesson and Topic Reference
4.3 Identify and label different components of medical interfaces.	
• HL7	Lesson 2, Topic D
■ Standard contents	Lesson 2, Topic D
■ Provider types	Lesson 2, Topic D
■ AL1	Lesson 2, Topic D
■ BLG	Lesson 2, Topic D
■ IN1	Lesson 2, Topic D
■ MSH	Lesson 2, Topic D
■ OBR	Lesson 2, Topic D
■ PID	Lesson 2, Topic D
■ SCH	Lesson 2, Topic D
• e-Prescribing	Lesson 2, Topic D
■ Medication reconciliation	Lesson 2, Topic D
■ Bedside medication verification	Lesson 2, Topic D
■ Allergy interactions	Lesson 2, Topic D
■ Formulary checking	Lesson 2, Topic D
• Billing	Lesson 2, Topics C and D
■ EMR/EHR outbound communication	Lesson 2, Topic C
■ Types of codes	Lesson 2, Topics C and D
■ Clearinghouse	Lesson 2, Topic C

Exam Objective	CompTIA Healthcare IT Technician Lesson and Topic Reference
4.4 Determine common interface problems and escalate when necessary.	
• HL7	Lesson 5, Topic C
■ Threads/nodes deactivated	Lesson 5, Topic C
■ Improperly formatted patient demographics	Lesson 5, Topic C
■ Communication link (fax, network, Internet)	Lesson 5, Topic C
• e-Prescribing	Lesson 5, Topic C
■ Improperly formatted patient demographics	Lesson 5, Topic C
■ Improperly formatted script	Lesson 5, Topic C
■ Deactivated medication	Lesson 5, Topic C

Exam Objective	CompTIA Healthcare IT Technician Lesson and Topic Reference
4.4 Determine common interface problems and escalate when necessary.	
■ Controlled substance	Lesson 5, Topic C
■ Communication link (fax, network, Internet)	Lesson 5, Topic C
● Medical devices	Lesson 5, Topic C
■ Power	Lesson 5, Topic C
■ Network	Lesson 5, Topic C
■ I/O	Lesson 5, Topic C
■ Configuration settings	Lesson 5, Topic C
● Billing	Lesson 5, Topic C
■ Improperly formatted patient demographics	Lesson 5, Topic C
■ Improperly formatted superbill	Lesson 5, Topic C
■ Communication link (fax, network, Internet)	Lesson 5, Topic C
■ I/O	Lesson 5, Topic C
■ Software configuration settings	Lesson 5, Topic C

Exam Objective	CompTIA Healthcare IT Technician Lesson and Topic Reference
4.5 Explain the basics of document imaging.	
● File types	Lesson 3, Topic D
■ TIFF	Lesson 3, Topic D
■ PDF	Lesson 3, Topic D
■ JPG	Lesson 3, Topic D
■ GIF	Lesson 3, Topic D
● Characteristics	Lesson 3, Topic D
■ Quality	Lesson 3, Topic D
■ Size	Lesson 3, Topic D
■ Resolution	Lesson 3, Topic D
■ Compression	Lesson 3, Topic D
● Scanning and indexing	Lesson 3, Topic D
■ Metadata	Lesson 3, Topic D
■ Storage and retrieval	Lesson 3, Topic D
● OCR and structured data	Lesson 5, Topic D

Exam Objective	CompTIA Healthcare IT Technician Lesson and Topic Reference
4.6 Given a scenario, determine common clinical software problems.	
● Locate the affected modules or fields	Lesson 5, Topic C
● Determine file/data types	Lesson 5, Topic C
● Escalation procedures to proper support tier	Lesson 5, Topic C
■ Vendor or local application support	Lesson 5, Topic C

Exam Objective	CompTIA Healthcare IT Technician Lesson and Topic Reference
4.7 Describe change control best practices and its system-wide effects.	
● Procedural systematic customization	Lesson 5, Topic E
● Governance board	Lesson 5, Topic E
● System patching/updates	Lesson 5, Topic E
● Appropriate scheduling	Lesson 5, Topic E
● Change control environments	Lesson 5, Topic E
■ Development	Lesson 5, Topic E
■ QA/test	Lesson 5, Topic E
■ User test	Lesson 5, Topic E
■ Production/live	Lesson 5, Topic E

Exam Objective	CompTIA Healthcare IT Technician Lesson and Topic Reference
Domain 5.0 Security	
5.1 Explain physical security controls.	
● Locations for:	Lesson 6, Topic A
■ Servers	Lesson 6, Topic A
■ Network hardware	Lesson 6, Topic A
■ Printers	Lesson 6, Topic A
■ Scanners	Lesson 6, Topic A
■ Copiers	Lesson 6, Topic A
● Access	Lesson 6, Topic A
■ Servers	Lesson 6, Topic A
■ Office	Lesson 6, Topic A

Exam Objective	CompTIA Healthcare IT Technician Lesson and Topic Reference
Domain 5.0 Security	
5.1 Explain physical security controls.	
■ Data closet	Lesson 6, Topic A
■ IDF/MDF	Lesson 6, Topic A
■ Backups	Lesson 6, Topic A
■ Keyfobs	Lesson 6, Topic A
■ Keyfobs	Lesson 6, Topic A
■ Biometrics	Lesson 6, Topic A
● Environmental	Lesson 5, Topic C Lesson 6, Topic A
■ HVAC	Lesson 6, Topic A
■ Security lighting	Lesson 6, Topic A
■ Surveillance	Lesson 6, Topic A
■ Fire suppression	Lesson 6, Topic A
■ Personnel	Lesson 6, Topic A
■ Generator	Lesson 5, Topic C
● Office hardware	Lesson 5, Topics B and C Lesson 6, Topic A
■ Locks	Lesson 6, Topic A
■ Door locks	Lesson 6, Topic A
■ Biometrics	Lesson 6, Topic A
■ Privacy screens	Lesson 6, Topic A
■ UPS	Lesson 5, Topics B and C Lesson 6, Topic A

Exam Objective	CompTIA Healthcare IT Technician Lesson and Topic Reference
Domain 5.0 Security	
5.2 Summarize the different encryption types and when each is used.	
● Types	Lesson 6, Topic A
■ SSL	Lesson 6, Topic A
■ DES	Lesson 6, Topic A
■ AES	Lesson 6, Topic A
■ 3DES	Lesson 6, Topic A

Exam Objective	CompTIA Healthcare IT Technician Lesson and Topic Reference
Domain 5.0 Security	
5.2 Summarize the different encryption types and when each is used.	
■ PGP	Lesson 6, Topic A
• Communication	Lesson 6, Topic A
■ Email	Lesson 6, Topic A
■ Chat	Lesson 6, Topic A
■ Smart phone	Lesson 6, Topic A
■ Collaboration sites	Lesson 6, Topic A
■ FTP sites	Lesson 6, Topic A
■ Phones	Lesson 6, Topic A
■ VoIP	Lesson 6, Topic A
■ Fax	Lesson 6, Topic A
• Storage	Lesson 6, Topic A
■ Flash drives	Lesson 6, Topic A
■ PCs	Lesson 6, Topic A
■ Laptops	Lesson 6, Topic A
■ SD cards	Lesson 6, Topic A
■ External drives	Lesson 6, Topic A
■ Servers	Lesson 6, Topic A
■ NAS	Lesson 6, Topic A
■ SAN	Lesson 6, Topic A
• Dissemination of PHI	Lesson 1, Topics A and D

Exam Objective	CompTIA Healthcare IT Technician Lesson and Topic Reference
5.3 Apply best practices when creating and communicating passwords.	
• Communication of passwords	Lesson 6, Topic B
• Storage of passwords	Lesson 6, Topic B
• Password strength (complexity/length)	Lesson 6, Topic B
• Password reuse	Lesson 6, Topic B

Exam Objective	CompTIA Healthcare IT Technician Lesson and Topic Reference
5.4 Classify permission levels based on roles.	
• Read	Lesson 6, Topic A
• Write	Lesson 6, Topic A
• Modify	Lesson 6, Topic A
• Full access	Lesson 6, Topic A

Exam Objective	CompTIA Healthcare IT Technician Lesson and Topic Reference
5.5 Identify different remote access methods and security controls.	
• RDC	Lesson 4, Topic B
• VPN	Lesson 6, Topic C
• Remote control applications	Lesson 4, Topic B
• Terminal emulation	Lesson 4, Topic C
• L2TP	Lesson 6, Topic C
• SSH	Lesson 6, Topic A
• HTTPS	Lesson 6, Topic A
• SFTP	Lesson 3, Topic B

Exam Objective	CompTIA Healthcare IT Technician Lesson and Topic Reference
5.6 Recognize wireless security protocols and best practices.	
• WEP	Lesson 6, Topic D
• WPA	Lesson 6, Topic D
• WPA2	Lesson 6, Topic D
• AES	Lesson 6, Topics A and D
• RADIUS	Lesson 6, Topic A
• SSID naming	Lesson 4, Topic D Lesson 6, Topic D
• MAC filtering	Lesson 4, Topic D Lesson 6, Topic D
• Site surveys	Lesson 4, Topic D
• Access point placement	Lesson 4, Topic D Lesson 6, Topic D

Exam Objective	CompTIA Healthcare IT Technician Lesson and Topic Reference
5.7 Implement best practices in secure disposal of electronic or physical PHI.	
• Secure shredding	Lesson 3, Topic D
• Degaussing	Lesson 3, Topic D
• Sanitizing	Lesson 3, Topic D

Exam Objective	CompTIA Healthcare IT Technician Lesson and Topic Reference
5.8 Implement backup procedures based on disaster recovery policies.	
• Deployment, configuration, and testing of back-ups	Lesson 6, Topic E
• Backup storage (offsite, courier, onsite)	Lesson 6, Topic E
• Methods of secure transfer	Lesson 6, Topic E
• Backup inventory	Lesson 6, Topic E

Exam Objective	CompTIA Healthcare IT Technician Lesson and Topic Reference
5.9 Identify common security risks and their prevention methods.	
• Social engineering – user training	Lesson 6, Topics A and B
• Phishing – user training	Lesson 6, Topic B
• Spamming – filters	Lesson 6, Topic B
• Malware – access control	Lesson 6, Topic B
• Spyware – anti-spyware	Lesson 6, Topic B

B CompTIA Acronyms

The following is a list of acronyms that may appear on the CompTIA Healthcare IT Technician exam. Candidates are encouraged to review the complete list and attain a working knowledge of all listed acronyms as a part of a comprehensive exam preparation program.

Acronym	***Associated Term***
ACL	access control list
AGP	accelerated graphics port
AMD	advanced micro devices
ARRA	American Reinvestment Recovery Act
ASC	Ambulatory Surgery Center
ATA	advanced technology attachment
BA	Business Associate
BAA	Business Associate Agreement
BIOS	basic input/output system
BP	Blood Pressure
CCD	Continuity of Care Document
CCR	Continuity of Care Record
CCU	Critical Care Unit
CD	compact disc
CDC	Centers for Disease Control
CD-ROM	compact disc-read-only memory
CD-RW	compact disc-rewritable
CDS	Cardiac Diagnostic Services
CFR	Code of Federal Regulation
CMOS	complementary metal-oxide semiconductor
CMS	Center for Medicare Services
CNA	Certified Nursing Assistant
CPOE	Computerized Physician Order Entry
CPT	Current Procedural Terminology
CPU	central processing unit
CRN	Clinical Resource Nurse
CSW	Clinical Social Worker

Acronym	Associated Term
CT	Computerized Tomography
DA	Dental Assistant
DB-25	serial communications D-shell connector, 25 pins
DB-9	9 pin D shell connector
DDOS	distributed denial of service
DDR	double data-rate
DDR RAM	double data-rate random access memory
DDR SDRAM	double data-rate synchronous dynamic random access memory
DHCP	dynamic host configuration protocol
DIMM	dual inline memory module
DLP	digital light processing
DMZ	demilitarized zone
DODNS	domain name service or domain name server
DO	Doctor of Osteopathy
DRP	Disaster Recovery Plan
DSL	digital subscriber line
DVD	digital video disc or digital versatile disc
DVD-RAM	digital video disc-random access memory
DVD-ROM	digital video disc-read only memory
DVD-R	digital video disc-recordable
DVD-RW	digital video disc-rewritable
E/M	Evaluation and Management Code
EEG	Electro Encephalogram
EHR	Electronic Health Record
EKG/ECG	ElectroCardiogram
EMI	electromagnetic interference
EMR	Electronic Medical Record
ENT	Ear, Nose, and Throat
EP	Eligible Provider
ePHI	Electronic Personal Health Information
ER	Emergency Room
ESD	electrostatic discharge
FAT	file allocation table
FAT32	32-bit file allocation table
FBC	Family Birthing Center
FDA	Food and Drug Administration
FQND	fully qualified domain name
FTP	file transfer protocol
FQDN	fully qualified domain name
Gb	gigabit

Acronym	Associated Term
GB	gigabyte
GHz	gigahertz
GUI	graphical user interface
H&P	History and Physical
HCL	hardware compatibility list
HDD	hard disk drive
HDMi	high definition media interface
HHS	Health and Human Services
HIPAA	Health Information Portability and Accountability Act
HITECH	Health Information Technology
HL7	Health Level 7
HTML	hypertext markup language
HTTP	hypertext transfer protocol
HTTPS	hypertext transfer protocol over secure sockets layer
HVAC	Heating Ventilation and Air Conditioning
I/O	input/output
ICD	International Code of Diseases
ICR	intelligent character recognition
ICU	Intensive Care Unit
IDE	integrated drive electronics
IDS	Intrusion Detection System
IEEE	Institute of Electrical and Electronics Engineers
IP	internet protocol
IPCONFIG	internet protocol configuration
IPSEC	internet protocol security
ISP	Internet Service Provider
Kb	kilobit
KB	Kilobyte or knowledge base
L&D	Labor and Delivery
LAN	local area network
LCD	liquid crystal display
LOINC	Logical Observation Identifiers Names and Codes
LPN	Licensed Practitioner Nurse
LVN	Licensed Vocational Nurse
MA	Medical Assistant
MAC	media access control / mandatory access control
Mb	megabit
MB	megabyte
MFD	multi-function device
MFP	multi-function product

Acronym	Associated Term
MHz	megahertz
MOU	Memorandum of Understanding
MP3	Moving Picture Experts Group Layer 3 Audio
MP4	Moving Picture Experts Group Layer 4
MPEG	Moving Picture Experts Group
MRI	Magnetic Resonance Imaging
MSCONFIG	Microsoft configuration
NAS	network-attached storage
NAT	network address translation
NDCID	National Drug Code Identifier
NIC	network interface card
NICU	Neonatal Intensive Care Unit
NIST	National Institute of Standards and Technology
NP	Nurse Practitioner
NTFS	new technology file system
OCR	optical character recognition
OB/GYN	Obstetrics and Gynecology
OBR	Observation Request
OCR	optical character recognition
OCR	Office of Civil Rights
ODBC	open database connectivity
OEM	original equipment manufacturer
ONC	Oncology
ONC	Office of the National Coordinator
ONC-ATCB	Office of the National Coordinator — Authorized Temporary and Certification Body
OR	Operating Room
OS	operating system
OT	Occupational Therapist
PA	Physician Assistant
PACS	Picture Archiving Communication System
PACU	Post Anesthesia Care Unit
PC	personal computer
PCI	peripheral component interconnect
PCIe	peripheral component interconnect express
PCIX	peripheral component interconnect extended
PCP	Primary Care Physician
PCT	Patient Care Technician
PCU	Progressive Care Unit

Acronym	Associated Term
PEDS	Pediatrics
PET	Positron Emission Tomography
PGP	Pretty Good Privacy
PHI	Protected Health Information
PHR	Personal Health Record
PKI	public key infrastructure
PM	Project Manager
PM	Practice Manager
POP3	post office protocol 3
POST	power-on self test
PPACA	Patient Privacy and Affordable Care Act
PS/2	personal system/2 connector
PT	Physical Therapist
QA	Quality Assurance
QC	Quality Control
RAID	redundant array of independent (or inexpensive) discs
RAM	random access memory
RDP	Remote Desktop Protocol
RF	radio frequency
RFI	radio frequency interference
RGB	red green blue
RISC	reduced instruction set computer
RJ	registered jack
RJ-11	registered jack function 11
RJ-45	registered jack function 45
RN	Registered Nurse
ROM	read only memory
RS-232 or RS-232C	recommended standard 232
RT	Respiratory Therapist
S.M.A.R.T.	self-monitoring, analysis, and reporting technology
SAN	storage area network
SATA	serial advanced technology attachment
SCSI	small computer system interface
SCSI ID	small computer system interface identifier
SD card	secure digital card
SDRAM	synchronous dynamic random access memory
SIMM	single inline memory module
SLA	Service-Level Agreement
SMTP	simple mail transport protocol
SNMP	simple network management protocol

Acronym	Associated Term
SoDIMM	small outline dual inline memory module
SOHO	small office/home office
SRAM	static random access memory
SSH	secure shell
SSID	service set identifier
SSL	secure sockets layer
STP	shielded twisted pair
SVGA	super video graphics array
TB	terabyte
TCP	transmission control protocol
TCP/IP	transmission control protocol/internet protocol
TCU	Transitional Care Unit
UA	Unit Assistant
UPS	uninterruptible power supply
URL	uniform resource locator
URO	Urology
USB	universal serial bus
VGA	video graphics array
VoIP	voice over internet protocol
VPN	virtual private network
WAN	wide area network
WAP	wireless application protocol
WEP	wired equivalent privacy
WIFI	wireless fidelity
WLAN	wireless local area network
WPA	wireless protected access

Solutions

Lesson 1

Activity 1-1

1. **Which of the following are true of protected health information? (Select all that apply.)**

   ✓ a) It is personally identifiable.

   ✓ b) It is protected by law.

   c) It is stored by the government.

   d) It is not accessible by the patient.

2. **Which one or more of the following are true of legal health records?**

   ✓ a) They are personally identifiable.

   b) They are the same everywhere.

   c) They are always on paper.

   ✓ d) They contain specific treatment information.

3. **True or False? EHRs often contain multiple EMRs.**

   ✓ True

   __ False

4. **What is the significance of the word "accountability" in the HIPAA acronym?**

   Because the Privacy Rule and Security Rule mandate how information is accessed and stored, accountability represents who is responsible for keeping that information secured.

5. **Visit any of the websites mentioned in this topic and spend some time exploring and researching the various core concepts. What were your findings?**

   Answers will vary, but may include locating information on HIPAA regulations.

Activity 1-2

1. **Which of the following are features of an EHR system? (Select all that apply.)**
   - a) Automated diagnosis
   - ✓ b) Note taking
   - ✓ c) Referral management
   - d) Staff recruiting
   - ✓ e) e-Prescribing
2. **Which of the following are benefits of an EHR system? (Select all that apply.)**
   - ✓ a) More complete patient profiles
   - b) Reduced potential for audits
   - ✓ c) Increased efficiency
   - ✓ d) Increased regulatory compliance
3. **Have you had any personal experience with an EHR system?**

   Answers will vary, but might include having a prescription submitted electronically.
4. **What potential road blocks do you foresee with an EHR implementation?**

   Answers will vary, but may include needing additional IT staff to support the system.

Activity 1-3

1. **HHS is responsible for which of the following? (Select all that apply.)**
   - ✓ a) Medicare
   - ✓ b) Medicaid
   - ✓ c) Healthcare IT regulation
   - d) Accrediting hospitals
2. **True or False? Most healthcare providers and facilities can be considered covered entities.**

   ✓ True

   __ False

Activity 1-4

1. **Which statements are true about ROI?**
   - ✓ a) It is subject to the HIPAA Privacy Rule
   - ✓ b) It is usually under the HIM department.
   - c) It is more concerned with security than privacy.

2. Research the HIPAA Privacy and Security Rules using the websites listed in this topic. What type of information did you find? Was anything familiar to you?

Answers will vary but may include a full description of the rules, as well as some background history information.

Lesson 2

Activity 2-1

1. A 67-year-old woman falls down in her home, breaking her hip and hitting her head, cutting it open. She is rushed to the hospital, where she is treated for the head wound and has hip replacement surgery, and is recovering well. Based on the knowledge of the different departments in an organization, which of the following departments would the woman likely come in contact with throughout her treatment? (Select all that apply.)

✓ a) ED

b) Cardiovascular department

✓ c) Perioperative Services

✓ d) Radiology

e) ICU

2. True or False? A public hospital cannot be a teaching hospital.

__ True

✓ False

3. A married couple needs to determine a healthcare plan for themselves that will suit their immediate needs and for the coming years. She was recently diagnosed with the onset of Alzheimer's disease, and he takes daily medication for diabetes management, but is otherwise mentally and physically healthy. Of the following healthcare organizations, which would make the best choice to fulfill their healthcare needs now and over time?

a) Nursing home

✓ b) Continuing care facility

c) Intermediate care facility

d) Home healthcare

Activity 2-2

1. Match the medical term on the left with the correct definition on the right.

a	Acuity	a.	The level of severity of a patient's illness or disease.
c	Preceptor	b.	A medical facility equipped to treat patients suffering from life-threatening injuries.
d	Scope of practice	c.	A senior, skilled medical staff member who serves as an instructor or supervisor to medical students or new hires in training.
b	Trauma center	d.	The procedures, processes, or actions, as defined by state and national licensing boards, that are permitted for an individual in a particular licensing area, usually driven by criteria such as specific education and experience requirements.

2. Dr. Michaels and two of his colleagues are opening a private practice. They went to move to a paperless system for their patients. Which software system would make the most sense for them to implement at their office?

a) Patient tracking

b) Order entry

✓ c) Practice management

d) Scheduling

3. Match the type of medical imaging process with the correct description on the right.

b	MRI	a. A radioactive chemical, called a radiotracer, is injected into the bloodstream and is absorbed by the organs and tissues and a scanner detects and records the radioactive energy given off by the radiotracer to create a three-dimensional image.
d	EEG	b. High-powered magnetic fields and radio frequencies are used to scan and create images of the body. Provides good contrast for soft tissues, making it an especially useful tool for imaging the brain, muscles, heart, other organs, and cancers.
f	EKG	c. A series of X-rays taken of the same area from different angles to generate a three-dimensional image of an area of the body,
a	PET	d. Electrodes are placed on the scalp to record the electrical activity of the brain produced with neural communications.
c	CT	e. High-frequency sound waves are used to reflect or echo off of a boundary within the body to create a two- or three-dimensional image.
e	Ultrasound	f. Electrodes are placed on the outer surface of the skin and a special machine detects and records the electrical activity of the heart produced with each heartbeat.

Activity 2-3

1. Of the following statements, which most accurately explains the importance of medical billing and coding in the healthcare industry?

a) Medical professionals need to get paid appropriately for the services they provide.

✓ b) There are so many different types of systems using various codes, there needs to be some consistent system for patient data and payment purposes.

c) Patients need to be able to feel comfortable that their information can be transferred between professionals with no mistakes.

d) Medical professionals need to be able to quickly and efficiently record and store pertinent patient information.

2. Match the type of medical coding systems to the correct description.

b	ICD-10	a.	Numeric codes used to describe a medical professional-patient interaction.
d	SNOMED CT	b.	Classification list of numeric codes used to describe diseases, signs and symptoms, etc.
c	NDC ID	c.	A unique numeric code used to identify registered drugs.
a	E/M Codes	d.	An organized collection of numeric codes correlating to clinical information.

3. **Which of the following describes the complete medical coding and billing process most accurately?**

✓ a) The codes for services rendered are determined. The claim is generated. The billing clearinghouse scrubs the claim. The claim is submitted to the insurance company. The insurance company accepts or rejects the claim.

b) The codes for services rendered are determined. The claim is generated. The claim is submitted to the insurance company. The insurance company accepts or rejects the claim.

c) The codes for services rendered are determined. The billing clearinghouse scrubs the claim. The claim is submitted to the insurance company. The insurance company accepts or rejects the claim.

d) The codes for services rendered are determined. The claim is generated. The billing clearinghouse scrubs the claim. The claim is submitted to the insurance company. The insurance company automatically accepts the claim.

Activity 2-4

1. **Match the prescription-related term on the left with the correct description on the right.**

c	Medication reconciliation	a.	The automatic process of checking a prescription for medication against a patient's known allergies (drug-allergy) and current medications for possible adverse interactions (drug-drug) immediately when it is prescribed in the e-prescription system.
b	Bedside medication verification	b.	A checks-and-balances system that ensures that a patient is receiving the correct medication, the correct dose of medication, at the correct time, from an authorized caregiver by requiring verification of patient, medication, and possibly dispensing personnel prior to the medication being dispensed.
a	Formulary checking	c.	A process that involves comparing a list of a patient's medication orders to a list of those that the patient has been taking to avoid any possible medication errors such as duplicated prescriptions, errors in dosage, or potentially hazardous drug interactions.

2. Which of the following steps would potentially take place during bedside medication verification? (Select all that apply.)

✓ a) The patient's wristband is scanned.

b) The ID of the dispensary personnel is scanned.

✓ c) The barcode on the medication label is scanned.

✓ d) The ID of the administering personnel is scanned.

e) The ID of the provider who prescribed the medication is scanned.

3. Match the interface-related term on the left with the correct description on the right.

d	HL7	a. A health record standard that was developed as a means of creating summary documents containing the most relevant and pertinent information about a patient that can be shared electronically between medical caregivers, regardless of their respective EMR or EHR software applications.
c	PACS	b. A health record standard designed to provide guidelines for creating summary documents containing the most pertinent patient information, which can be shared electronically between medical caregivers regardless of their respective EMR or EHR system, but uses standards from both HL7 and ASTM.
b	CCD	c. An application system where medical images of almost all kinds, including MRIs, CAT scans, ultrasounds, mammograms, etc., can be stored and retrieved electronically.
a	CCR	d. Healthcare industry standards and a framework concerning the exchange and integration of a patients's electronic information between software systems.

Lesson 3

Activity 3-1

1. **One of the medical facilities you support has contacted you because they cannot connect the EMR/EHR system to access the patient billing web-based application. When you arrive at the office and check out the situation, you determine that she can connect to the Internet, but not the billing application. You determine that the issue has to do with the EMR/EHR in-house server. Who should you contact for server issues?**

   a) Security administrator

   b) Network administrator

   c) DBA

   ✓ d) Systems administrator

2. **When is break glass access necessary in a medical setting?**

   Break glass access is necessary when a clinician must access information that has been classified as highly sensitive within the EMR/EHR system. This can happen in an emergency situation, when a clinician needs to check a patient's medical record for medication reactions and other pre-existing medical conditions.

3. **In the hospital where you work as an IT support technician, there has been a breach in security within the ED. Someone has reported that a laptop has been stolen. The laptop was a shared device for updating and tracking all ED patient information. What medical roles will this impact?**

   Because this environment is limited to the ED, most likely the medical personnel impacted are MDs, RNs, PAs, and LPNs.

Activity 3-2

1. **Match each communication skill or behavior with the appropriate example.**

f	Verbal communication	a.	Allow the user to complete statements without interruption.
g	Non-verbal communication	b.	Project professionalism by being neat and clean.
a	Listening skills	c.	Do not use information gained during a service call for your personal benefit.
e	Respect	d.	Keep sensitive client information to yourself.
c	Ethical behavior	e.	Ask permission before sitting down in a user's chair or touching a user's computer.
d	Confidentiality	f.	Use clear, concise, and direct statements.
b	Appearance	g.	Maintain the proper amount of eye contact.

2. **Which are examples of displaying respect during a service call?**

   ✓ a) Asking permission before changing display settings

   b) Asking "What happened just before you noticed the problem?"

   c) Sitting in a user's chair without permission

   ✓ d) Silencing your pager or mobile phone

3. **You have been informed that starting next week, you will be supporting a new medical facility with their EMR/EHR implementation. You will be onsite all day for a whole week helping the front-end office staff with setting up and configuring their workstations. Your supervisor has warned you that the environment may be uncomfortable and unsettling due to the medical facility with a low-income provider and its location being in a known problem area of the city, where drugs are a constant problem. How should you prepare yourself for working in this type of setting?**

   Start by reviewing the medical office ethics policies and make sure to adhere to them while on the job. When you are in the situation, stay calm and be patient. Do not let non-verbal communication cues appear judgmental. Recognize that this is already an area of high anxiety and that stress may be increased because of having to adapt to a new system.

Activity 3-3

1. **One of the medical offices that you support is in the process of transitioning from a traditional paper file-based system to an electronic EMR/EHR system. There are a number of patient files that have not been accessed in over a year. What time of storage factors should be considered when deciding whether to enter the files into the system?**

   The time of storage factors will vary depending on a specific medical facility, but state and federal laws, case laws, medical board policies, and the patient's age may all be considered in this situation.

2. **True or False? One of the doctors in the medical practice where you work has been accused of malpractice by a patient. The patient is claiming that the doctor prescribed him a medication that he was allergic to, even though the medication is documented as being problematic in his file. The patient has suffered severe asthma symptoms and has been hospitalized because of the reaction to the medication. In this scenario, the doctor potentially could be held liable for the outcome of this patient's health.**

   ✓ True

   __ False

3. **What is the correct description for each agreement document?**

c	BAA	a. Lists all agreed upon actions and services between two parties.
b	SLA	b. An agreement between a service provider and a customer that stipulates the precise services and support options the vendor must provide.
a	MOU	c. Defines the authorized uses of PHI.

4. **The hospital where you work has just re-configured the main entrance and reception area to make it more accessible to wheelchairs and walkers. In doing this, you discover that the reception computer displays can now be seen by anyone sitting in the waiting area. What PHI practice would you suggest in this scenario to prevent anyone from seeing sensitive information on those computers?**

   The first choice in this scenario is to either move the computers to block the view, or position the waiting area so that no one can see the computer screens. Additional measures can include enabling the screen saver and time lockout options on all front desk computers, or installing privacy screens.

Activity 3-4

1. **Sam, the office manager for a large medical practice, is in charge of getting all patient files from hardcopy to digital copies to store in the EMR system. He is currently in the process of adding keywords to each scanned file so that the files can be found quickly during a search. What phase of the process is this?**

   a) Preparation and transport

   b) Scanning

   c) Output

   ✓ d) Indexing

   e) Storage and retrieval

2. **What part of the EMR/EHR scanning process is the most challenging?**

   The preparation and transport phase is generally the most challenging phase, because of the manual labor required to physically prep all hard copy documents, record, and X-rays. The process of removing staples and clips from the hard copies alone can be tedious and time consuming.

3. **What are some of the system implications of scanning and storing hard copy medical files?**

   The main concern for scanning and storing medical files is having the storage space required. The wide range of file types used and the size of the files can demand additional IT hardware installations.

Activity 3-5

1. **As an IT technician working in various medical environments, what are some steps you can take to prevent the spread of disease and illness while working with IT and medical equipment?**

   Follow proper hand washing guidelines, wear protective gear when necessary, regularly disinfect equipment, and follow specific cleaning guidelines for each medical area.

2. **True or False? Shared computer equipment within a medical facility is at a high risk for spreading disease to medical staff.**

   ✓ True

   __ False

3. **How can you mitigate the risk of spreading diseases through shared IT equipment in a medical facility?**

   Set up daily cleaning and disinfecting guidelines and enforce good hand washing habits among medical and IT personnel.

Lesson 4

Activity 4-1

1. **Identify the computer components in the graphic.**

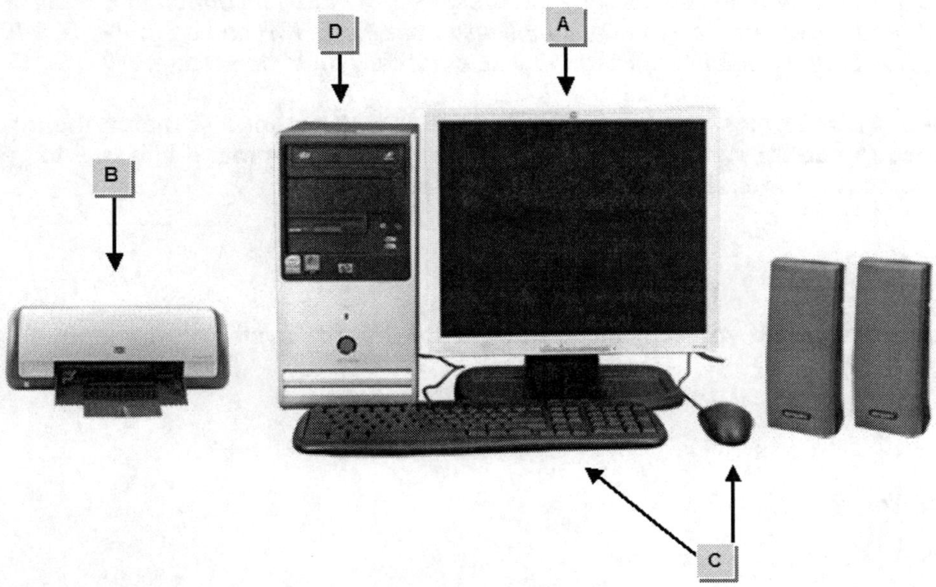

d	B	a.	System unit
a	D	b.	Display device
c	C	c.	Input device
b	A	d.	External device

2. **Match each external device with its function.**

d	Microphone	a.	Provides audio output
a	Speaker	b.	Provides graphical input
b	Scanner	c.	Provides text and graphical output
c	Printer	d.	Provides audio input
e	External drive	e.	Provides additional data storage

3. **What are the main categories of personal computer components?**

   ✓ a) System unit

   ✓ b) Display device

   ✓ c) Input devices

   d) Network devices

Activity 4-4

1. On your network, users connect from individual workstations to access the EMR/ EHR system running within a data center. Your network uses which network model?

a) Ad-hoc

b) Mixed mode

✓ c) Client/server

d) Centralized

2. You have been called to one of the outpatient care centers because the office staff cannot connect to the Internet. Once you arrive, you verify that the DHCP server is functional, but in the TCP/IP properties of the workstation, an IP address has been assigned statically. What is the issue, and how would you go about fixing it?

The issue is that the Internet connection set up for all office computers is established through DHCP. A manually assigned address is likely to be incorrect. In this configuration, the IP addresses are assigned automatically from the DHCP server. In the TCP/IP properties, the option to obtain an IP address automatically must be selected.

3. True or False? Once you have changed the TCP/IP settings to match the Internet connection setup method, you can use the ipconfig command line tool to verify that the computer is receiving a valid IP address.

_✓_ True

__ False

4. What utility would you typically use to verify that the system can communicate with other computers?

a) ipconfig/all

✓ b) Ping

c) Tracert

d) FTP

Activity 4-10

1. What is the correct description for each type of imaging device?

_*f*_	Barcode reader	a. Used to scan a patient's driver licenses or insurance card.
_*e*_	Document scanner	b. Used to fax prescriptions or to print out prescription information from the EMR/EHR system.
_*a*_	Card/badge scanner	c. Used to capture a patient's signature.
_*b*_	Fax printer	d. In diagnostics, used to capture an image that will then be analyzed.
_*d*_	Camera	e. Used to convert paper to an electronic format.
_*c*_	Signature pads	f. Used to scan and identify patients using information included on their ID wrist band.

2. When placing a new router within an existing infrastructure, what should you consider before installing and configuring the device?

Things to consider are: the location of the nodes that the router will be connected to, the location of the power source, how the device will be secured, if there will be any interference and range issues, and if the device is near a network drop.

3. One of the doctors in the medical office that you are supporting asks you for a quick way to transfer patient notes taken on his smartphone to his laptop. He would like to be able to transfer data after each patient once he gets back to his office. What connection method would work well for these devices in this situation?

a) FireWire

b) USB

✓ c) Bluetooth

d) Serial

Lesson 5

Activity 5-6

1. A doctor calls you, complaining that he cannot turn on his computer. It worked fine yesterday, but this morning he cannot get it to turn on. What is the first thing you should do?

a) Use compressed air to remove dirt and debris from the fan.

b) Replace the monitor.

✓ c) Check all the power sources to the computer.

d) Check the network connections to the machine.

2. You receive a call from a practice manager who reports that she is unable to access any websites in Microsoft® Internet Explorer®. While talking with this user, you verify that none of the other users in the office can connect to websites in Internet Explorer. What might be the problem?

a) Her computer is configured with the wrong default gateway address.

✓ b) Her ISP's DNS server is down.

c) Her computer is configured with the wrong subnet mask.

d) Her ISP's default gateway server is down.

3. You receive a call from an nurse practitioner who is having trouble with his laptop. He ran out of battery power during a meeting, and when he tried to turn it back on using the power cord, it still would not turn on. What are some of the possible causes of this issue?

✓ a) The power outlet he was plugged into was not working.

✓ b) The power supply in the laptop has failed.

c) The battery contacts are dirty.

✓ d) The power cord or AC adapter has failed.

4. **You receive a call from a physician's assistant who has been having ongoing issues with her keyboard. Sometimes it works fine; other times, when she presses certain keys, there is no input or the wrong characters are input. What is the most likely explanation for this issue?**

   a) The keyboard is plugged into the wrong port.

   b) There is interference between the keyboard and the computer.

   c) The device driver needs to be updated.

   ✓ d) There is foreign matter under the keys.

5. **You receive a call from a client who is experiencing an issue with one of her software applications. Every time she tries to launch the program, it will start to load but then a window pops up prompting her to go to an outside website and download antivirus software. She cannot close the window and access the program.**

   What is the most logical cause and solution to her issue?

   a) She is running an outdated version of the program and you need to install a software update.

   b) She is experiencing conflicts with another program that is open and you need to uninstall one of the programs.

   c) She accidentally blocked the program and you need to change the firewall settings to allow the program to run.

   ✓ d) She likely downloaded something with a virus or malware and you need to scan the system and remove it.

Activity 5-7

1. **Which of the following are common causes of issues in many medical software systems? (Select all that apply.)**

   a) The superbill or prescription is not properly formatted.

   ✓ b) Patient demographics are formatted incorrectly or missing necessary information.

   c) Necessary nodes needed for proper communication have been deactivated.

   ✓ d) The communication link between systems is not working or is disconnected.

2. **You receive a call from a physician's assistant (PA), Sherri, who is having problems with the e-prescription service. Today is her first day working for the practice, and she is having difficulty sending any prescriptions. After talking with Sherri for a minute, you know that her colleagues are not having the same issues. One colleague even checked her work for some of the possible formatting errors, and she couldn't find anything that might be causing the problem.**

   Based on this information, what is the most likely cause of the problem?

   a) The pharmacy Sherri selected to receive the prescription does not accept e-prescriptions.

   b) The e-prescription was not filled out completely or was formatted improperly.

   ✓ c) Sherri has not been assigned the necessary privileges in the system to be able to send e-prescriptions.

   d) Sherri was trying to send a prescription for a controlled substance.

3. **Though you were able to troubleshoot Sherri's problem, you do not have the authorization to provide the solution.**

   What should you do?

   a) Have another employee send the e-prescriptions for Sherri.

   b) Contact the manufacturer and make sure they are aware of the problem with the system.

   c) Contact the system administrator for the system, who can provide Sherry the privileges she needs.

   ✓ d) Have another employee send the e-prescription for Sherri while you contact the system administrator to provide Sherri with the necessary privileges.

4. **What should you do if the issue you have been called to troubleshoot is outside of the realm of your knowledge or skills?**

   Figure out who is better suited to troubleshoot the problem: it may be another IT professional within the organization employed specifically to serve as support for the device or program, or it may be the manufacturer or vendor. Know who to escalate a problem to if you cannot solve it yourself.

Activity 5-8

1. **Your medical practice is in the process of selecting a vendor for the EMR implementation planned for early next year. You have been asked to take part in the demonstrations given by the top three choices. What phase of the process does this occur in?**

   This occurs within the vendor evaluation phase when the practice needs are compared to the vendor's offerings.

2. **How does the size of a medical environment effect the EMR implementation process?**

   The size can effect how the EMR system hardware is installed and distributed throughout the facility. It can also effect how the system rollout is completed and how much support will be needed.

3. **A small private practice is looking to move their traditional patient record system to an EMR. They do not want to purchase additional computer equipment other than the three workstations they use at the front desk. The office manager also does not want to have to hire an administrator to manage the system onsite. What implementation option would best suit the needs of the small office?**

   a) A client-server implementation

   ✓ b) An ASP implementation

4. **What are the three general types of EMR/EHR clients?**

   A browser-based client, an application-based client, and a terminal or remote access client.

5. **What phase of the EMR project lifecycle is described?**

b	Planning	a.	Environment readiness is determined.
c	Selection	b.	The scope of the EMR installation is determined.
a	Implementation	c.	Purchase agreements are created.
f	Configuration	d.	Goals and objectives are verified against the EMR plan.
d	Post implementation	e.	EMR resources are distributed to users of the system.
e	Training	f.	Processes are aligned with the EMR system.

Activity 5-9

1. **True or False? When considering how a system-wide EMR/EHR update will affect users, you should plan for all types of responses, including any negative reactions to the updates.**

   ✓ True

   __ False

2. **What are the four environments where change must be controlled?**

   Development, quality assurance, user testing, and production live.

3. **Why is controlling change of great importance in the healthcare environment?**

   Change control is important in the healthcare environment because you are dealing with important and sensitive information about a person's health. It is important to control change in an EMR/EHR environment in a timely manner, and in a way that will protect the security and validity of patient information.

Lesson 6

Activity 6-2

1. **Any employee gets to work and realizes that he forgot his laptop in the car. Upon exiting the building, he props the door open with a rock so he won't have to use his swipe card to get back in. Does this pose a security threat to the company?**

   ✓ a) Yes. Leaving an otherwise locked door open allows anyone to enter the building and access systems and data.

   b) No. He is just running to his car and will be fast enough to ensure that no one else will have a chance to enter the building.

2. **Why is it better to create groups instead of managing individual user accounts?**

   Because so many permission assignments must be duplicated for users with similar roles and because individual users' roles and needs can change so frequently.

3. **Match the type of security threat with its correct definition.**

b	Social engineering	a. An attack that targets a computer's physical components and peripherals.
c	Physical security	b. An attack that uses deception and trickery to convince unsuspecting users to provide sensitive data or to violate security guidelines.
a	Hardware attacks	c. These can be internal, external, natural or man made.
d	Environmental threats	d. Threats include fire, hurricanes and tornadoes, floods, extreme temperatures and extreme humidity.

4. Which of the following are ways you can protect your environment from social engineering attacks? (Select all that apply.)

✓ a) Do not give out passwords over the phone or in email.

b) Users should immediately answer phone callers who make unusual requests.

c) Organizations should implement security policies but don't need to train users to follow them.

✓ d) Users should report possible attacks.

✓ e) Users should employ common sense. If anything sounds forced, too good to be true, or otherwise unusual, it is best to err on the side of caution.

Activity 6-9

1. Which are common components that should be in a medical facility's DRP? (Select all that apply)

a) A list of employees' personal items.

✓ b) Contact information for key individuals.

✓ c) An inventory of important hardware and software.

✓ d) Plans to reconstruct the network.

2. Assume that Ristell Health Center is located in a climate and location identical to the company you work for now. What are some unique geographical or weather-related conditions you might need to account for, but that might not be a consideration for other companies?

Answers will vary, but you some locales might particularly be concerned with natural disasters such as hurricanes, tornados, river flooding, ice storms, heavy snowfall, and so on.

3. Assume that a high-level manager has expressed some dissatisfaction with the notion of a "fire drill" to test the clinic's preparedness for a disaster; it seems he is leery of so much paid time being used in an unproductive way, and he wonders if you cannot just write a detailed plan instead. What are some things you can mention to help persuade him that such an unannounced drill is necessary?

Answers will vary, but should contain some reference to the cost of being unprepared. If a company were to never test their DRP or BCP, then how does one really know if they will work? A company might be spending a lot of money on non-billable projects during a "fire drill," but such a drill could ensure that business is actually able to continue if disaster struck the clinic. You can also mention the legal ramifications or liability exposure of being unprepared for a disaster situation.

4. **Once you have the DRP and other components in place, what do you do to make sure it works smoothly?**

   Answers may vary, but you can perform a walkthrough or parallel testing, and when you are sure it all works well, you can even perform a cutover. Also make sure there is a system in place to review the plan annually and make any maintenance-level changes.

Glossary

802.11
A family of specifications developed by the IEEE for wireless LAN technology.

802.11a
A fast, secure, but relatively expensive protocol for wireless communication. The 802.11a protocol supports speeds up to 54 Mbps in the 5 GHz frequency.

802.11b
Also called Wi-Fi, short for "wired fidelity," 802.11b is probably the most common and certainly the least expensive wireless network protocol used to transfer data among computers with wireless network cards or between a wireless computer or device and a wired LAN. The 802.11b protocol provides for an 11 Mbps transfer rate in the 2.4 GHz frequency.

802.11g
A specification for wireless data throughput at the rate of up to 54 Mbps in the 2.4 GHz band that is a potential replacement for 802.11b.

802.11i
A standard that adds AES security to the 802.11 standard.

802.11n
A wireless standard for home and business implementations that adds QoS features and multimedia support to 802.11a and 802.11b.

802.1x
An IEEE standard used to provide a port-based authentication mechanism for wireless communications using the 802.11a and 802.11b protocols.

access point
See AP.

Active Server Pages
See ASP.

acuity
The acuteness, or level of severity, of an illness or disease.

ad hoc
A type of network that is established spontaneously through a peer-to-peer wireless connection.

Address Resolution Protocol
See ARP.

Advanced Technology Attachment
See ATA.

adware
Unwanted software loaded onto a system for the purposes of presenting commercial advertisements to the user.

ambulatory care
Any medical treatment or services provided on an outpatient basis.

American Recovery and Reinvestment Act
See ARRA.

antivirus software
A software program that scans a computer or network for known viruses, Trojans, worms, and other malicious software.

AP
(access point) A hardware device or a computer software program that acts as a communication hub to provide heightened wireless security and extend the physical range of a wireless local area network (LAN).

API
(Application Programming Interface) Application code that enables various applications to communicate with each other.

Application Programming Interface
See API.

application server
A server that runs applications for client use or is used by developers to store and share application components that can be used in web applications.

applications
Software components that allow users to perform specific tasks and job functions on a computer.

archive flag
A file property that essentially indicates whether the file has been modified since the last back up.

ARP poisoning
A method in which an attacker with access to the target network redirects an IP address to the MAC address of a computer that is not the intended recipient.

ARP
(Address Resolution Protocol) The mechanism by which individual hardware MAC addresses are matched to an IP address on a network.

ARRA
(American Recovery and Reinvestment Act) U.S economic stimulus legislation; provisions include funding of some healthcare initiatives and the creation of the HITECH Act.

ASP
(Active Server Pages) A server-side programming language developed by Microsoft to provide a method to create dynamic web pages.

assisted living facility
A residential facility or community for patients who may need assistance with some functions of daily living, such as bathing or medication reminders, but can otherwise remain mostly independent.

ATA
(Advanced Technology Attachment) The official ANSI term for IDE drives.

availability
The fundamental security goal of ensuring that systems operate continuously and that authorized persons can access data that they need.

BAA
(business associate agreement) A document that defines the authorized uses of PHI, and how the information is to be used and managed.

barcode scanner
A wired or wireless device that is used to scan and identify patients using the unique barcode located on their ID wrist band.

bedside medication verification
A checks-and-balances system that ensures that a patient is receiving the correct medication, the correct dose of medication, at the correct time, from an authorized caregiver by requiring that barcodes storing information about the patient, medication, and possibly the administering personnel be scanned and verified prior to the medication being dispensed.

billing and coding software
Software that provides one location where charges are entered, codes can be checked, insurance claims and statements can be generated and sent, claim denials can be managed, and payments can be posted and processed.

billing clearinghouse
The intermediary between the medical biller at the healthcare organization and the paying insurance company who ensures that the claim has no errors before it is transmitted to the insurance company.

biometrics
Authentication schemes based on individuals' physical characteristics.

bluejacking
A method used by attackers to send out unwanted Bluetooth signals from mobile phones, smartphones, tablets, and laptops to other Bluetooth-enabled devices.

bluesnarfing
A process in which attackers gain access to unauthorized information on a wireless device using a Bluetooth connection.

Bluetooth
A short-range wireless radio network transmission medium usually used between two personal devices, such as between a mobile phone and wireless headset.

Bluetooth
A wireless connection method that is used to communicate from one device to another in a small area, usually less than 30 feet.

break glass access
Temporary and specific emergency access to specifically locked PHI data in order to gain access to information which enables task completion.

business associate agreement
See BAA.

camera
A device used to take pictures of patients, because some EMR/EHR systems allow for a patient picture to be tied to their electronic record.

card/badge scanner
A device used often to scan patient's driver licenses or insurance card to store within the EMR/EHR system.

CCD
(Continuity of Care Document) A healthcare record standard, similar to CCR but more robust as it was developed by both the HL7 and American Society for Testing and Materials (ASTM), as a means of creating summary documents containing the most relevant and pertinent information about a patient that can be shared electronically between medical caregivers regardless of their respective EMR or EHR software applications.

CCHIT
(Certification Commission for Health Information Technology) A not-for-profit organization that promotes the adoption of healthcare IT systems, as well as certifies health record technology.

CCMP
(Counter Mode with Cipher Block Chaining Message Authentication Code Protocol) An AES cipher-based encryption protocol used in WPA2.

CCR
(Continuity of Care Record) A health record standard that was developed by a number of American healthcare organizations as a means of creating summary documents containing the most relevant and pertinent information about a patient that can be shared electronically between medical caregivers regardless of their respective EMR or EHR software applications.

Centers for Medicare and Medicaid Services
See CMS.

centralized
A network in which a central host computer controls all network communication and performs the data processing and storage on behalf of network clients.

Certification Commission for Health Information Technology
See CCHIT.

certified EHR system
An EHR system that has been certified by ONC.

change management
A systematic way of approving and executing change in order to assure maximum security, stability, and availability of information technology services.

CIA triad
(confidentiality, integrity, availability) The three principles of security control and management: confidentiality, integrity, and availability. Also known as the information security triad or triple.

client-server
A computer model where functionality is divided into two roles: a server computer which provides services and controls network operations, and a client computer, which uses the services provided by the servers.

cloud computing
A method of computing that relies on the Internet to provide the resources, software, data, and media needs of a user, business, or organization.

CMS
(Centers for Medicare and Medicaid Services) A U.S. federal agency responsible not only for overseeing its named services but also for administering a children's insurance program, some portions of HIPAA, and other programs.

coaxial cable
A type of cable that features a central conductor surrounded by braided or foil shielding. A dialectric insulator separates the conductor and shield and the entire package is wrapped in an insulating layer called a jacket. The data signal is transmitted over the central conductor. The outer shielding serves to reduce electromagnetic interference.

Code Blue
Term used to communicate that a patient has gone into cardiac arrest, and immediate medical attention/rapid response is needed to resuscitate the patient.

computerized physician order entry
See CPOE.

confidentiality
The fundamental security goal of keeping information and communications private and protecting them from unauthorized access.

continuing care facility
A residential facility with "steps" of care based on the residents' needs; residents can start out with more independence through assisted living, with the comfort of knowing nursing home care is available at the same facility when they can no longer remain independent.

Continuity of Care Document
See CCD.

Continuity of Care Record
See CCR.

controlled substance
Any drug or chemical substance that is regulated by the federal government in its production, possession, or use, including illegal and prescription drugs.

Counter Mode with Cipher Block Chaining Message Authentication Code Protocol
See CCMP.

covered entity
Any healthcare provider that conducts certain transactions in electronic form, a healthcare clearinghouse, or a health plan. All covered entities fall under the HHS Administrative Simplification standards adopted as part of HIPAA. All covered entities must adhere to the HIPAA Privacy Rule and Security Rule.

CPOE
(computerized physician order entry) Software that allows for electronic entry of all medical orders/instructions for treatment for a patient from their licensed caregiver, which can then be accessed by other medical staff.

CPT
(Current Procedural Terminology) A list of descriptions and accompanying five-digit numeric codes used for reporting medical services and procedures, which is published every year by the American Medical Association.

Current Procedural Terminology
See CPT.

custodian
The role, department, or individual that is formally responsible for a health record.

daily backup
A backup that backs up all selected files on a daily basis.

data sanitation
The method used to repeatedly delete and overwrite any traces or bits of sensitive data that may remain on a device after data wiping has been done.

data wiping
A method used to remove any sensitive data from a mobile device and permanently delete it.

database administrator
See DBA.

database server
A server that provides database services to other computers in a network.

DBA
(database administrator) An IT role that is responsible for designing, implementing, maintaining, and repairing databases. Usually also responsible for the security of an organization's database system and all the data stored on the systems.

DC
(Domain Controller) A Windows Server computer that runs the Active Directory service. Directory information is automatically replicated between the DCs in a given forest.

DDoS
(Distributed Denial of Service attack) A network attack in which an attacker hijacks or manipulates multiple computers (through the use of zombies or drones) on disparate networks to carry out a DoS attack.

degaussing
A method used to remove data from magnetic media. Degaussing changes the magnetic alignment of data, so that it cannot be recovered.

Denial of Service
See DoS attack.

desktop support
An IT role that is responsible for assisting end users and attempts to restore normal service to users as quickly as possible.

DHCP server
A server that contains at least one DHCP scope.

DHCP
(Dynamic Host Control Protocol) A protocol used to automatically assign IP addressing information to IP network computers.

differential backup
A backup that backs up all files in a selected storage location that have changed since the last full backup.

display devices
Personal computer components that enable users to view the text and graphical data output from a computer.

Distributed Denial of Service
See DDoS attack.

DNS server
A server that consists of databases that store domain name information and translate and resolve fully qualified domain name requests from clients.

DNS
(Domain Name System) The service that maps names to IP addresses on most TCP/IP networks, including the Internet.

document imaging
Electronic conversion of hard copy documents to digital form.

document scanner
A device used to convert paper to electronic format and then associates the file with the proper patient.

Domain Controller
See DC.

Domain Name System
See DNS.

DoS
(Denial of Service attack) A network attack in which an attacker disables systems that provide network services by consuming a network link's available bandwidth, consuming a single system's available resources, or exploiting programming flaws in an application or operating system.

drone
Unauthorized software introduced on multiple computers to manipulate the computers into mounting a DDoS attack. Also called a zombie.

DRP
(disaster recover plan) A policy that defines how people and resources will be protected in a natural or man-made disaster, and how the organization will recover from the disaster.

drug allergy
Any adverse reaction to a medication being taken.

Dynamic Host Control Protocol
See DHCP.

e-prescribing
The transmission of a patient's prescription for medication electronically from the prescriber's computer to the pharmacy's computer.

E/M Codes
(Evaluation and Management Codes) Five-digit CPT codes used to describe a medical professional-patient interaction, such as an office visit or a hospital, to facilitate in the billing process.

EAP
(Extensible Authentication Protocol) An authentication protocol that enables systems to use hardware-based identifiers, such as fingerprint scanners or smart card readers, for authentication.

eavesdropping
A network attack that uses special monitoring software to gain access to private communications on the network wire or across a wireless network. Also known as a sniffing attack.

ED
(Emergency Department) An area of the facility where those needing immediate medical treatment arrive and are provided with initial care for their medical illness or injury, before being admitted for further treatment by another department.

EHR
(Electronic Health Record) The consolidation of all of the recorded health information about a person stored within a given network. EHRs generally contain multiple EMRs collected from various facilities and providers within a provider network or umbrella organization.

Electronic Health Record
See EHR.

Electronic Medical Record
See EMR.

eligible provider
A healthcare provider that meets legally defined criteria and thus is eligible for incentive payments for the implementation of EHR systems.

email
Electronic messages sent between users or groups.

Emergency Department
See ED.

EMI
(electromagnetic interference) Disturbances caused by electromagnetic radiation emitted from any external source, which may interrupt, obstruct, degrade, or limit the performance of an electrical circuit.

EMR
(Electronic Medical Record) A computerized record of a health encounter. EMRs are specific to a facility (doctor's office, treatment facility, etc.) and its computer system.

encryption
A process in which information is transcribed into an unreadable form by anyone who does not have the encryption code.

Evaluation and Management Codes
See E/M Codes.

Examination Room
A private room where a patient is examined and diagnosed by a medical practitioner.

Extensible Authentication Protocol
See EAP.

eXtensible Markup Language
See XML.

external devices
Devices that provide alternative input or output methods or additional data storage through a connection to the system unit via cable or a wireless connection.

fax printer
A device used to fax prescriptions or to print out prescription information from the EMR/EHR system.

fax server
A device that manages all fax messages sent within a network.

fax server
A server or software program that enables users to send and receive fax messages through a network connection.

FDA
(Food and Drug Administration) The federal agency that oversees the regulation of food safety, tobacco products, prescription and over-the-counter medications, dietary supplements, vaccines, medical devices, sanitation requirements, and other related public health products and services.

fiber
A type of cable in which one or more glass or plastic strands, plus additional fiber strands or wraps, are surrounded by a protective outer jacket. Light pulses carry the signal through fiber optic cable.

file server
A server that is primarily used to share, store, and access files.

File Transfer Protocol
See FTP.

Final Rule
An effort to set standards, specifications, and criteria for the implementation, use, and security of healthcare IT systems.

fire suppression
A system that extinguishes fires using special gases.

firewall
A software or hardware device that protects a system or network by blocking unwanted network traffic.

FireWire connection
A high-speed serial bus developed by Apple and Texas Instruments that allows for the connection of up to 63 devices. Originally a trademarked term for IEEE 1394, but is now used interchangeably.

Flash
An Adobe platform that allows developers to create animations, videos, and other interactive components using the ActionScript programming language.

Float Room
Any room used to temporarily house patients when they are in transition between their patient room and another location, such as before or after tests or surgeries.

Food and Drug Administration
See FDA.

for-profit hospital
An investor-owned hospital, usually owned by a corporation or group of private individuals, that aims to gain profits for the services provided which are then paid to those invested in the ownership.

formulary checking
The automatic process of checking a prescription for medication against a patient's known allergies for possible drug-allergy reactions, and against current medications for possible adverse drug-drug interactions.

FTP server
A server that uses the File Transfer Protocol (FTP) to exchange files over an Internet connection.

FTP
(File Transfer Protocol) A communications protocol that enables the transfer of files between a user's workstation and a remote host.

full backup
A backup that backs up all selected files regardless of the state of the archived bit.

general/community hospital
A hospital that treats a wide variety of medical issues including emergencies and inpatient/outpatient care, and performs general surgeries.

grayware
A general classification for any unwanted software that produces harmful or annoying effects.

hardware attack
An attack that targets a computer's physical components and peripherals, including its hard disk, motherboard, keyboard, network cabling, or smart card reader.

HDD
(hard disk drive) A personal computer storage device that uses fixed media and magnetic data storage.

Health Information Technology for Economic and Clinical Health Act
See HITECH.

Health Insurance Portability and Accountability Act
See HIPAA.

HHS
(U.S. Department of Health and Human Services) The U.S. agency charged with protecting the health of the population and providing various human services.

HIPAA
(Health Insurance Portability and Accountability Act). A U.S. law that established rules for the governance of health information privacy, security, breach notification, administrative simplifications, and enforcement.

HITECH
(Health Information Technology for Economic and Clinical Health Act) The part of the ARRA that promotes the adoption and meaningful use of healthcare IT through enhanced enforcement and extension of HIPAA policies.

HL7
Specific healthcare industry standards and a framework concerning the exchange and integration of patients's electronic information between software systems, which are adhered to by vendors developing interfaces, ensuring that the disparate software applications are used by healthcare organizations and the interfaces that communicate between them are all speaking the same electronic language to accurately exchange patient medical data.

hoax
Any message containing incorrect or misleading information that is disseminated to multiple users through unofficial channels.

home healthcare
A wide variety of medical services that are provided in a patient's home by an accredited home health aide, often including physical therapy and medication delivery through more complicated methods like injections, intravenous therapy, etc.

hospice care
A residential facility for terminally ill patients who have reached the end stages of their condition. Hospice care is designed to provide comfort and care for patients and support for the patient's family during end-of-life.

host computer
A powerful, centralized computer system that performs data storage and processing tasks on behalf of clients and other network devices.

HTML
(HyperText Markup Language) The standard language that defines how web pages are formatted and displayed.

HTTPS
(Hypertext Transfer Protocol Secure) A secure version of HTTP that supports e-commerce by providing a secure connection between a web browser and a server.

human interface devices
Hardware components that enable users to interact with computers.

HyperText Markup Language
See HTML.

Hypertext Transfer Protocol Secure
See HTTPS.

IaaS
(Infrastructure as a Service) A method that uses the cloud to provide any or all infrastructure needs.

ICD-10
(International Statistical Classification of Diseases and Related Health Problems, 10th revision) One of several internationally endorsed medical coding classifications lists which gives a numeric code to diseases, signs and symptoms, possible complaints, abnormalities, and possible causes of injuries and diseases.

ICMP
(Internet Control Message Protocol) A service added to the IP protocol that attempts to report on the condition of a connection between two nodes.

IDF
(Intermediate Distribution Frame) Systems that store networking hardware and provide networking services to local area networks within a medical environment.

IDS
(intrusion detection system) A software and/or hardware system that scans, audits, and monitors the security infrastructure for signs of attacks in progress.

IEEE 1394
See FireWire connection.

IEEE
(Institute of Electrical and Electronic Engineers) Pronounced "I-triple-E." An organization of scientists, engineers, and students of electronics and related fields whose technical and standards committees develop, publish, and revise computing and telecommunications standards.

IM
(instant messaging) A type of communication service which involves a private dialogue between two persons via instant-text-based messages over the Internet.

Imaging Center
An area where all medical imaging procedures are conducted.

imaging
The use of various technologies to create images of the human body for use in the clinical field, such as diagnosis, treatment, and tracking of a disease or medical issue within the body.

incremental backup
A back up that backs up all files in a selected storage location that have changed since the last full or differential backup.

information security triad
See CIA triad.

Infrastructure as a Service
See IaaS.

initialization vector
See IV.

inpatient treatment
Treatment provided when a patient's medical condition requires being admitted a healthcare facility for anywhere from an overnight stay to a long-term stay, due to the fact that the patient's condition must be closely monitored.

input devices
Personal computer components that enable users to enter data or instructions into a computer.

instant messaging
See IM.

Institute of Electrical and Electronic Engineers
See IEEE.

integrity
The fundamental security goal of ensuring that electronic data is not altered or tampered with.

interference
Within wireless networking, the phenomenon by which radio waves from other devices interfere with the 802.11 wireless signals.

intermediate care facility
A residential facility for individuals with persistent medical conditions who are currently unable to live independently, but do not need constant medical care or supervision.

Intermediate Distribution Frame
See IDF.

International Statistical Classification of Diseases and Related Health Problems, 10th revision
See ICD-10.

Internet Control Message Protocol
See ICMP.

Internet modem
A network device that modulates digital information onto an analog signal at one end, and demodulates the analog signal back to digital data, used for dial-up Internet connections.

Internet Service Provider
See ISP.

intrusion detection system
See IDS.

ipconfig
A command line utility used to display the connection-specific DNS suffix, IP address, subnet mask, and default gateway.

Isolation Room
An area within a medical facility designed to prevent the spread of airborne infections through the use of negative pressurization control of the air inside and outside the room.

ISP
(Internet Service Provider) A company that provides access to the Internet.

IV attack
An attack where the attacker is able to predict or control the IV of an encryption process, thus giving the attacker access to view the encrypted data that is supposed to be hidden from everyone else except the user or network.

IV
(initialization vector) A technique used in cryptography to generate random numbers to be used along with a secret key to provide data encryption.

Joint Commission
See The Joint Commission.

keyfob
A portable electronic security token that contains biometric user data, or other identification information.

L2TP
(Layer Two Tunneling Protocol) The de facto standard VPN protocol for tunneling PPP sessions across a variety of network protocols such as IP, frame relay, or ATM.

LAN
(Local Area Network) A LAN implementation in which nodes use a wireless network card to connect to other stations.

Layer Two Tunneling Protocol
See L2TP.

LEAP
(Lightweight Extensible Authentication Protocol) Cisco Systems' proprietary EAP implementation.

legal health record
The official record that an organization would release if requested.

Level I Trauma Center
A trauma center that can provide the highest possible level of surgical care to trauma patients, with a full range of specialists and technology available 24 hours a day. It is required to have an ongoing research program and trauma education/prevention services.

Level II Trauma Center
A trauma center that can provide essential trauma care 24 hours a day with all available specialties, personnel, and equipment. It provides comprehensive trauma care and clinical assistance to a Level I facility as needed. It is differentiated from Level I because it is not required to have ongoing research programs or surgical residency.

Level III Trauma Center
A trauma center that can provide treatment, surgery, and intensive care to most trauma patients, but does not have all available specialists and their equipment in facility. It has transfers agreements with a Level I or II facility for the treatment of severe injuries that the Level III cannot treat.

Level IV Trauma Center
A trauma center that can provide initial evaluation, stabilization, and diagnosis of a trauma patient but then the patient must be transferred to a Level I, II or III facility for treatment and care. It is required to provide services 24 hours a day.

Level V Trauma Center
A trauma center that can provide initial evaluation, stabilization, and diagnosis of a trauma patient, but then the patient must be transferred to a Level I, II or III facility for treatment and care. It is differentiated from Level IV because it is not required to have services available 24 hours a day, but must have an after-hours trauma response plan in place.

liability waiver
A legal document that may be signed by a patient (or those acting legally on behalf of a patient) to acknowledge the risks involved in a specific medical procedure or medication.

liability
The condition of being actually or potentially subject to a legal obligation based on one's actions or omissions.

Lightweight Extensible Authentication Protocol
See LEAP.

Local Area Network
See LAN.

logic bomb
A piece of code that sits dormant on a user's computer until it is triggered by a specific event, such as a specific date. Once the code is triggered, the logic bomb "detonates," erasing and corrupting data on the user's computer.

logical access control
Protection mechanisms used to identify, authenticate, and authorize access to computers and their corresponding systems.

logical security
Software protection systems in an organization.

long-stay facility
A facility that provides long-term services, such as rehabilitation, that address more permanent or long-term medical conditions like mental illness.

mail server
A server that receives email requests from hosts on a network, and redirects them to the intended recipient.

Main Distribution Frame
See MDF.

mainframe
See host computer.

man-in-the-middle
A form of eavesdropping where the attacker makes an independent connection between two victims and steals information to use fraudulently.

mantrap
A physical security control system that has a door at each end of a secure chamber.

MDF
(Main Distribution Frame) A hardware rack that holds networking equipment to provide connections from public lines coming into the physical building, generally from the ISP, to all the IDFs located throughout the medical facility.

meaningful use
A regulatory concept describing the ideal of effectively and efficiently leveraging EHR technology in the medical workplace.

Medicaid
The U.S. federal program to provide healthcare for certain low-income individuals and families.

medical billing
The process of submitting and tracking claims made by healthcare providers or organizations to insurance companies on behalf on the insured patient in order to receive payment for services rendered.

medical coding
The process of assigning a universally recognized and used medical code number to a specific medical diagnosis or procedure.

medical interfaces
Software systems solutions developed using specific industry standards and rules that allow all the myriad medical systems to communicate as seamlessly as possible with one another.

medical record controls
Mechanisms that are put in place to limit access to electronic health information.

Medicare
A federal health insurance program for the elderly and some disabled individuals in the United States, with three main parts: Part A for inpatient, Part B for outpatient, and prescription drug coverage.

medication reconciliation
A process in which a list of a patient's medication orders is compared to a list of those that the patient has been taking in order to avoid any possible medication errors such as duplicated prescriptions, errors in dosage, or potentially hazardous drug interactions.

memorandum of understanding
See MOU.

metadata
Data that is added to a patient EMR to allow for quick searching and file location.

mixed mode
A network that displays characteristics of more than one of the three standard network models.

MOU
(memorandum of understanding) A document that lists agreed upon actions between two parties.

NAC
(Network Access Control) The compilation of protocols, policies, and hardware that govern access on devices to and from a network.

NAS
(Network-Attached Storage) A specialized file server that is designed and dedicated to support only data storage needs.

National Drug Code Directory
A list of all NDC identification numbers, compiled and published by the Food and Drug Administration.

National Drug Code Identification
See NDC ID.

National Institute of Standards and Technology
See NIST.

NDC ID
(National Drug Code Identification) A unique, 10-digit, three-segment numeric code assigned to each registered drug manufactured, processed, and distributed by registered drug manufacturers.

network administrator
An IT role that is responsible for the network infrastructure and components within an organization.

Network Interface Card
See NIC.

Network-Attached Storage
See NAS.

NIC
(Network Interface Card) A device that provides network connectivity capabilities for computer systems.

NIST
(National Institute of Standards and Technology) An agency of the U.S. Department of Commerce. NIST's mission is to promote U.S. innovation and industrial competitiveness by advancing measurement science, standards, and technology in ways that enhance economic security and improve our quality of life

non-profit hospital
A hospital owned by a not-for-profit organization, religious organization, or government organization. Profits do not go to individual investors, but are reinvested back into the hospital or the community.

nursing home
A residential facility for patients who need constant medical or nursing care and supervision.

OCR
(optical character recognition) The process of transforming handwritten, scanned images of text or typed text into machine-encoded text.

Office of the National Coordinator for Health Information Technology
See ONC.

ONC
(Office of the National Coordinator for Health Information Technology) A part of the U.S. Department of Health and Human Services, ONC is charged with encouraging, administering, and regulating the advancement of IT in healthcare.

Operating Room
See OR.

optical character recognition
See OCR.

optical disk
A personal computer storage device that stores data optically, rather than magnetically.

OR
(Operating Room) An area where surgical procedures are performed in a sterile environment.

outpatient treatment
Medical services that can be provided to a patient without the need for the patient to be admitted to any type of healthcare facility.

P2P
(peer-to-peer) A network that has a broadcast application architecture that distributes tasks between peer systems who have equal privileges, and in which resource sharing, processing, and communications controls are decentralized.

PaaS
(Platform as a Service) A method that uses the cloud to provide any platform-type services.

packet sniffing
An attack on wireless networks where an attacker captures data and registers data flows in order to analyze what data is contained in a packet.

PACS
(Picture Archiving and Communications System) Application system where medical images of almost all kinds, including MRIs, CAT scans, ultrasounds, mammograms, etc., can be stored and retrieved electronically by various members of a healthcare organization.

PAN
(Personal Area Network) A network that connects wireless devices in very close proximity but not through a wireless access point.

Parallel Advanced Technology Attachment
See PATA.

parallel connection
A personal computer connection type that transfers data, usually 8 bits at a time, over eight wires and is often used for a printer.

PATA connection
(Parallel Advanced Technology Attachment) A personal computer connection that provides a parallel data channel from a disk controller to the disk drives. Also referred to as ATA, IDE, EIDE, or UDMA.

patient tracking software
Software that allows staff to track a patient's flow of care in the system from registration, through treatment, and during and after discharge.

PCP
(primary care physician) A doctor who serves as the first contact for a patient for a variety of medical services, including physicals or well-visits, and who also serves as either the diagnosing doctor or the referring doctor when a patient presents a medical condition that he or she cannot treat.

PEAP
(Protected Extensible Authentication Protocol) Similar to EAP-TLS, PEAP is an open standard developed by a coalition made up of Cisco Systems, Microsoft, and RSA Security.

peer-to-peer
See P2P.

permission
A security setting that determines the level of access a user or group account has to a particular resource.

Personal Area Network
See PAN.

Personal Health Information
See PHI.

Personal Health Record
See PHR.

PGP
(Pretty Good Privacy) A method of securing emails created to prevent attackers from intercepting and manipulating email and attachments by encrypting and digitally signing the contents of the email using public key cryptography.

pharming
A type of social engineering attack where a request for a website, typically an e-commerce site, is redirected to a similar-looking, but fake, website.

PHI
(Personal Health Information) Information about an individual held by parties that are involved in the healthcare and billing process.

phishing
A common type of email-based social engineering attack where the attacker sends an email that seems to come from a respected bank or financial institution.

PHP
A server-side programming language used to develop dynamic web pages by embedding its code into an HTML pages.

PHR
(Personal Health Record) A patient maintained health record that can be shared with medical professionals. Generally not a part of a Legal Health Record.

physical security controls
Implemented security measures that restrict, detect, and monitor access to specific physical areas or assets.

physical security
The implementation and practice of various control mechanisms that are intended to restrict physical access to facilities.

Picture Archiving and Communications System
See PACS.

ping
A TCP/IP utility used to verify the network connectivity of a computer.

Platform as a Service
See PaaS.

Point-to-Point Protocol
See PPP.

Point-to-Point Tunneling Protocol
See PPTP.

port scanning
An attack where an attacker scans your systems to see which ports are listening in an attempt to find a way to gain unauthorized access.

PPP
(Point-to-Point Protocol) The VPN protocol that is an Internet standard for sending IP datagram packets over serial point-to-point links.

PPTP
(Point-to-Point Tunneling Protocol) A VPN protocol that is an extension of the PPP remote access protocol.

practice management software
An all-encompassing solution of many other IT-based pieces that streamlines the workflow processes of all activities needed to run a practice or facility while providing the ability to become a paperless office, including patient tracking, medical coding and billing, payment collection, rules compliance, and reporting capabilities.

preceptor
A senior, skilled medical staff member who serves as an instructor or supervisor, providing experience and feedback, to medical students or newly hired employees still in training.

Pretty Good Privacy
See PGP.

primary care physician
See PCP.

print server
A device that distributes and manages print jobs sent from client computers.

Privacy Rule
The section of HIPAA that establishes a ruleset to govern the use and disclosure of PHI by covered entities. The goal of the Privacy Rule is to protect a person's health information while allowing adequate transfer of information to promote efficiency and better patient outcomes.

private health insurers
Private, non-government businesses that contract with individuals or employers to help pay medical expenses. These insurers also have separate contracts with many health organizations that specify negotiated rate structures for that health organization's services. Patients usually pay a portion of the fee in the form of a co-payment or deductible.

private health record
Records that are not for public consumption and require appropriate releases before they can be shared.

private practice
An independent medical practice opened by one or more accredited medical practitioners of any specialty area in an office environment.

Procedure Room
An area where minor procedures are performed, including minor surgeries not requiring anaesthesia and post-operative care.

Protected Extensible Authentication Protocol
See PEAP.

protected health information
Individually identifiable health information that is transmitted or maintained in any form or medium by a covered entity or business associate.

proxy server
A server that isolates internal networks from the Internet by downloading and storing Internet files on behalf of internal clients.

public health record
Records that are released for public viewing.

public hospital
A hospital owned and operated by a federal, state, or city government. Typically provides subsidized medical services to patients unable to pay for medical services.

RADIUS
(Remote Authentication Dial-in User Service) A standard protocol for providing centralized authentication and authorization services for remote users.

RDP
(Remote Desktop Protocol) A protocol used to connect to and access a remote computer.

Recovery Room
An area where patients are housed after a surgical procedure or any procedure requiring anaesthesia and are closely monitored for any indications of post-operative complications.

Regional Health Information Organization
See RHIO.

Release of Information
See ROI.

remote access
The ability to connect to systems and services from an offsite or remote location using a remote access method.

Remote Authentication Dial-In User Service
See RADIUS.

Remote Desktop Protocol
See RDP.

replay
A type of network attack where an attacker captures network traffic and stores it for retransmission at a later time to gain unauthorized access to a network.

Request for Proposal
See RFP.

RFP
(Request for Proposal) An invitation for vendors to submit a plan and bid for the delivery of a product or service.

RHIO
(Regional Health Information Organization) A health information organization comprised of key stakeholders in the healthcare industry within a specific geographical region who oversee the health information exchange of healthcare providers in the area.

rogue access point
An unauthorized wireless access point on a corporate or private network, which allows unauthorized individuals to connect to the network.

ROI department
A department within a medical organization dedicated to handling ROI requests for EMR/EHR information release.

ROI
(Release of Information) An approved process for releasing PHI to appropriate parties while preserving patient confidentiality.

router
A device that connects multiple networks that use the same protocol.

SaaS
(Software as a Service) A method that uses the cloud to provide application services to users.

sanitizing
See data wiping and data sanitization.

SATA connection
(Serial ATA connection) A personal computer connection that provides a serial data channel between the drive controller and the disk drives.

Schedule I Controlled Substance
Classification for a drug or substance that has a high potential for abuse; currently has no accepted medical use in treatment in the United States; and has a lack of accepted safety for use under medical supervision.

Schedule II Controlled Substance
Classification for a drug or substance that has a high potential for abuse; is currently accepted for medical use in treatment in the United States; and abuse of which may lead to severe psychological or physical dependence.

Schedule III Controlled Substance
Classification for a drug or substance that has less potential for abuse than those categorized as Schedule I or II; is currently accepted for medical use in treatment in the United States; and abuse of which may lead to moderate or low physical dependence or high psychological dependence.

Schedule IV Controlled Substance
Classification for a drug or substance that has a low potential for abuse as compared to those categorized in Schedule III; is currently accepted for medical use in treatment in the United States; and abuse of which may lead to limited to physical or psychological dependence, especially in comparison to those categorized in Schedule III.

Schedule V Controlled Substance
Classification for a drug or substance that has a lower potential for abuse as compared to those categorized in Schedule IV; is currently accepted for medical use in treatment in the United States; and abuse of which may lead to limited to physical or psychological dependence, especially in comparison to those categorized in Schedule IV.

scheduling software
Online or electronic software that provides a start-to-finish workflow from the time a patient is scheduled through their checkout after their appointment, including insurance verification, check-in, check-out, and payment.

scope of practice
The procedures, processes, or actions, as defined by state and national licensing boards, that are permitted for an individual in a particular licensing area, usually driven by criteria such as specific education and experience requirements.

SCSI
(Small Computer System Interface) An older personal computer connection standard hat provides high-performance data transfer between the SCSI device and the other components of the computer. Pronounced "scuzzy."

secure chat
An instant messaging service that uses strong encryption to send and receive secure messages.

Secure File Transfer Protocol
(Secure FTP) A secure version of FTP that uses SSH as an encryption method to transfer, access, and manage files.

secure shredding
A method used to securely remove data from hard drives and other electronic storage devices.

Secure Socket Tunneling Protocol
See SSTP.

Secure Sockets Layer
See SSL.

security administrator
An IT role that is responsible for ensuring that an organization's security policies are being followed by employees and that sufficient controls are in place to prevent unauthorized access to systems and facilities.

security policy
A formalized statement that defines how security will be implemented within a particular organization.

Security Rule
The section of HIPAA that establishes national standards for the security of personal electronic health information maintained by a Covered Entity.

sensitivity label
A security designation that determines the clearance for an information zone within the EHR system.

Serial ATA connection
See SATA connection.

serial connection
A personal computer connection that transfers data one bit at a time over a single wire and is often used for an external modem.

server load
The amount of work a server performs on a regular basis.

server utilization
The management of performance levels of servers to ensure that critical operations are highly available to resources.

service-level agreement
See SLA.

session hijacking
An attack where the attacker exploits a legitimate computer session to obtain unauthorized access to an organization's network or services.

short-stay facility
Also known as an acute care facility. This facility provides services aimed to resolve immediate and short-term medical conditions like pregnancy or a heart attack.

signature pads
A device used for patient billing to capture an electronic signature.

site survey
An analysis technique that determines the coverage area of a wireless network, identifies any sources of interference, and establishes other characteristics of the coverage area.

SLA
(service-level agreement) A contractual agreement between a service provider and a customer that stipulates the precise services and support options the vendor must provide.

Small Computer System Interface
See SCSI.

sniffing
A network attack that uses special monitoring software to gain access to private communications on the network wire or across a wireless network. Also known as an eavesdropping attack.

SNOMED CT
(Systemized Nomenclature of Medicine–Clinical Terms) An organized collection of numeric codes correlating to clinical information such as diseases, procedures, microorganisms, medications, and so forth that may be used in a patient's records.

social engineering attack
A type of attack where the goal is to obtain sensitive data, including user names and passwords, from network users through deception and trickery.

Software as a Service
See SaaS.

software hotfix
A package of files used to address a specific problem, often specific to a particular customer's problem and not released to all customers at large.

software patch
A piece of software created to fix problems with or provide updates to a program or application. This may include fixing known vulnerabilities or bugs, or improving functionality or performance.

software update
A piece of software created to fix problems with or provide updates to a program or application. This may include fixing known vulnerabilities or bugs, or improve functionality or performance.

solid state storage
A personal computer storage device that stores data in non-volatile special memory instead of on disks or tape.

spam
Originally, frequent and repetitive postings in electronic bulletin boards; more commonly, unsolicited or distasteful commercial email from anonymous sources.

specialized hospital
A hospital specialized to treat a specific disease or condition or a specific type of patient.

spyware
Unwanted software that collects personal user data from a system and transmits it to a third party.

SQL
(Structured Query Language) A programming and query language common to many large-scale database systems.

SSH
(Secure Shell) A protocol for secure remote logon and secure transfer of data.

SSL
(Secure Sockets Layer) A security protocol that uses certificates for authentication and encryption to protect web communication.

SSTP
(Secure Socket Tunneling Protocol) A protocol that uses the HTTP over SSL protocol and encapsulates an IP packet with a PPP header and then with an SSTP header.

stat
Derived from the Latin "statim," a term used to connote immediacy or urgency.

storage server
A server that stores files and programs.

strong password
A password that meets the complexity requirements that are set by a system administrator and documented in a password policy.

structured data
Data that fits into a well-defined data model.

Structured Query Language
See SQL.

superbill
An itemized form containing all the information needed to file a claim, including patient information and services rendered for a visit, that is compiled by the healthcare provider's medical biller and supplied to the insurance company as the source for the claim.

surgical center
A healthcare facility that performs surgical procedures that does not require hospitalization. Surgeries are usually outpatient, meaning the surgery performed does not require an overnight or extended hospital stay for recovery.

switch
A device that has multiple network ports and combines multiple physical network segments into a single logical network.

Systemized Nomenclature of Medicine–Clinical Terms
See SNOMED CT.

systems administrator
An IT role that is responsible for the maintenance of an organization's hardware systems, networks, and server systems.

tape drive
A personal computer storage device that stores data magnetically on a removable tape.

TCP/IP
(Transmission Control Protocol/Internet Protocol) A non-proprietary, routable network protocol suite that enables computers to communicate over all types of networks.

teaching hospital
A hospital affiliated with a nearby medical school, allowing medical students and residents to gain hands-on learning and obtain real world experience by working in the hospital environment

Temporal Key Integrity Protocol
See TKIP.

The Joint Commission
An independent, non-regulatory, not-for-profit organization that provides accreditation and certification for healthcare organizations in the United States.

time server
A server that provides the most accurate actual time to all clients in a computer network.

Time to Live
See TTL.

TKIP
(Temporal Key Integrity Protocol) A security protocol created by the IEEE 802.11i task group to replace WEP.

tracert
A utility used to determine the route data takes to get to a particular destination.

tracking and auditing software
Software that provides a single system for tracking and managing compliance with medical claims audits that are performed by both government and commercial healthcare (insurance) organizations.

transitive access
Access given to certain members in an organization to use data on a system without the need for authenticating themselves.

Transmission Control Protocol/Internet Protocol
See TCP/IP.

trauma center
A facility equipped to treat patients suffering traumatic injuries.

treatment team
A team of clinicians assigned to work with a specific patient at any given time.

Trojan horse
Malicious code that masquerades as a harmless file. When a user executes it, thinking it is a harmless application, it destroys and corrupts data on the user's hard drive.

TTL
(Time to Live) A value that determines how many hops an IP packet can travel before being discarded.

twisted pair
A type of cable in which multiple insulated conductors are twisted together and clad in a protective and insulating outer jacket.

U.S. Department of Health and Human Services
see HHS.

Universal Serial Bus
See USB.

UPS
(Uninterruptible Power Supply) A battery backup device that is intended to save computer components from damage due to power problems such as power failures, spikes, and sags.

urgent care facility
An outpatient facility where treatment can be provided for medical problems or conditions that need immediate medical attention, but are not an emergency.

USB connection
A personal computer connection that enables you to connect multiple peripherals to a single port with high performance and minimal device configuration.

USB
(Universal Serial Bus) A hardware interface standard designed to provide connections for numerous peripherals.

virtual private network
See VPN.

virtualization
A class of technology that separates computing software from the hardware it runs on via an additional software layer, allowing multiple operating systems to run on one computer simultaneously.

virus
A sample of code that spreads from one computer to another by attaching itself to other files. The code in a virus corrupts and erases files on a user's computer, including executable files, when the file to which it was attached is opened or executed. The term is often used as an umbrella term to refer to many types of malicious software.

Voice over IP
See VoIP.

VoIP
(Voice over IP) An implementation in which voice signals are transmitted over IP networks.

VPN protocol
A protocol that provides VPN functionality.

VPN
(virtual private network) A private network that is configured within a public network, such as the Internet.

WAN
(Wide Area Network) A network that spans multiple geographic locations, connecting multiple LANs using long-range transmission media.

war chalking
Using symbols to mark off a sidewalk or wall to indicate that there is an open wireless network which may be offering Internet access.

war driving
The act of searching for instances of wireless LAN networks while in motion, using wireless tracking devices like mobile phones, smartphones, tablets, or laptops.

web server
A server that displays web pages to clients.

WEP
(Wired Equivalency Protocol) A protocol that provides 64-bit, 128-bit, and 256-bit encryption using the RC4 algorithm for wireless communication that uses the 802.11a and 802.11b protocols.

WHO
(World Health Organization) A division of the United Nations that manages the authority of international public health.

Wide Area Network
See WAN.

Wired Equivalency Protocol
See WEP.

wireless security
Any method of securing your wireless LAN network to prevent unauthorized network access and network data theft while ensuring that authorized users can connect to the network.

Wireless Transport Layer Security
See WTLS.

World Health Organization
See WHO.

worm
A piece of code that spreads from one computer to another on its own, not by attaching itself to another file. Like a virus, a worm can corrupt or erase files on your hard drive.

WTLS
(Wireless Transport Layer Security) The security layer of a WAP and the wireless equivalent of TLS in wired networks.

XML
(eXtensible Markup Language) A widely adopted markup language used in many documents, websites, and web applications.

zombie
Unauthorized software introduced on multiple computers to manipulate the computers into mounting a DDoS attack. Also called a drone.

Index

085710 S3PB rev 1.0
ISBN-13 978-1-4246-1874-3
ISBN-10 1-4246-1874-6
90000
9 781424 618743